Pathfinders, Pioneers, & Patriots
(Volume 2, Edition 1)
(1800 - 1900)

Copyright © 2020 by Danny Dixon

All rights reserved. No part of this publication may be reproduced, distributed, or transmitted in any form or by any means, including photocopying, recording, or other electronic or mechanical methods, without the prior written permission of the publisher, except in the case of brief quotations embodied in critical reviews and certain other noncommercial uses permitted by copyright law.

Self-Published by Danny Dixon
Printed and Available Through Lulu Press (lulu.com)
Morrisville, North Carolina, 27560

Front Cover Picture: "The Bush Mill" in Nickelsville, Virginia, 24271
                       Photographer – Mike Dixon

Volume 2 of a two-part series – "Pathfinders, Pioneers, & Patriots".

Volume 1 (1500 - 1800) and Volume 2 (1800 - 1900) are available from the Printer (lulu.com), several regional outlets, or the Author:

Danny Dixon
190 Kilgore Street
Nickelsville, Virginia 24271
echo@mounet.com

Foreword:

<u>"Pathfinders, Pioneers, & Patriots"</u> Volume 2, Edition 1 (1800 - 1900)

Any attempt to record all the significant problems, accomplishments, conflicts, etc. of any given century is doomed to failure before it even begins. There is simply to much time and material to cover, and no one can possibly know or dig up all the relevant information that should be recorded. For that reason, I make no claim that this work is comprehensive, in any sense. Not every person, event, discovery, struggle, etc. that deserves recognition or preserving is included or even known to me. But, having said that, every person, event, challenge, struggle, etc. that I have included is, in my mind, more than worthy of our recognition and appreciation.

As in my first work, <u>"Pathfinders, Pioneers, and Patriots"</u> - Volume One, Edition One, you will find a Historical Timeline to help keep the events covered in proper sequence and tie everything contextually together. And you will find stories about many fascination people and interesting events. A considerable amount of the material will focus on the Appalachian Frontier or on illustrating how national events impacted life here. Some of the stories will cover well known historical people and events. In such cases I have tried to uncover additional, often intriguing information that helps us better understand what we have read elsewhere, or to point out "the rest of the story".

Sound interesting? I certainly hope so. It was very interesting to me as I regularly encountered historical gems I didn't know about, discovered new mysteries to ponder, and was constantly impressed by our amazing ancestors and all the challenges they faced and overcame.

Introduction:

By 1800, many of the most pressing challenges settlers of the Appalachian Mountains had faced since the first explorers entered the region, had essentially been met and at least partially overcome. But soon it became apparent that the new ones they faced were also daunting, in new and significantly different ways. In some cases, they would find themselves even less prepared for what lay ahead.

They would soon find that addressing the problems of growing communities, developing necessary infrastructure, dealing effectively with governance and public safety, providing for the education of young people, dealing with growing national divisions, etc. would sorely tax their wisdom and endurance.

And they would discover that unexpected events can be counted on to show up and often bring out the best and the worst in the people affected. The new century would certainly present its own special challenges.

Pathfinders, Pioneers, & Patriots
(Volume 2, Edition 1)

1800's

1800 - (May 14) **John Watts**, chief of the Cherokee Nation, leads a war party against another tribe to the west of the Mississippi River (probably Creek).
 - (June 15) The U.S. capital is moved from Philadelphia to Washington, DC.
 - A **Private Turnpike** is completed between Knoxville and Spartanburg, S.C. following the French Broad River through Saluda Gap.
 - (4/23) **The Natchez Trace** post route, following an old trail running from Nashville, Tennessee to Natchez, Mississippi, is established by an Act of Congress.
 - **Duncan's Mill** is built by John Duncan on Cove Creek (sometime in the early 1800's) in the edge of Rye Cove, Va. (Scott County). He operated the mill until 1857 when he turned it over to his son-in-law, George W. Johnson.
 - **Alley's Mill** is built by Thomas Alley (sometime in the late 1790's) on present day Jessee Branch, about 3 miles east of Nickelsville, Va. He operates the mill for several years until it is taken over by his son.
 - (8/4) **The second census** of the United States is conducted. The total population of the USA was 5,308,483 and the center of its population was 18 miles west of Baltimore, Maryland.
 - (11/1) **U.S. President John Adams** is the first President to live in the White House, then known as the Executive Mansion and sixteen days later, the United States Congress holds its first session in Washington, D.C.
 - (11/17) **Gabriel Prosser**, an enslaved African American blacksmith, organizes a slave revolt intending to march on Richmond, Virginia. The conspiracy is uncovered, and Prosser and a number of the rebels are hanged. Virginia's slave laws are consequently tightened.

1801 – (3/4) **Thomas Jefferson** is inaugurated as the third president in Washington, DC
 - According to family tradition, James O'Brien takes the first flatboat loaded with iron from the mouth of the North Fork of the Holston River to New Orleans.
 - (5/10) **Tripoli** declares war against the United States. The United States had refused to pay additional tribute to commerce raiding corsairs from Arabia.

1802 – (10/2) War ends between Tripoli and Sweden, but continues with the United States, despite a negotiated peace, due to compensation disagreements.
 - William King buys the first lots available in Christianville, Tn., at the mouth of the North Fork of the Holston River. By this time King had leased the Preston Salt Works in Saltville, Va. and was producing 10,000 tons of salt annually.

1803 – British begin to impress American sailors and force them to work on British

Ships.
On his newly acquired property, King builds a warehouse and loading docks on the Holston River. He sends his long-time friend, John Lynn, to operate his boat yard. Lynn soon develops Christianville Boat Yard, which is situated at the head of navigation on the Holston, into a thriving commercial center. The boarding house he builds there, overlooking the area, is heavily used by boatmen and travelers, and is eventually sold to Richard Netherland (1818) and is known then and today as The Netherland Inn. The boat yard is often referred to as King's Port during its early years and in 1822, when Christianville and adjacent Rossville combine, the new Town is called **Kingsport, Tn.**

- (1/30) Discussions to buy New Orleans begins when Monroe and Livingston sail to Paris, ending with the complete purchase of the Louisiana Purchase three months later.
- (4/30) France and the U.S. sign a treaty setting up the **Louisiana Purchase**. President Thomas Jefferson doubles the size of the United States of America with his purchase of the Louisiana Territory from Napoleon's France, thus paving way for the western expansion that would mark the entire history of the 19th century from Missouri to the Pacific Coast. The price of the purchase includes bonds of $11,250,000 and $3,750,000 in payments to United States citizens with claims against France.
- (9/23) **John Sevier** is inaugurated for his second term as Gov. of Tennessee.
- Daniel Boone is seriously injured in a hunting accident. He moves to son's farm.
- (12/20) **The Louisiana Purchase** is completed and the land transferred to the U.S. Almost immediately, because of pressure from several states, the President recommends to Congress that they begin proceedings to re-locate all Indians to land acquired beyond the Mississippi. A number of silent and shady deals were advocated and carried out with pseudo leaders of the Cherokee Nation.
- (12/28) The General Assembly of Va. approves the building of a **Turnpike** between Abingdon and Saltville.

1804 - (11/13) **Jonathan Wood Sr.** (a very early Scott Co. Va. Pioneer) dies.
- (5/14) **Lewis and Clark** set out from St. Louis, Mo., on expedition to explore the West and find a route to the Pacific Ocean - <u>**The Corps of Discovery**</u>.
- (7/11) The duel between Alexander Hamilton and Vice President Aaron Burr, longtime political rivals, occurs in Weehawken, New Jersey, culminating in the death of Hamilton.
- (10/1) The attack on **Sitka, Alaska** by Russians and their allies in the Aleut community siege a Tlingit Indian fort. One week later, the siege was complete with the driving out of Tlingit forces.
- (10/26) **The Lewis and Clark Expedition** arrives at the confluence of the Knife and Missouri Rivers, in what is now the state of North Dakota, where they camp until the spring of 1805 at the hospitality of the Mandan and Minitari Indian villages.
- Trading Posts are established in the West to facilitate trade with the Native Americans.

1805 - (3/20) **David Jessee**, a future S.W. Va. Minister is born in Russell County, Va.
- **Doublehead**, a leading Cherokee culprit in the illegal deals between the Cherokee and the Federal Gov., is assassinated by Council order. Other signers flee west for safety. Official Members of the Cherokee Council go to Washington to protest the illegal treaties, but Congress ratifies them inspite of their objections.
- (4/27) **American Marines and Berbers** attack the Tripoli city of Derna. Land and naval forces battle against Tripoli until peace is concluded with the United States on June 4, 1805.
- (6/13) **Meriweather Lewis** and four companions confirm their correct heading by sighting the Great Falls of the Missouri River, as the Lewis and Clark expedition continues west.
- (10/22) **Davy Crockett** applies for a marriage license, but his fiance' (Margaret Elder) gets cold feet and calls the wedding off.
- (12/5) Members of the **Lewis and Clark Expedition** upon sighting the Pacific Ocean on November 15, build Fort Clatsop, a log fort near the mouth of the Columbia River in present-day Oregon. They spend the winter of 1805-1806 in their newly constructed fort.

1806 – (January) James Madison delivers a report regarding British interference and impressment of sailors.
- **Davy Crockett** takes out a license in Jefferson County to marry Polly Findley.
- **Stand Watie**, future Cherokee Chief and Civil War General is born in Georgia.
- **The 1st Newspaper** is printed in Washington Co. Va. ("The Holston Intelligencer & Abingdon Advertiser")
- (3/23) **Explorers Lewis and Clark and the Corps of Discovery** begin the several thousand mile trek back to St. Louis, Missouri from their winter camp near the Pacific Ocean.
- **Tecumseh & Tenskwatawa** (The Prophet) seek to unite 1000's of Indians against the whites. Their following begins to grow among many different tribes.
- **Daniel Boone** appears before the Federal Land Commission seeking confirmation of his Spanish Land Grant.
- (7/15) **A second exploratory expedition** led by U.S. **Army Lieutenant Zebulon Pike** begins from Fort Bellefountaine near St. Louis. Later that year, during a second trip, he reaches the distant Colorado foothills of the Rocky Mountains and discovers Pike's Peak.
- (9/23) **The Lewis and Clark Expedition** to map the northwest United States ends.

1807 – (3/2) Congress passes an act that prohibits the importation of slaves into any port within the confines of the United States from any foreign land. It was to take effect on the 1st of January 1808.
- (June) - The American ship Chesapeake is fired upon by the British ship Leopard causing an international incident.
- (8/17) The first practical steamboat journey is made by **Robert Fulton** in the steamboat Clermont, who navigated the Hudson River from New York City to Albany in thirty-two hours, a trip of 150 miles. This becomes the first commercial

steamboat service in the world.
- Through the tireless efforts of **William Wilberforce** in England over many years, The British Parliament finally abolishes their slave trade and, in 1833, they Abolish slavery itself everywhere in the British Empire.
- (December) **Thomas Jefferson** imposes an embargo on Great Britain but it results in economic disaster for American merchants and is discontinued in 1809.

1808 – (1/1) The importation of slaves is outlawed, although between 1808 and 1860, more than 250,000 slaves are illegally imported.
- (2/11) **Anthracite coal** is first burned, in an experiment, as fuel.
- (6/3) **Jefferson Davis**, future President of the Confederacy,,is born in Todd Co., Ky
- (Summer) **General Meigs** encourages the Cherokees to swap their Eastern land holdings for western land. A large number of Cherokee become resigned to the inevitable and move west.
- **Robin Kilgore** is ordained and becomes the first Pastor of the Copper Creek Church of Christ (Nickelsville, Va.) -serves for 45 years.
- (11/4) **James Madison** is elected as the 4th President of the United States
- (12/18) **Joseph Martin** dies in Henry County, Va. (age 68)
- (12/29) **Andrew Johnson**, future President of the U.S. is born in Raleigh, N.C.

1809 - (1/19) **Robert E. Lee**, future Commander in Chief of the Confederacy is born in Stratford, Va.
- (2/12) **Abraham Lincoln**, future 16th Pres. of the U.S. is born in Hardin Co. Ky.
- **The Treaty of Ft. Wayne** is signed ceding 3 million acres of Indian land to the U.S. (Rejected by Tecumseh and his followers.)
- (March) **James Madison** is inaugurated President of the United States.
- (12/7) Col. James L. Shoemaker is born near Lebanon, Russell Co., Va.
- (12/24) **Kit Carson**, trapper, frontiersman, and soldier is born in Madison Co. Ky.

1810 - **Tecumseh & the Creek Medicine-man, Seekaboo**, travel to the Southern Nations to drum up their support against the whites. Many Native American, from several different nations join him.

1811 - **The Battle of Tippecanoe** - Gov. Harrison leads 1,000 soldiers against The Shawnee at Prophet's Town and soundly defeats them. The Indian Confederation falls into disarray.
- (12/16) **A Great Earthquake** (centered near New Madrid, Missouri) shakes the whole Southeastern United States. (estimated to be over 8.4 on the Richter Scale)
- Col. Arthur Campbell dies at his home in Middlesboro, Ky.

1812 – (4/11) As tension with England grows **Wash. Co. troops muster at Abingdon**
- (5/2) a tremendous hail storm hits the area.
- (6/18) **The U.S. declares War on Great Britain. (War of 1812)**
- (June – Aug) - Riots break out in Baltimore in protest of the war.
- **The Capitol of Tennessee** is moved to Nashville, Tenn. (from Knoxville)

- **David Campbell** of Wash. Co., is commissioned a major in the 12 Reg. of Infantry and ordered to raise all recruits possible and proceed to Winchester, Va.
- (April, May, & June) Calls go out for volunteers to muster at Abingdon to organize troops for Cavalry, Infantry, and Artillery Companies.
- (July) **General William Hull** enters Canada, the first of three failed attempts made by the U.S. to invade Canada. The British force the surrender of **Fort Michilimackinac** (in present-day Michigan).
- (8/19) The **USF Constitution** defeats the British Ship, HMS Guerriere
- **General William Hull** surrenders to General Isaac Brock at Detroit.
- (Oct) General Isaac Brock is killed at the **Battle of Queenston Heights (Canada).**

1813 - (1/7) **Gen. Andrew Jackson** leads a march to Natchez with 1,500 men to help defend New Orleans from the British.
- British and their Indian allies repel American troops at the **Battle of Frenchtown** (present-day Michigan). American survivors are killed the following day in the **Raisin River Massacre**.
- (Feb) His Majesties fleet, under the command of **Rear Admiral George Cockburn**, arrives off the entrance to the Chesapeake Bay and raids towns along the bay from Norfolk, VA to Havre de Grace in MD. Later, the British blockade is extended along the entire Eastern coast, effectively limit shipping into and out of the bay.
- (3/18) **Rebecca Boone** dies.
- (4/27) U.S. troops capture and burn the city of **York** (present-day Toronto).
- (May) The siege of **Fort Meigs** (present-day Ohio)
- William Gray marries Nancy Green Stallard and soon afterward builds his log house in a bend of Clinch River, a short distance downriver from present day Dungannon in Scott Co., VA, where his wife's two grandfathers had carved out a home on the frontier when it was still plagued by hostile Indian activity..
- (6/22) The **Battle of Norfolk, Va** takes place.
- (8/10) A party of Creek Indians attack **Ft. Mims**. The Cherokee send 600 Braves to assist Gen. Andrew Jackson in his battle to destroy the Red Sticks.
- (9/10) **Oliver Hazard Perry** leads the American forces to victory at Lake Erie.
- (Oct.) The warrior **Tecumseh** is killed at the **Battle of the Thames** (Canada).
- (Nov) The Battle of **Crysler's Farm** (Canada).

1814 - **The Red Stick War** breaks out in Alabama. Creeks angered by U.S. policy and encouraged by Tecumseh attack Creek Villages allied with the U.S. and Ft. Mims, where they kill most of the U.S. citizens living there.
- (March)- Several hundred Cherokee assist the U.S. Army against the Creeks in The **Battle of Horseshoe Bend** .(over 900 Creeks are killed) This event does much to convince the Cherokees of the futility of trying to resist the whites. Chief Junaluska, of the Cherokees, later said that if he had known what Andrew Jackson would later do to the Cherokee, he would have killed him himself at that battle.(22 million acres of Indian land is ceded to the U.S. Gov.)
- Congress grants Boone a tract of Missouri land.

- (July) **The Battle of Chippawa** (Canada).
  The Battle of Lundy's Lane (present-day Niagara Falls, Ontario, Canada).
- (8/25) **British Troops attack Washington D.C.**, burn the Capitol and the White House. **President James Madison** flees the Capital.
- (9/11) The Americans win the **Battle of Lake Champlain.**
- (9/15) British fleet attacks **Ft. McHenry** protecting the entrance to Baltimore Harbor but fails to force its surrender. Observing the battle, Francis Scott Key pens the **"Star Spangled Banner"**, which was later adopted as our National Anthem.
- (11/21) **Scott County Virginia** is formed from Washington County. (Named for Gen. Winfield Scott, a popular hero of the War of 1812.
- (12/24) **The Treaty of Ghent** is signed ending the War of 1812, (but word is slow to cross the Atlantic and one more great battle is fought).

1815 - (1/8) **General Andrew Jackson** defeats the British at New Orleans (the closing battle of the War of 1812 - 15 days after the treaty was signed).
- (2/14) **The first court is held in Scott County** and John Anderson is made Sheriff.
- The **Seminole Wars** begin.
- (9/24) **John Sevier** dies while serving on a Congressional Comm. in Alabama.
- The first settlers arrive in future Lawrence Co., Tenn. (near Henryville on Big Buffalo River)- including **Davy Crockett.**

1816 - (12/4) **James Monroe** is elected 5th President of the U.S.
- (10/16) **John Anderson** (prominent early settler of Scott Co.) dies.
- (11/27) **The Seminole Indian War** begins after U.S. soldiers attack a village in Florida.

1817 - **A party of unidentified Indians** march down the Stone Mountain Trail (from Ohio and across High Knob) (Chief Benge's notorious favored trail) to Scott County, Virginia, adjacent to where Fort Blackmore stood - the site of an ancient Indian Mound. While the confused and fearful inhabitants look on, they conduct a mysterious silent ritual and depart West through the group of onlookers.
- **The Cherokee Council** meets in Cleveland Tenn. **John Ross**, one of the Cherokee leaders is instructed to write a formal letter to the commissioners strongly protesting the proposed cessions of their land.
- (May 7) The Tribal-Clan form of rule is formally replaced by the Cherokees with an Executive, Legislative, and Judicial process, similar to the U.S. system.
- **The First Seminole War** breaks out in Florida.
- The first Court House is built on the public square (in present day Gate City, Va.)
- (7/8) **The Cession of Cherokee Land** formally begins. Through bribery, coercion, and out right lies, the vast Cherokee Empire lying East of the Mississippi River is systematically taken from them. The Cherokee who Actually "sign" the agreement flee west for their lives.
- The remaining Shawnees are relocated to a small reservation west of the Mississippi River.

1818 - (2/13) **George Rogers Clark** dies in Louisville, Ky.
   - **Frederick Ross** (son of David Ross) builds **"Ross's Bridge"** across the N. Fork of the Holston River and reroutes the Stage Road to cross it. There he builds his mansion known as Rotherwood. He also lays out a new Town, Rossville, along the river beside Christianville.
   - (4/18) Andrew Jackson defeated a force of Indians and African Americans at the **Battle of Suwanee**, ending the First Seminole War.
   - (10/19) **Andrew Jackson and Isaac Shelby** sign a treaty with the Chickasaw Indians.
   - **Tusculum College**, Tenn. is founded by Presbyterian Clergyman, Dr. Samuel Doak.
   - (November 19) **Nancy Ward**, The Cherokee Rose dies at her brother's home, (Long Fellow), near the Ocoee River.

1820 - **The Cherokee Nation** is divided into 8 Districts and John Ross is elected President.
   - (9/26) **Daniel Boone** dies at the home of his son, Nathan. (86 yrs. old)
   - (March) **The Missouri Compromise** became law in the United States. The landmark legislation effectively pushed the issue of slavery aside for the next few decades.
   - **James Monroe** faces virtually no opposition and is reelected president of the United States.

1821 - **The Cherokee alphabet** is completed by **Sequoyah** and adopted as the official written language of the tribe.
   - American traders began using the **Santa Fe Trail**.

1822 - **Denmark Vesey**, an enslaved African American carpenter who had purchased his freedom, plans a slave revolt with the intent to lay siege on Charleston, South Carolina. The plot is discovered, and Vesey and 34 coconspirators are hanged.
   - The first group of freed slaves being resettled in Africa by the American Colonization Society arrive in **Liberia** and found the town of Monrovia, named for President James Monroe.

1823 – (12/2) **Monroe Doctrine**: In his annual address to Congress, President Monroe declares that the American continents are henceforth off-limits for further colonization by European powers

1824 - The U.S. presidential election of 1824 is deadlocked with no clear winner and becomes known as **"The Corrupt Bargain."**

1825 – A road is built from Pound, Va. to Pikeville, Ky.
   - (2/9) The election of 1824 was settled by a vote in the U.S. House of Representatives, which elected **John Quincy Adams** as president. Supporters of Andrew Jackson claimed a "Corrupt Bargain" had been struck between Adams

and Henry Clay.
- (10/26) The entire length of the **Erie Canal** was officially opened across New York, from Albany to Buffalo. The engineering feat had been the brainchild of DeWitt Clinton.

1826 - **John Adams** died in Massachusetts and **Thomas Jefferson** died in Virginia, on the 50th anniversary of the signing of the Declaration of Independence.

1827 - **The Concord Coach** is first built. Served as the preferred Stage Coach used in the area.

1828 - **John Ross** is elected Principal Chief of the Cherokee Nation, a position he held until his death.
- The first issue of the **Cherokee Phoenix** rolls off the presses on February 21, and has an immediate international circulation. (the Official Newspaper of the Cherokee Nation)
- (2/2) **Patrick Hagan** is born in Ireland. He comes to America when he was 16.
- The first steamboat to reach the mouth of the Holston River (at Knoxville, Tn.) is the Atlas, under Captain S. D. Conner.
- (7/4) Construction is begun on the **Baltimore and Ohio Railroad**, the first public railroad in the U.S.
- (Fall) The election of 1828 was preceded by perhaps the dirtiest campaign ever, with supporters of Andrew Jackson and John Quincy Adams hurling shocking accusations. **Andrew Jackson** is elected president of the United States.

1829 - The old Court House in Scott Co. is replaced by a brick structure (part of present building).
- **Gold is discovered** on Cherokee land in north Georgia resulting in pressure on Congress to open up the Cherokee land for speculators and settlers.
- Drury S. Godsey is born.
- (3/29) **Andrew Jackson** was inaugurated as president of the United States, and raucous supporters nearly wreck the White House.

1830 - Pressures increase in Georgia and the Carolinas to take over the Cherokee's land and Congress passes <u>the "Indian Removal Act"</u> with the backing of Pres. Andrew Jackson. (Provided for the removal of all Eastern Indians - west of the Mississippi)
- Francis Preston moves to Abingdon, Va. in 1830and begins building on his mansion-like home, now known as the Martha Washington Inn.
- The **"Underground Railroad"** is established.

1831 - **Nat Turner**, an enslaved African American preacher, leads the most significant slave uprising in American history. He and his band of about 80 followers launch a bloody, day-long rebellion in Southampton County, Virginia. The militia quells the rebellion, and Turner is eventually hanged. As a consequence, Virginia institutes much stricter slave laws.

- (Summer) **Cyrus McCormick**, a Virginia blacksmith, demonstrates a mechanical reaper which revolutionizes farming in America and eventually worldwide.

1832 - **The Fincastle Turnpike** is authorized by the Va. General Assembly. From Fincastle (above Roanoke) to Pearisburg, through the Narrows of the New River to Tazewell, to Lebanon, to Dickensonville, to Castlewood, down Sinking Creek to Porter's Fort area, across the Clinch River, to Ft. Blackmore, on to Rye Cove, Duffield, through Lee County and to Cumberland Gap.
- (2/23) **Smyth County** is formed from Washington & Wythe Counties.
- Andrew Jackson is elected to his second term as president of the United States.
- Daniel Ramey establishes a Ferry at Osborne's Ford (later Dungannon, Va.)

1833 – Joseph Hagan begins to buy large tracks of land in the Hunter's Valley of Scott County, Va. including land near the Sulphur Spring on which Hagan Hall would later be built.

1835 – (1/30) In the first assassination attempt on an American president, a deranged man shot at **Andrew Jackson** in the rotunda of the U.S. Capitol.
- **The Second Seminole War** breaks out. U.S. troops battle Seminoles in the swamps of Florida but without conclusive results. The second and most terrible of three wars between the US government and the Seminole people was also one of the longest and most expensive wars in which the US army was ever engaged. Thousands of troops were sent, 1,500 men died, and between 40-60 million dollars were spent to force most of the Seminole to move to Indian Territory – more than the entire US government's budget for Indian Removal. The Seminole leader, Osceola, is eventually deceived and captured.
- **Treaty of New Echota** - A portion of the Cherokee nation agree to give up Cherokee lands in the Southeast in exchange for land and removal to Indian Territory. A larger group of the Cherokee do not accept the terms of this treaty and refuse to move westward.
- A campaign to mail abolitionist pamphlets to the South leads to mobs breaking into post offices and burning the anti-slavery literature in bonfires.
- William Gray builds a corn mill on his farm near Dungannon, Va.

1836 - (3/1) **Texas declares its independence from Mexico.**
- (3/6) Texan defenders of the **Alamo** are all killed during a siege by the Mexican Army. The Battle of the Alamo ended with the deaths of Davy Crockett, William Barrett Travis, and James Bowie.
- (4/21) Texans, led by Sam Houston defeat Mexicans at **San Jacinto,** the decisive battle of the War with Mexico.
- **Martin Van Buren** is elected President of the United States.

1837 – **A major economic depression** sweeps the nation and lasts until 1843.
– (5/20) The first steamboat ascends the Big Sandy as far as Prestonsburg, Ky.
- Depression begins with the "Panic of 1837".

1838 - (Winter) - **The "Trail of Tears"**, forced removal of over 15,000 Cherokee, begins. They receive no compensation for their land and at least 4,000 of them perish along the way. Approx. 1,000 escape to the mountains of North Carolina where a reward is offered for their capture - dead or alive. Will Thomas, a white trader, helps secure clemency for them and they are granted 57,000 acres of land, most of which becomes the Eastern Reservation known as the **Qualla Boundary**.
- **Seminole leader Osceola** dies from complications of malaria at Fort Moultrie, South Carolina.

1839 - A slave rebellion brakes out aboard the ship Amistad.

1840 - The timber trade starts in earnest in the Big Sandy Valley.
- The 1840 presidential campaign was the first to prominently feature songs and slogans. **William Henry Harrison** won the presidency thanks to his "Log Cabin and Hard Cider" campaign, and the slogan "Tippecanoe and Tyler Too!"

1841 – The first coal mine is established at Abbott Shoal in Floyd County, KY.
- Forty-eight wagons arrive in Sacramento by way of the Oregon Trail, one of the earliest large groups to make this journey.
- (3/4) **William Henry Harrison** is inaugurated as president of the United States. He delivers a two-hour inaugural address in very cold weather. He catches pneumonia, from which he never recovers. He dies after only one month in office. He was the first American president to die in office, and was succeeded by the vice-president, **John Tyler**.

1843 - Summer: "Oregon Fever" gripped America, and 1843 marked the beginning of mass migration westward on the Oregon Trail.

1844 – (5/24) The first telegram is sent from the U.S. Capitol to Baltimore. Samuel F.B. Morse wrote, "What hath God wrought."
- **James Knox Polk** defeated Henry Clay in the U.S. presidential election.

1845 - Peter Brickey builds **Brickey's Mill**, north of Ft. Blackmore.
- (3/1) **The U.S. annexes Texas** by joint resolution of Congress.
- A delegation from Kentucky disinters the Boone graves and moves them to Frankfort, Kentucky.
- A large tannery (John Dils'?) is established in Pike County, KY.
- The Irish potato famine, which would become known as The Great Famine, began with widespread failures of the potato crop.

1846 – The General Assembly of Va. votes to build the **Southwestern Turnpike** (MacAdemized surface) from Salem to Christiansburg, Newbern, Wytheville, Marion, and Abingdon and on to the Tenn. Line (not less than 22 feet wide) (authorizes $75,000 to complete the project).
- (4/25) Mexican troops ambush and killed a patrol of US soldiers. Reports of the incident inflame tensions between the two nations.

- (5/13) **War begins with Mexico**. U.S. declares war on Mexico in an effort to gain California and other territory in the Southwest.
- **The Wilmot Proviso**, introduced by Democratic representative David Wilmot of Pennsylvania, attempts to ban slavery in territory gained in the Mexican War The proviso is blocked by Southerners, but continues to enflame the debate over slavery.
- (6/14) In the **Bear Flag Revolt**, settlers in northern California declare their independence from Mexico.
- (December) **The Donner Party**, a party of American settlers in wagon trains, became stranded in the snow-covered Sierra Nevada Mountains in California and resort to cannibalism to survive.

1847 – **The first steamboat successfully navigates the Holston to Kingsport, TN**. A large crowd gathers at the Netherland Inn to welcome **the Casandra**'s arrival from Knoxville.
- **Westward migration** begins along the Oregon Trail through Plains Indian country. Thomas H. Hardy, Superintendant of Indian Affairs in St. Louis, warns of trouble from declining buffalo herds.
- (2/22) U.S. troops commanded by General Zachary Taylor defeated a Mexican Army at the **Battle of Buena Vista** in the Mexican War.
- (3/29) U.S. troops commanded by General Winfield Scott captured **Veracruz** in the Mexican War.
- (Late Summer) The potato famine continued in Ireland, and the year became known as "Black '47."
- (9/13-14) U.S. troops entered Mexico City and effectively ended the Mexican War.
- (12/6) Abraham Lincoln takes his seat in the U.S. House of Representatives. After serving a single two-year term he returns to Illinois.

1848 – (2/2) **War with Mexico** concludes with the signing of the Treaty of Guadalupe Hidalgo. Mexico recognizes Rio Grande as new boundary with Texas and, for $15 million, agrees to cede territory comprising present-day California, Nevada, Utah, most of New Mexico and Arizona, and parts of Colorado and Wyoming.
- (7/12-19) A conference at Seneca Falls, New York, organized by **Lucretia Mott** and **Elizabeth Cady Stanton** took up the issue of **Women's Rights** and plant the seeds of the suffrage movement in the US.
- **Zachary Taylor**, Whig candidate and a hero of the Mexican War, is elected president of the United States.

1849 – (January) Heavy rains bring flooding to northern and eastern Kentucky. Many mills are washed away or severely damaged.
- (1/24) James Marshall discovers gold near Sutter's Fort, California. News of the find begins the **California Gold Rush of 1849.**
- **Harriet Tubman** escapes from slavery and becomes one of the most effective and celebrated members of the Underground Railroad.

1850 - **Gladeville** (which became Wise in 1928 and originally called Big Glades), is chartered.
 - **The Peach Orchard Coal Company** begins operation.
 - Tobacco becomes more important as a crop in the western-most counties of Virginia.
 - There are an estimated 20,000,000 buffalo on the plains between Montana and Texas.
 - The continuing debate whether territory gained in the Mexican War should be open to slavery is decided in the **Compromise of 1850**: California is admitted as a free state, Utah and New Mexico territories are left to be decided by popular sovereignty, and the slave trade in Washington, DC, is prohibited. It also establishes a much stricter fugitive slave law, than the original, passed in 1793.
 - (7/9) **President Zachary Taylor** dies in the White House. His vice president, Millard Fillmore, ascends to the presidency.

1851 - **An enormous exhibition of technology** opened in London with a ceremony attended by Queen Victoria and the event's sponsor, her husband Prince Albert. Prize-winning innovations shown at the Great Exhibition included photographs by Mathew Brady and the reaper of Cyrus McCormick.
 - (9/11) In what became known as the Christiana Riot, a Maryland slave-owner is killed when he attempts to capture a runaway slave in rural Pennsylvania.

1852 - Harriet Beecher Stowe's novel, **Uncle Tom's Cabin** is published. It becomes one of the most influential works to stir anti-slavery sentiments.
 - **Franklin Pierce** is elected President of the United States.

1853 – (7/8) **Commodore Matthew Perry** sailed into Japanese harbor near present day Tokyo with four American warships, demanding to deliver a letter to the emperor of Japan.

1854 - The legislation **repeals the Missouri Compromise** of 1820 and renews tensions between anti- and proslavery factions.
 - (5/30) The Kansas-Nebraska Act is signed into law. The legislation, designed to lessen the tension over slavery, actually has the opposite effect.

1856 - **The Virginia and Tennessee Railroad** (as it was known in Virginia) is completed from Lynchburg, through Roanoke to Bristol, Va/Tn (with a nine mile stretch to Saltville). From there it continued to Knoxville, Tn. It was the first railroad in the S.W. Va./N.E. Tennessee Region.
 - **James Buchanan** is elected president of the United States.

1857 - **Dred Scott v. Sanford**: Landmark Supreme Court decision holds that Congress does not have the right to ban slavery in states and, furthermore, that slaves are not citizens.

1858 - **The Preston** home (in Abingdon) is purchased by the Martha Washington College

for Women. The first session of classes held there run from March to July 1860. The College is converted to a field hospital during the Civil War and closed permanently in 1931, due to the effects of the Depression on the region.
- Abraham Lincoln comes to national attention in a series of seven debates with Sen. Stephen A. Douglas during the Illinois state election campaign.

1860 - **Patrick Hagan** builds Hagan Hall in Hunter's Valley near present day Dungannon, Va..
- (11/6) **Abraham Lincoln**, who had declared "Government cannot endure permanently half slave, half free..." is elected president, the first Republican, receiving 180 of 303 possible electoral votes and 40 percent of the popular vote. (Dec) - South Carolina secedes from the Union.

1861- (2/4) **The Va. General Assembly** meets to consider secession from the Union. Most of the people of the southwestern region oppose it at first. Even so, when Va. votes to secede, the citizens of the area volunteer in large numbers to fight for the Confederacy. To them the issue is "State's Rights" rather than slavery, for in most counties in western Virginia, fewer than 10% of white families own slaves, and in no counties did more than 20%, a stark contrast to the counties in the eastern part of the state.
- (2/9) **The Confederate States of America** is formed with Jefferson Davis, a West Point graduate and former U.S. Army officer, as president.
- (4/12) At 4:30 a.m. Confederates under **Gen. Pierre Beauregard** open fire with 50 cannons upon **Fort Sumter in Charleston, South Carolina**. *The Civil War begins.*
- (4/15) **President Lincoln** issues a Proclamation calling for 75,000 militiamen, and summoning a special session of Congress for July 4. Robert E. Lee, son of a Revolutionary War hero, and a 25 year distinguished veteran of the United States Army and former Superintendent of West Point, is offered command of the Union Army. Lee declines the offer.
- (4/17) **Virginia secedes from the Union**, followed within five weeks by Arkansas, Tennessee, and North Carolina, thus forming an eleven state Confederacy with a population of 9 million, including nearly 4 million slaves. The Union will soon have 21 states and a population of over 20 million.
- **Colonel James F. Preston** became leader of the **Washington Mounted Riflemen**. He led his troops from Abingdon to Saltville to protect the valuable salt mines.
- (4/19) **President Lincoln** issues a **Proclamation of Blockade** against Southern ports. For the duration of the war the blockade limits the ability of the rural South to stay well supplied in its war against the industrialized North.
- (4/20) **Robert E. Lee** resigns his commission in the United States Army. "I cannot raise my hand against my birthplace, my home, my children." Lee then goes to Richmond, Virginia, is offered command of the military and naval forces of Virginia, and accepts.
- (7/21) The Union Army under **Gen. Irvin McDowell** suffers a defeat at **Bull Run** 25 miles southwest of Washington. **Confederate Gen. Thomas J. Jackson** earns

the nickname "Stonewall," as his brigade resists Union attacks. Union troops fall back to Washington. President Lincoln realizes the war will be long. "It's damned bad," he comments.
- (11/8) **Battle at Ivy Mountain**, Pike County, KY.
- (11/9) **Skirmish at Pikeville**, Pike County, KY.
- (12/26) **Union Col. Garfield** reports the strength of the Rebels located at Paintsville at around 2,500 and remarks that they have thrown up breastworks in preparation for battle.
- **The Scott County Court** appoints two men to monitor Federal Troop movements through the passes of the Big Sandy River. (The same ones Clinch Scouts had watched for hostile Indian bands in earlier years.)
- (6/3) Early in the morning, the little village of **Gladeville,** (now Wise, Va.) hears the first call to arms in defense of the Southern Confederacy. Mustered and under the command of **Capt. Logan H. N. Salyers**, 101 brave men, calling themselves the **"Yankee Catchers"**, march away to the defense of their beloved South.
- **Union General Stephen Burbridge**, marches up the Levisa Fork and attacks the Saltworks at Saltville. Defeated, he leads his weary troops homeward through the Pound Gap.
- (7/13) <u>**The Nickelsville Spartan Band**</u> marches to Abingdon to join Gen. Stonewall Jackson's Army to fight for the Confederacy.
- (9/1) Two troop trains collide about one mile west of Abingdon (2nd Reg. of Polish Brigade from Louisiana) (1 are killed and 17 wounded)
- (11/8) The beginning of an international diplomatic crisis for President Lincoln as two Confederate officials sailing toward England are seized by the U.S. Navy. England, the leading world power, demands their release, threatening war. Lincoln eventually gives in and orders their release in December. "One war at a time," Lincoln remarks.
- The threat of **guerilla warfare in the region**, especially in East Tennessee, keeps civilians in fear as marauders representing both sides use wartime chaos as an excuse to steal and intimidate. "As law and order collapsed in the chaos of a lingering war, southerners became trapped in a style of conflict that did not differentiate between combatant and civilian. The unpredictability of when violence might occur added to the horror, as neighbor turned against neighbor and communities split over political differences." (Karissa Martin, Liberty Univ.)

1862 - The Confederate Virginia Government in Richmond passes the **Home Guard Act** to provide organized defenses for towns in Virginia, help increase the state's military power, and control local slave populations. They had to furnish their own guns, but the state agreed to provide food and ammunition. Many of the participants were too young or old to fight in the regular army, although partially disabled veterans and soldiers convalescing or on leave occasionally lent a hand in an emergency. The Washington County Home Guard remains alert for potential threats to come from Tennessee, while the one in Scott County keeps pickets along the Big Sandy River to sound the alert against any invading forces.
- **The Fortieth Ohio Infantry** is encamped at Pikeville, KY.
- (1/7) **Battle of Jenny's Creek**, near Paintsville

- (1/10) **Battle of Middle Creek**, near Prestonsburg.
- (2/6) Victory for **Gen. Ulysses S. Grant** in Tennessee, capturing Fort Henry, and ten days later Fort Donelson. Grant earns the nickname "Unconditional Surrender" Grant.
- (2/22) **The Big Sandy Valley** floods, particularly around Piketon. The region is devastated.
- (March) - **Confederate General Humphrey Marshall**, who had his headquarters at Gladeville, leads his army through the Pound Gap into Kentucky, occupying territory near Prestonsburg. Many of his men become ill with mumps and measles. He is attacked by Union forces and driven back several miles. Many of his troops dessert, some of them going over to the Union side. Eventually he is ordered back to Pound Gap.
- (3/5) **Col. J. A. Garfield** orders Capt. Garrard of the 22nd Kentucky Volunteers to ride to Elkhorn Creek and drive out the Rebels under Menifee.
- (3/7) **Col. Garfield** reports that a change in favor of the Union has occurred in Buchanan County, Va. Community meetings have been held where the participants have expressed their favor for the Union, and a delegation was even sent to Garfield to express such sentiments and to invite the regiment to move into the area.
- (3/8 & 9) The Confederate Ironclad **'Merrimac'** sinks two wooden Union ships then battles the Union Ironclad **'Monitor'** to a draw. Naval warfare is thus changed forever, making wooden ships obsolete
- (3/14) **Confederate Brigadier General Marshall** orders the Kentucky-Virginia border closed.
- (3/16) **Col. Garfield** begins his approach and attack on **Pound Gap**. The Confederate defenders quickly melt away into the dense mountain underbrush. The Union forces find and destroy their camp but most of the troops escape.
- Following the attack at Pound Gap, Marshall calls out the militia of most of the Southwest Virginia counties. He refers to Buchanan as a "very bad district."
- (4/ 6 & 7) Confederate surprise attack on **Gen. Ulysses S. Grant**'s unprepared troops at **Shiloh** on the Tennessee River results in a bitter struggle with 13,000 Union killed and wounded and 10,000 Confederates, more men than in all previous American wars combined. The president is then pressured to relieve Grant but resists. "I can't spare this man; he fights," Lincoln says
- (4/10) **Gen. Marshall** sends Col. Bowen to Buchanan County to recruit 300 men. He gets 100. At the same time he sends his militia men home to plant their crops.
- (4/16) The Confederate Congress passes the first draft bill.
- (4/24) Union ships under the command of **Flag Officer David Farragut** move up the Mississippi River then take New Orleans, the South's greatest seaport. Later in the war, sailing through a Rebel mine field Farragut utters the famous phrase "Damn the torpedoes, full speed ahead!"
- (5/3) The Confederate War Department declares **martial law in Buchanan County, Va.**.
- (5/12) The river is so low that Union forces at Pikeville are in danger of running out of supplies.
- (5/14) **Gen. Marshall** issues an order for the local militia units in Southwest

Virginia to form and make themselves available for deployment into the field. At the same time he issues orders dealing with espionage and sympathizers.

- (5/31) **The Battle of Seven Pines** as **Gen. Joseph E. Johnston**'s Army attacks McClellan's troops in front of Richmond and nearly defeats them. But Johnston is badly wounded.
- (6/1) **Gen. Robert E. Lee** assumes command, replacing the wounded Johnston. Lee then renames his force the Army of Northern Virginia. McClellan is not impressed, saying Lee is "likely to be timid and irresolute in action."
- (6/25 – 7/1) **The Seven Days Battles** as Lee attacks McClellan near Richmond, resulting in very heavy losses for both armies. McClellan then begins a withdrawal back toward Washington.
- (6/27) **Col. Samuel V. Fulkerson**, of the 37th Reg., is mortally wounded near Richmond and dies the next day.
- (7/1) **The first attack on the town of Gladeville** (now Wise, Va.), Federal troops make a raid on the town and capture both Morgan T. Lipps, County Clerk, and Alexander Smith, Commonwealth's Attorney. Mr. Smith is released immediately, but Elder Morgan T. Lipps, a Primitive Baptist preacher, is taken to Pikeville and later to Louisa, Kentucky, and remains a prisoner for three months before he is released.
- (8/3) **John Dils' store in Piketon** is plundered by soldiers under Moore and Menifee. This action is cited by Osborne as the first cross-border action involving the Virginia State Line.
- (8/14) Rebels Troops take over Pike County, Ky, but the Home Guards (under John Dils?) there resists them and capture a rebel Captain.
- (8/29 & 30) 75,000 Federals under **Gen. John Pope** are defeated by 55,000 Confederates under **Gen. Stonewall Jackson and Gen. James Longstreet** at the **second battle of Bull Run** in northern Virginia. Once again the Union Army retreats to Washington. The president then relieves Pope.
- (9/1) John Dils receives his commission as commander of the 39th Kentucky.
- (9/4-9) **Gen. Lee invades the North** with 50,000 Confederates and heads for Harpers Ferry, located 50 miles northwest of Washington. The Union Army, 90,000 strong, under the command of **Gen. McClellan**, pursues Lee.
- (9/17) **The bloodiest day in U.S. military history** as **Gen. Robert E. Lee** and the Confederate Armies are stopped at **Antietam** in Maryland by **Gen. McClellan** and numerically superior Union forces. By nightfall 26,000 men are dead, wounded, or missing. Lee then withdraws to Virginia.
- (11/5) **The 39th Kentucky** encamps at Piketon.
- (11/7) The president replaces McClellan with **Gen. Ambrose E. Burnside** as the new Commander of the Army of the Potomac. Lincoln had grown impatient with McClellan's slowness to follow up on the success at Antietam, even telling him, "If you don't want to use the army, I should like to borrow it for a while."
- (12/4) **The 39th Kentucky** is beaten badly at Wireman's Shoals, KY.
- (12/5) Elements of the 39th led by **Colonel Dils** are again defeated at Bull Gap, near Prestonsburg, KY. and are driven from Pike County back to Lawrence County, KY.
- (12/13) In the heat of an argument, an officer from the 34 Virginia Cavalry shoots

Lt.-Col. James Harrison of the 2d Virginia State Line. Lt.-Col. Harrison is only wounded and the other officer is never held accountable for the assault and battery.
- **The Army of the Potomac under Gen. Burnside** suffers a costly defeat at **Fredericksburg** in Virginia with a loss of 12,653 men after 14 frontal assaults on well entrenched Rebels on Marye's Heights. "We might as well have tried to take hell," a Union soldier remarks. Confederate losses are 5,309. "It is well that war is so terrible - we should grow too fond of it," states Lee during the fighting.
- By the end of 1862, **Confederate Gen. John B. Floyd**, who had fallen from favor after several unsuccessful commands, returns to his native southwest Virginia to put together a militia for the defense of the area. His local connections and his promise that he was raising solely a defensive company rallied many remote mountaineers to his cause, several of whom had resisted the draft and refused to join any other company. Called **the Virginia State Line**, the company remained in existence answering only to the Adjunct General and Governor of the Commonwealth, until the Partisan Ranger Act was revoked in 1864, when it was dissolved.

1863 - (Jan 1) President Lincoln issues **the final Emancipation Proclamation** freeing all slaves in territories held by Confederates and emphasizes the enlisting of black soldiers in the Union Army. The war to preserve the Union now becomes a revolutionary struggle for the abolition of slavery.
Nathaniel Menifee is relieved of his command in the 4th Virginia State Line.
- **The Old Sulphur Springs Baptist Church** is established early in 1863 just north of present-day Hurley, in Buchanan County, Va.
- (1/17) Buchanan County and the surrounding counties come under the command of **C.S.A. General D. S. Donelson** and the Department of East Tennessee.
- (1/25) The president appoints **Gen. Joseph (Fighting Joe) Hooker** as Commander of the Army of the Potomac, replacing Burnside.
- (1/29) Gen. Grant is placed in command of the **Army of the West**, with orders to capture Vicksburg.
- (3/3) **The U.S. Congress enacts a draft**, affecting male citizens aged 20 to 45, but also exempts those who pay $300 or provide a substitute. "The blood of a poor man is as precious as that of the wealthy," poor Northerners complain.
- (3/24) **General Humphrey Marshall's** Confederate infantry attempts to take the town of Louisa, Lawrence County, attacking a portion of General White's Federal forces and is repulsed when the Federals are reinforced.
- (Late in March) **Humphrey Marshall's** forces form outside Louisa ready to give battle. Inexplicably, he refuses to do so, leaving his position overnight.
- (4/1) The 39th Kentucky and the 10th Kentucky (USA) set out after Marshall's supply train.
- (5/1-4) The Union Army under Gen. Hooker is decisively defeated by Lee's much smaller forces at the **Battle of Chancellorsville** in Virginia as a result of Lee's brilliant and daring tactics. **Confederate Gen. Stonewall Jackson is mortally wounded by his own soldiers**. Hooker retreats. Union losses are 17,000 killed, wounded and missing out of 130,000. The Confederates, 13, 000 out of 60,000.

- (5/10) The South suffers a huge blow as **Stonewall Jackson dies** from his wounds, his last words, "Let us cross over the river and rest under the shade of the trees." "I have lost my right arm," Lee laments.
- (June) The Northwestern counties of Virginia break away from the rest of Virginia and form the loyalist state of **West Virginia**.
- (6/3) **Gen. Lee** with 75,000 Confederates launches his second invasion of the North, heading into Pennsylvania in a campaign that will soon lead to Gettysburg.
- (6/28) President Lincoln appoints **Gen. George G. Meade** as commander of the Army of the Potomac, replacing Hooker. Meade is the 5th man to command the Army in less than a year.
- (7/1-3) The tide of war turns against the South as the Confederates are defeated at **the Battle of Gettysburg** in Pennsylvania.
- (7/4) **Vicksburg,** The last Confederate stronghold on the Mississippi River, surrenders to Gen. Grant and the Army of the West after a six week siege. With the Union now in control of the Mississippi, the Confederacy is effectively split in two, cut off from its western allies**.**
- (7/7) **The Second Ohio and 10th KY CAV USA** march through the Big Sandy River Pass and Pound Gap and invade Gladevillle (Wise) about daylight capturing both Morgan T. Lipps, County Clerk, and Alexander Smith, Commonwealth's Attorney. Mr. Smith is released immediately, but Elder Morgan T. Lipps, a Primitive Baptist preacher, is taken to Pikeville and later to Louisa, Kentucky, and remains a prisoner for three months before he is released.
- (7/13-16) Anti-draft riots in New York City include arson and the murder of blacks by poor immigrant whites. At least 120 persons, including children, are killed and $2 million in damage caused, until Union soldiers returning from Gettysburg restore order.
- (7/17) **Molly Tynes** rides across the mountains from Tazewell to Wytheville to warn the town of an attack by Federal forces under Colonel J. T. Toland.
- **The Federal cavalry raids Wytheville** in Wythe County, Virginia, the people of the town grab their guns and engaged them.
- At dawn on July 20, 1863 the Confederate Cavalry of **Maj. Andrew J. May** surprises a Union raiding party led by **Lt. Col. Freeman E. Franklin**. Aroused from his bivouac in Brown's Meadow, where it was preparing to burn the Falls Mill, the Union cavalry flees north toward Abb's Valley. Brig. Gen. John S. Williams' Confederate Cavalry strikes the raiders as they withdrew up the valley, compelling them to abandon captured livestock and contraband slaves.
- (7/31) **Gen. Burnside** declares martial law in Kentucky.
- (8/21) At Lawrence, Kansas, pro-Confederate **William C. Quantrill** and 450 pro-slavery followers raid the town and butcher 182 boys and men.
- (9/19-20) A decisive Confederate victory by **Gen. Braxton Bragg's Army** of Tennessee at **Chickamauga** leaves **Gen. William S. Rosecrans' Union Army of the Cumberland** trapped in Chattanooga, Tennessee under Confederate siege.
- (10/16) The president appoints **Gen. Grant** to command all operations in the western theater.
- (11/19) President Lincoln delivers a two minute **Gettysburg Address** at a ceremony dedicating the Battlefield as a National Cemetery.

- (11/23-25) **The Rebel siege of Chattanooga** ends as Union forces under Grant defeat the siege army of Gen. Braxton Bragg. During the battle, one of the most dramatic moments of the war occurs. Yelling "Chickamauga! Chickamauga!" Union troops avenge their previous defeat at Chickamauga by storming up the face of **Missionary Ridge** without orders and sweep the Rebels from what had been thought to be an impregnable position. "My God, come and see 'em run!" a Union soldier cries.
- (12/7) **The 39th Kentucky** is involved in action at Pound Gap.
- (12/10) **Col. John Dils, Jr.** is dismissed from command of the 39th Kentucky.

1864– (2/15) **Elements of the 39th Kentucky with the 14th** capture **Col. Ferguson and portions of the 16th Virginia Cavalry at Laurel Creek, WV.**
- (March) **Jack May** reassumes command of the **10th Kentucky Cavalry**, but finds that all five of the Buchanan County companies have deserted and returned to their homes.
- (3/9) **President Lincoln** appoints **Gen. Grant** to command all of the armies of the United States.
- (April) **Marauders** infiltrate the **Big Moccasin Valley** of Scott County.
  From the Ironton Register, April 14, 1864: "Private dispatches are to the effect, that the rebels, emboldened by the continued inactivity of the Union troops, up Sandy, had previous to that time (April 4th) penetrated their lines as far as Peach Orchard, at which place they robbed Col. Dill's store of about $700 worth of goods, and the clerk of $43; Captain Soward's store of $500. Henry Danby, agent of the Great Western Mining Company, was robbed of $200. The number killed, taken prisoner and captured horses is as stated in the dispatch, but it was locking the door after the thief had departed. Guerrillas are reported on the increase, and stirring times are apprehended in that quarter."
- (May) In the west, **Gen. Sherman**, with 100,000 men begins an advance toward Atlanta to engage **Gen. Joseph E. Johnston's** 60,000 strong Army of Tennessee.
- (5/4) The beginning of a massive, coordinated campaign involving all the Union Armies. In Virginia, **Grant with an Army of 120,000 begins advancing toward Richmond to engage Lee's Army of Northern Virginia**, now numbering 64,000, beginning a war of attrition that will include major battles at the **Wilderness** (May 5-6), **Spotsylvania** (May 8-12), and **Cold Harbor** (June 1-3).
- (June) - **Gen. John H. Morgan**, on his Kentucky raid, forces Pound Gap from the Virginia side, capturing and destroying much property.
- (6/15) Union forces miss an opportunity to capture **Petersburg** and cut off the Confederate rail lines. As a result, a nine month siege of Petersburg begins with Grant's forces surrounding Lee.
- (9/2) **Atlanta is captured by Sherman's Army**. "Atlanta is ours, and fairly won," Sherman telegraphs Lincoln. The victory greatly helps President Lincoln's bid for re-election.
- (9/3) **Gen. John H. Morgan** is betrayed and murdered by Federal Troops while in the residence of Mrs. Dr. Williams, in Greeneville, Tenn.
  Burbridge moves from Pikeville up the Big Sandy to Grundy, VA. From there he proceeds over the mountains through Richlands by the end of the month.

- (9/28) **Burbridge's** forces move through Buchanan County on their way to Saltville.
- (10/2) **The Battle of Saltville, VA.** - outnumbered Confederate cavalry troops repulse the advance of Union troops, including members of the 5th U.S. Colored Cavalry.
- (10/3) **The "Saltville Massacre"** takes place. According to some accounts, Confederate soldiers kill from five to seven wounded prisoners who are members of the 5th U.S. Colored Cavalry, along with a white lieutenant.
- (10/19) A decisive Union victory by **Cavalry Gen. Philip H. Sheridan** in the Shenandoah Valley over **Jubal Early's troops.**
- (11/4) A large body of guerrillas, under **Witcher and Bill Smith**, makes a raid on **Peach Orchard, Lawrence Co**, Ky., 45 miles from the mouth of Big Sandy River, captures Col. Dills, of the 39th Ky., burns two little steamers and some houses, and pillages the stores.
- (11/15) After destroying Atlanta's warehouses and railroad facilities, **Gen. Sherman,** with 62,000 men begins a **March to the Sea**. President Lincoln on advice from Grant approved the idea. "I can make Georgia howl!" Sherman boasts.
- (11/21) **Elements of the 39th** refuse to leave the region when the unit is ordered to make an expedition into Virginia against Saltville and the lead works at Austinville, south of Wytheville, Va.
- (12/13) **The Battle of Kingsport** takes place at Ross's Bridge when Federal Troops, on their way to Saltville, are confronted by Confederate Troops guarding the bridge across the North Fork of the Holston River. The Confederates are heavily outnumbered but manage to delay the column for a time before being forced to give way.
- (12/15) **Abingdon** is burned by Federal Troops.
- (12/15-16) **Hood's Rebel Army** of 23,000 is crushed at Nashville by 55,000 Federals including Negro troops under **Gen. George H. Thomas**. The Confederate Army of Tennessee ceases as an effective fighting force.
- **Union General George Stoneman** captures Saltville, destroying the town's salt mines which are crucial in supplying provisions for the Confederate army. The damage is quickly repaired and the salt production back in operation.
- (12/21) **Gen. Sherman** reaches Savannah in Georgia leaving behind a 300 mile long path of destruction 60 miles wide all the way from Atlanta. Sherman then telegraphs Lincoln, offering him Savannah as a Christmas present.
- (12/24) **"Rebel" Bill Smith** completes organization of at least six to eight hundred men into **"Smith's Battalion."**

1865-For four years **the border between Kentucky and Virginia** is no-man's land. Soldiers from both armies pass through looking for food or patrolling the area. As deserters congregate in bands and use the mountains to conceal themselves, they frequently turn their military training on civilians to survive, adding to the instability of the region. The region itself is largely pro-Confederate, but many of the men who live in this contested area remain at home to fight the war in their own way, often forced to use bushwhacking tactics to protect their families.

- (1/31) The U.S. Congress approves the **Thirteenth Amendment to the United States Constitution,** to abolish slavery. The amendment is then submitted to the states for ratification.

- (2/3) **A peace conference occurs as President Lincoln meets with Confederate Vice President Alexander Stephens** at Hampton Roads in Virginia, but the meeting ends in failure - the war will continue.

- Only Lee's Army at Petersburg and Johnston's forces in North Carolina remain to fight for the South against Northern forces now numbering 280,000 men.

- (3/4) **Inauguration ceremonies for President Lincoln** in Washington. "With Malice toward none; with charity for all...let us strive on to finish the work we are in...to do all which may achieve and cherish a just, and a lasting peace, among ourselves, and with all nations," Lincoln says.

- (3/25) **The last offensive for Lee's Army of Northern Virginia** begins with an attack on the center of Grant's forces at Petersburg. Four hours later the attack is broken.

- (4/2) Grant's forces begin a general advance and break through Lee's lines at **Petersburg**. **Confederate Gen. Ambrose P. Hill** is killed. Lee evacuates Petersburg. The Confederate Capital, Richmond, is evacuated. Fires and looting break out. The next day, Union troops enter and raise the Stars and Stripes.

- (4/9) **Gen. Robert E. Lee surrenders his Confederate Army to Gen. Ulysses S. Grant at the village of Appomattox Court House** in Virginia. Grant allows Rebel officers to keep their sidearms and permits soldiers to keep horses and mules. "After four years of arduous service marked by unsurpassed courage and fortitude the Army of Northern Virginia has been compelled to yield to overwhelming numbers and resources," Lee tells his troops.

- (4/14) The Stars and Stripes is ceremoniously raised over Fort Sumter. That night, Lincoln and his wife Mary see the play "Our American Cousin" at Ford's Theater. At 10:13 p.m., during the third act of the play, **John Wilkes Booth shoots the president in the head**. Doctors attend to the president in the theater then move him to a house across the street. He never regains consciousness

- (4/15) **President Abraham Lincoln dies** at 7:22 in the morning. **Vice President Andrew Johnson assumes the presidency.**

- (4/26) **John Wilkes Booth** is shot and killed in a tobacco barn in Virginia.

- (May) **Remaining Confederate forces surrender.** The Nation is reunited as the Civil War ends. Over 620,000 Americans died in the war, with disease killing twice as many as those lost in battle. 50,000 survivors return home as amputees.

- (12/6) **The Thirteenth Amendment to the United States Constitution,** passed by Congress on January 31, 1865, is finally ratified. Slavery is abolished.

1866 - The 16 year old son of **Valentine Bush** is shot and killed from ambush, by an unknown assassin, at the forks of Amos Branch, East of where Bush's Mill is later built, outside Nickelsville, Va..

1867 – (3/30) The U.S. acquires **Alaska** from Russia for the sum of $7.2 million

1870 - **Scott County, Va.** is laid out into 7 Magisterial Districts.
   -(November) The first public (free) schools are opened in Scott County.

1871 – (10/8-9) **The Chicago fire** kills 300 and leaves 90,000 people homeless.

1875 - Members of the **James gang** pay a visit to the bank in Huntington, WV, "withdrawing" between ten and twelve thousand dollars.

1876 – (6/25) **Lt. Col. George A. Custer's** regiment is wiped out by Sioux Indians under Sitting Bull at the Little Big Horn River, Mont

1877 - **The first telephone line** is built from Boston to Somerville, Mass.; the following year, President Hayes has the first telephone installed in the White House.

1880 – **Commercial Rafting begins on the Clinch River, in Virginia**. Used primarily for shipping timber, the practice continued until the railroads eventually replaced the river as the preferred mode of transportation.
   - Beginning during the 1880's, the Southern Appalachian mountains become the scene of a major logging boom which continues until the 1920's. Such companies as the Kentucky Coal and Timber Company of New York; the Chicago Lumber Company; the American Associates Ltd of London, England; Burt and Babb Lumber Company of Michigan; the Yellow Popular Lumber Company of Ohio; and W.M. Ritter of Pennsylvania – made large fortunes denuding large swathes of the Appalachian Forest.
   - **James Garfield** defeates Winfield Hancock in the U.S. presidential election.

1881 - **James A. Garfield** is inaugurated as the 20th president (March 4). He is shot (July 2) by Charles Guiteau in Washington, DC, and later dies from complications of his wounds in Elberon, N.J. (Sept. 19). Garfield's vice president, **Chester Alan Arthur**, succeeds him in office.
   - (10/26) The **Gunfight at the O.K. Corral** takes place in Tombstone, Arizona.

1882 – (4/3) **Outlaw Jesse James** is shot and killed by Robert Ford.
   - (9/5) The first commemoration of **Labor Day** was held in New York City when 10,000 workers held a march.

1884 - In the presidential election of 1884 **Grover Cleveland**, despite a paternity scandal, defeated James G. Blaine, whose gaffe about "rum, Romanism, and rebellion" probably cost him the presidency.

1885 – (3/4) **Grover Cleveland** is inaugurated as the 22nd president.

1886 – (10/28) **The Statue of Liberty** is dedicated.
   - (6/2) **President Grover Cleveland** married Frances Folsom in the White House, thus becoming the only president to be married in the executive mansion.

1887 - The first passenger train reaches **Bratton's Switch** (Gate City).
- **The Abingdon Coal and Iron Railroad Company** is organized and builds the **Virginia Creeper Line**.

1888 - **Big Stone Gap**, originally known as Three Forks, is chartered as a Town. (2/23)
- **The Louisville and Nashville Railroad's (L & N) Cumberland Valley Division** is built from Cumberland Gap to Norton, Va., into the coal fields.

1889 – (3/4) **Benjamin Harrison** is inaugurated as the 23rd president.

1890 – **The South Atlantic & Ohio Rail Road (SA & O)**, owned by the Virginia, Tennessee & Carolina Steel and Iron Company), is opened from Bristol to Big Stone Gap, Va. Via the "Natural Tunnel".
- **Battle of Wounded Knee** – 200 Native American women and children are massacred by U.S. troops.
- Sometime in the 1890's William Gray builds a school on his property near Dungannon.

1893 – **The Clinch Valley Division of the N & W Railroad** is opened from Bluefield to Norton, Va.
- **The Holston Salt and Plaster Corp.**, is sold to **the Mathieson Alkali Works** and the company ultimately dominates the town of Saltville, owning most of the land, it operates the utilities, pays the salaries of the police and teachers, etc.
- **Grover Cleveland** is inaugurated a second time, as the 24th president.

1894 - **The Town of Coeburn, which was originally called Gist's Station,** is chartered at the site where, according to legend, one of Christopher Gist's exploring camps was established in 1750.

1895 – (Feb) **Cuba fights for independence from Spain.** As Cuba struggles to win its freedom from Spain, American newspapers publish sensational stories about Spain's brutality toward the Cubans. Some Americans begin to call for the U.S. to get involved in the fight.

1896 - Construction is begun on **Bush's Mill** on Amos's Branch outside of Nickelsville, Va. (completed in Sept. 1897) The first bushel of corn was ground 9/24/1897. by W.T. Frazier and Frank Stewart. Jim Stewart, the first mill-right, builds the original wheel from wood. The first owners are W.T. Frazier and his brothers-in-law, Steve and Bill Bush.
- **The Interstate Railroad** (1896 – 1923) is built to serve the emerging coal fields of Southwestern Virginia, carrying coal to other railroads for distribution.
- (5/18) **Plessy v. Ferguson**: Landmark Supreme Court decision holds that racial segregation is constitutional, paving the way for the repressive **Jim Crow laws** in the South.

1897 - **Drayton S. Hale** has a 300' x 7' x 7' tunnel dug through a narrow ridge on Copper

Creek, called "the dog's tail". The job takes 7 years and creates a sluice through which part of the creek is diverted and powers his rolling mill, corn mill, saw mill, and rock crusher. The mill is in operation until Hale's death in 1916.
- (3/4) **William McKinley** is inaugurated as the 25th president

1898 – (2/15) The battleship the **U.S.S. Maine** explodes and sinks in a Havana harbor. The cause is not known, but many blame Spain.
- (4/9) Spain agrees to an armistice, which will halt the fighting with Cuba. However, Spain only agrees to allow Cuba to have limited self-government and the U.S. Congress gives President William McKinley the right to use force against Spain.
- (4/11) **President McKinley** reluctantly asks Congress to declare war on Spain. Even though McKinley hoped to avoid war, he asks Congress to declare war on Spain. McKinley is pressured by American newspapers that call him a weak president for not standing up to Spain.
- (4/20) Congress passes the **Teller Amendment**. Congress responds to McKinley's war speech with the Teller Amendment. The amendment, which McKinley signs, says that the U.S. cannot annex Cuba.
- (4/24) **Spain declares war against the United States**. Although they are not ready for a war with the U.S., Spain declares war on the United States. The U.S. declares war against Spain the next day.
- (5/1) In the first battle of the war, the U.S. destroys Spain's fleet of ships in the **Battle of Manila Bay**. Four hundred Spanish sailors are killed, while only six Americans are wounded.
- (7/1) **U.S forces attack Spain on the southern coast of Cuba**. Spanish troops at **San Juan Hill** and **Kettle Hill** are overwhelmed by U.S. troops, including the **Rough Riders, led by Teddy Roosevelt**. The win permits the U.S. to launch a siege of Santiago de Cuba.
- (7/7) U.S. annexes **Hawaii** by an act of Congress
- (7/17) The Spanish fleet in the Caribbean is destroyed in the **Battle of Santiago**. After a relatively easy fight with Spain, the U.S. and Spain agree to stop fighting and sign a cease-fire agreement. The war unofficially comes to an end.
- (8/13) **U.S. troops capture Manila in a mock battle**. U.S. and Spanish troops stage a mock battle in the Philippine capital of Manila. It was predetermined that Spain would surrender and allow the U.S. to take control of the Philippines.
- (12/10) The U.S. and Spain sign the **Treaty of Paris**. The Spanish-American War officially ends when the U.S. and Spain sign the Treaty of Paris. The U.S. takes possession of Guam, the Philippines, and Puerto Rico for $20 million.

1899 - **The Philippines** declares itself an independent republic. The Philippines rejects U.S. rule and declares itself an independent republic, beginning the Philippine-American war. After the U.S. defeats the Philippines, revolution leader Emilio Aguinaldo is captured and forced to pledge allegiance to the American government.
- (12/2) U.S. acquires **American Samoa** by treaty with Great Britain and Germany.

1900 - **The Foraker Act** establishes the structure of government in Puerto Rico. After the U.S. takes possession of Puerto Rico, it is necessary to set up a government. The Foraker Act calls for elements including a governor, a House of Representatives, and a Supreme Court.

1902 – **The Treaty of Paris** calls for Cuba to be independent from the U.S and American troops withdraw. Cuba will experience years of turbulent leadership the decades to come.

Tecumseh

On a starry night in 1768 a Shawnee woman labored in a birth hut near present day Chillicothe, in south-central Ohio. As the male child made his way into the world a bright yellow/green meteor streaked across the sky lighting up the camp before it crashed somewhere over the horizon. The Shawnee believed that within the first ten days of a baby's life the great spirit would send a sign that would indicate the name it should be given. They were to be very observant for the sign (unsoma) that would give them this important information – and this clearly must be a powerful sign. His father exclaimed, "Oh what a man this will be, with such a sign as that." They named him Tecumseh (Panther in the Sky)! He grew up surrounded by the almost constant border warfare that ravaged the Ohio Valley in the last quarter of the 18th century.

His father, Puckeshinwa (Hard Striker) a minor war chief, was killed in the Battle of Point Pleasant during the French and Indian War, when Tecumseh was six. As he lay dying he supposedly told his son, Chiksika, to never make peace with the Virginians and to supervise the warrior training of his other male children. Tecumseh's mother, Methoataske (Turtle Mother), later migrated with other Shawnee to Missouri and left him to be raised by his older sister, Tecumpease (Sky Watcher) who had also observed the meteor the night he was born.

During his teenage years Tecumseh joined a confederation of Native Americans led by Mohawk Chief Joseph Brant. Brant encouraged tribes to pool their resources and defend their territory against the white mans' encroachment. Tecumseh led a raiding party attacking white settlers' boats making their way down the Ohio River and was successful in cutting off river travel for a time. However, Tecumseh was appalled by the brutality displayed by both white and Native Americans, and after witnessing a white man burned at the stake, Tecumseh vehemently chastised his fellow tribesmen for their actions.

The Shawnee continued to wage war against the encroaching white-men they felt were settling on their land, and in 1788, Tecumseh's older brother Chiksika was fatally wounded while attacking a stockade in present-day Tennessee.

In the fall of 1790, the Shawnee and Miami tribes repelled an assault on their villages near todays Fort Wayne, Indiana killing 183 U.S. troops in the process. President George Washington authorized a new campaign the following year with Governor Arthur St. Clair of the Northwest Territory in charge of some 2,300 men. On the march north from modern Cincinnati hundreds of them deserted as the weather worsened and food supplies ran low. For nearly two months the remaining troops failed to make contact with the native tribes and grew complacent. On November 3 the soldiers set up camp along the Wabash River in western Ohio. Washington had advised St. Clair to "beware of surprise" but he posted few guards and built no barricades. The next morning as the soldiers prepared breakfast a force of Native Americans attacked and immediately overran them. Poorly trained militiamen fled and the regulars who kept their position were decimated. When the battle was over, a few hours later, at least 623 American soldiers and dozens of camp followers were dead and hundreds more were wounded.

The victory over St. Clair and the white-men proved to be short lived and their defeat in 1794, at the Battle of Fallen Timbers, forced the Native Americans to give up most of present-day Ohio and part of Indiana. Another of Tecumseh's brothers, Sauwauseekau, was shot and killed during the battle. Tecumseh was so bitter about the defeat that he refused to attend the subsequent negotiations or to acknowledge the Treaty of Greenville. He sharply criticized the "peace" chiefs who signed away land that he believed wasn't theirs to give, asserting that the land was like the air and water, a common possession of all Native Americans. He proclaimed that every tribal leader who signed them "should have his thumb cut off." He began to envision a confederacy that would bring all of the remaining Native tribes together—even longtime enemies—to resist the whites' insatiable desire for Indian land.

In 1806 Tecumseh traveled with a small contingency of a few hundred tribesmen to what is now Indiana and joined his brother, Tenskwatawa, who had recently become a prominent Native American religious leader known as the Prophet. Using his superior oratory skills over time Tecumseh transformed his brother's religious following into a political movement that discouraged Native Americans from assimilation into the white world. That same year Tecumseh met with British officials in Canada. He then traveled widely in the Midwest gaining followers among such tribes as the Seneca, Wyandot, Sac, Fox, Winnebago, Potawatomi, Kickapoo, Chippewa, Ottawa, Delaware, Miami and, of course, Shawnee. Tecumseh even made it as far south as present-day Alabama and Mississippi, where he preached with limited success to Chickasaws, Choctaws and Creeks. "I have heard many great orators, but I never saw one with the vocal powers of Tecumseh or the same command of the muscles in his face," recalled a white soldier who saw one of his speeches.

And the speeches of Tecumseh were drawing Native Americans of all tribes to join him. This collection of Indians with a common bond greatly concerned the expanding white settlers. The country was growing quickly and the Ohio River was an important component of that expansion. Having an "enemy" so close was not a comfortable situation. Although each side talked of peace, each also made maneuvers to undermine the other both politically and in minor battles. William Henry Harrison was looking for a way to discredit the brothers in the eyes of the Indians. The Prophet claimed to have almost divine powers, so Harrison decided to put forth a challenge. Perhaps drawing from his Christian upbringing as a base he wrote an open letter to the Indians gathered at Tippecanoe. "If he (the Prophet) is really a prophet ask him to cause the Sun to stand still or the Moon to alter its course, the rivers to cease to flow, or the dead to rise from their graves". In other words, he wanted to see them produce a miracle of biblical proportions. What he did not expect was the reaction of the Indians to this request. For them this request had a different meaning.

This letter was presented to the brothers when they were visiting a friend along the White River. One story has the two of them going inside to meet in private. After an hour had passed the Prophet requested that all in the village be assembled for him to deliver his response. He said he had consulted with the Great Spirit and that he was not happy about Harrison's request. Thus the Great Spirit had agreed to give a sign that the Prophet could share with others in advance to demonstrate just how closely related they were. The Prophet spoke in a loud and confident voice saying that: "Fifty days from this day there will be no cloud in the sky. Yet, when the Sun has reached its highest point, at that moment will the Great Spirit take it into her hand and hide it from us. The darkness of night will thereupon cover us and the stars will shine round about us. The birds will roost and the night creatures will awaken and stir."

At around noon on the appointed day, June 16th 1806, a total solar eclipse crossed the region stretching from near the southern tip of Lake Michigan to just north of Cincinnati encompassing most of the lands inhabited by Tenskwatawa's followers. In Greenville where Tenskwatawa and Tecumseh waited for the event close to a thousand had gathered to see the Prophet's sign. The Prophet waved his arms towards the eclipse at the appropriate time and the people were truly impressed.

While Tecumseh was traveling through the south in the fall of 1811 William Henry Harrison, then governor of the Indiana Territory, decided to march on Prophetstown. Tecumseh had told his brother to avoid war with the Americans but when soldiers advanced to within a mile of the town on November 6, the Prophet greenlighted a preemptive strike. He assured his followers that white bullets could not hurt them and during the next morning's fighting he purportedly sat on a rock singing incantations. In the end, though the Native Americans likely suffered fewer casualties than their opponents in the Battle of Tippecanoe, they were forced to retreat and abandon Prophetstown. Harrison then burned it to the ground.

Upon returning home in January 1812 Tecumseh found his brother's reputation destroyed and his confederacy badly weakened. When the War of 1812 began in June Tecumseh assembled his followers and joined the British forces at Fort Malden on the Canadian side of the Detroit River. There he brought together perhaps the most formidable force ever commanded by a North American Indian, an accomplishment that was a decisive factor in the capture of Detroit and 2,500 U.S. soldiers.

Fired with the promise of triumph after the fall of Detroit Tecumseh departed on another long journey to arouse the tribes. His speeches resulted in the uprising of the Alabama Creeks though the Chickasaws, Choctaws, and Cherokees rebuffed him. He returned north and joined British General Henry A. Procter in his invasion of Ohio. Together they besieged Fort Meigs held by William Henry Harrison on the Maumee River above Toledo. Tecumseh intercepted and destroyed a brigade of Kentuckians under Col. William Dudley that had been coming to Harrison's relief. He and Procter failed to capture the fort however and were put on the defensive by Oliver Hazard Perry's decisive victory over the British fleet in the Battle of Lake Erie (September 10, 1813). Seizing the opportunity Harrison invaded Canada. Tecumseh and his Indian force reluctantly accompanied the retreating British who Harrison pursued to the Thames River in present-day southern Ontario. There on October 5, 1813 the British and Indians were routed and Harrison won control of the Northwest. Tecumseh directing most of the fighting was killed. His body was carried from the field and buried secretly in a grave that has never been discovered.

(This article was inspired by stories in: "A Sorrow in our Heart: The Life of Tecumseh" and "The Frontiersmen", by Allan Eckert, and "Panther In The Sky" by James Alexander Thom, each of which are excellent semi-fictional works, and the Encyclopedia Britannica, The History Channel, Ohiohistory.org, and "Tecumseh and the Eclipse Chasers" by Bill Kramer.)

The Lead Mines In Austinville, Virginia

In 1756 Colonel John Chiswell, a British Officer and a native of Wales, was exploring the area between the New River and what is now Wytheville, Virginia. According to oral traditions he encountered an Indian Raiding Party and in an effort to allude them hastily hid himself in a small cave on a bluff on the south side of the river. When the danger had passed he began to investigate the cave and found a vein of lead along one of its walls. Realizing the importance of his discovery he made arrangements to purchase the property around the cave and he and William Byrd soon began to mine the valuable resource. In 1758 a fort was built about 9 miles north of the lead mine by Byrd and named Fort Chiswell in his honor. Famous visitors to the lead mines during colonial days included Daniel Boone, General Andrew Lewis, and Thomas Jefferson.

On June 3, 1766 Col. Chiswell, a Loyalist, was involved in a drunken altercation with a "Scotch gentleman" named Robert Routledge at Mosby's Tavern near Richmond, Va.. After calling him "a fugitive rebel, a villain who came to Virginia to cheat and defraud men of their property, and a Presbyterian fellow", Col. Chiswell ordered him to leave. When Routledge refused Chiswell drew his sword and stabbed him through the heart. He was shortly arrested but soon released to his own home on bail causing a public outcry of favoritism. On October 14, 1766, Col. Chiswell was found dead in his home in Williamsburg. The coroner called it suicide from "an attack of his nerves".

The lead mine was in continuous private operation until the time of the Revolutionary War when it was taken over by the State and used to provide lead for Washington's Army. In 1780 the lead works were sold by the state at auction to two Austin brothers, Moses and Stephen. The Austin family operated the mine until 1800. By 1798 the community at the mines had become known as Austinville and Moses' son, Stephen F. Austin, later to become the "Father of Texas," had been born. The Austin family left Virginia for Missouri in 1800 to seek their destiny in the West. Thomas Jackson, an English immigrant who arrived in the Lead mines area in 1785, and two other partners acquired the lead mines from the state at auction in 1806.

In 1820 a shot tower was built about three and one-fourth miles northeast of the mines. It was located on a bluff on the south bank of New River at Jackson's Ferry overlooking the junction of Shorts Creek. Lead from the nearby Austinville Mines was melted in a kettle atop the 75-foot tower and poured through a sieve. The molten lead fell through the tower and an additional 75-foot shaft beneath the tower into a kettle of water. As the lead fell it cooled and was formed into almost perfectly round balls, an ingenious and efficient method still in use today.

OLD SHOT SHAFT AT THE LEAD MINES
AUSTINVILLE, VIRGINIA

As the Civil War loomed ever closer on the horizon it was obvious to war planners that certain mined resources were absolutely essential - salt, iron, niter (saltpeter), and lead. Salt was essential to pack and preserve meat and other foodstuffs; iron was needed for implements, armaments, and railroads; niter was the main ingredient for gunpowder; and lead was used to make bullets, which at that time were cast lead projectiles of approximately 50 caliber size. No state was more crucial to the Confederate war effort from the standpoint of providing these materials than Virginia (Boyle, 1936). The Old Dominion ranked first in the production of each of these resources except iron, where she was a close second to Alabama. Virginia also had the most railroad track mileage of any southern state over which these vital materials could move. Of all her mineral contributions to the Confederacy Virginia's production of lead might be the most significant.

Within a short time after the war began the Confederate government demanded that the management of the lead mines either work the mines to their utmost capacity or surrender them for operation by the government. The directors of the company, fearing that the property would be destroyed if it were managed by government officials, agreed to the first alternative. The government, in time, made it possible for the mines to have a supply of labor sufficient to maintain production. Dependable estimates are hard to arrive at but reports after the war by Confederate Ordnance officers indicate that around 3,500,000 pounds of lead were produced at the Wythe County mines during the war. This constitutes about one-third of the estimated 10,000,000 pounds of lead consumed by the entire Confederacy in the manufacture of 150,000,000 cartridges used by its armies (Robertson, 1993).

During the war years the South had three principal sources of lead: that which was domestically produced, supplies stockpiled before the war began, and stores smuggled in through the Federal blockade. So valuable was it to the resource-strapped South that southern soldiers actually scoured the battlefields after engagements to recover spent lead ammunition. Civilians were asked to contribute lead in the form of utensils, pipes, roofing, and even window weights. In the later years of the conflict, as pre-war stockpiles and smuggled quantities became increasingly scarce, the Confederacy came to rely almost exclusively on the one significant lead mining operation in the entire South - the lead mines in Wythe County, Virginia.

During the first two years of the Civil War there was little military action in southwestern Virginia. One of the most significant events during that time was the Federal capture of nearby West Virginia. West Virginia remained firmly in Union hands from 1862 on and served as an important launching point for periodic Union raids into southwestern Virginia. By spring of 1863 Federal strategists had begun to recognize the military significance of the salt and lead operations in this area as well as the importance of the Virginia and Tennessee Railroad. This great railroad, running from Lynchburg westward to Big Lick (Roanoke) and then down the Great Valley of Virginia to Bristol and beyond, provided the most direct rail link between Richmond and the western theater battlefronts (Noe, 1994). Both troops and wartime commodities, including Wythe County lead, moved along this vital railroad.

Early in July, 1863 Lee was beaten at Gettysburg and in retreat. Federal high command in West Virginia decided that this was a good time to attack southwestern Virginia, in particular, the salt works at Saltville (Walker, 1985). On July 13 Union Colonel John Toland left Charleston with about 1,000 calvary and mounted infantry. Coming into Virginia through Abbs Valley Toland met and defeated a small rebel outpost in a brief skirmish there. Fearing that Saltville and its several hundred defenders would be forewarned, Toland switched his plans to an assault on Wytheville, hoping to destroy the railroad "High Bridge" west of town over Reed Creek. He also anticipated mounting an attack on the lead mines. By late afternoon on July 18 Toland was within sight of Wytheville. A small group of rebel defenders had been hastily assembled, consisting of local armed citizens and about 130 troops from the Confederate Department of Southwest Virginia, that had arrived from Dublin by train. A sharp fight broke out along the streets of downtown

Wytheville and Colonel Toland was killed. In about 45 minutes the Union forces overpowered the southern defenders and the Battle of Wytheville was over. But the Union command was decimated and the surviving ranking officer gathered his troops and retreated to West Virginia.

The damage created by Toland's raid was minimal. Parts of Wytheville were burned and some railroad track was damaged taking about an hour to repair. The crucial High Bridge was untouched and the lead mines never attacked. Indeed the lead mines home guard, consisting of two companies of miners, was called out to help defend Wytheville but arrived too late to join the battle. They simply turned around and went back home (Donnelly, 1959.

No real threats to the lead mines re-emerged until a year later. By May, 1864 Union Commander-in-Chief General Ulysses S. Grant had Federal forces on the move throughout Virginia (Marvel, 1992). In particular General Benjamin Butler was moving up the James River toward Richmond, General Franz Sigel was advancing southward in the Shenandoah Valley, and Grant himself was moving from the north toward the Wilderness area and ultimately Richmond. As part of this grand strategy a Union force under General George Crook advanced into southwestern Virginia again from West Virginia. This time the principal objectives were to attack Saltville and destroy the railroad "Long Bridge" over the New River at Central (Radford). Crook sent General William Averell and his cavalry to wreck the salt works. But Averell learned that Saltville was defended by General John Hunt Morgan and his fearsome cavalrymen and decided to move on to Wytheville and perhaps the lead mines. Morgan's troops caught up to Averell at Crockett's Cove near Wytheville and inflicted serious losses. Eventually Averell and Crook returned to West Virginia without doing serious damage to the railroad or getting anywhere near the salt and lead operations (McManus, 1989).

December, 1864 - the rapidly weakening Confederacy was on the brink of defeat. Grant was slowly and steadily closing the ring around Richmond and Lee's encircled Army of Northern Virginia. In southwestern Virginia Union scouting parties roamed at will and the citizens of the region faced not only Federal troops but outlaw bands of bushwhackers, murderers, and deserters from the Confederate army as well (Walker, 1985). But even at this late stage in the war the three great military targets of the region - the lead mines, the salt works, and the Virginia and Tennessee railroad – almost miraculously remained intact and operational.

General George Stoneman, an ambitious Union commander in eastern Tennessee, was determined to change all this. Stoneman left Knoxville, which by now was in Union hands, on December 10 with 5,500 men plus artillery pieces. Stoneman's troops moved northeastward along the Virginia and Tennessee railroad entering Virginia at Bristol. Advancing up the Great Valley Stoneman drove the Confederate forces before him (Evans, 1993). Railroad trestles, rolling stock and depots were eventually burned from Bristol to 10 miles north of Wytheville.

On December 16 Wytheville itself was taken by Stoneman's troops and partly burned. The next day Stoneman sent two regiments of soldiers to attack the lead mines (Walker, 1985; Marvel, 1992). The Union raiders of December 17, 1864 met no resistance at the lead mines as the small Confederate force assigned that task retreated at the approach of Stoneman's troops. The biggest obstacle to the Yankee soldiers was crossing the frigid New River to get to the mines. They successfully accomplished the crossing and in only two hours the mine offices, storehouses, stables, crushing machine, bellows, furnaces, and even the sawmill and gristmill went up in flames (Marvel, 1992).

Even with this much damage the mines were back again in production on March 22, 1865. By this time all the accumulated reserves of lead had been used up and the eastern armies of the Confederacy were completely dependent upon the day-to-day production of the Wythe County mines (Donnelly, 1959). With his objectives accomplished Stoneman withdrew from southwestern Virginia and returned to Knoxville on December 29. Behind him lay ruined railroad engines, cars, depots, and bridges, as well as the wrecked salt and lead production.

Surprisingly before the end of the war both the salt and lead works were back in operation and some traffic was moving on the railroad. On March 21, 1865 Stoneman returned to southwestern Virginia to complete its devastation. Federal troops once again attacked the lead mines on April 7 and destroyed the partially rebuilt plant as well as the assembled repair materials (Donnelly, 1959). But by then it didn't really matter. Two days later Lee surrendered at Appomattox and the bloodiest war in American history was over.

After the war Colonel William Broun of the Confederate Ordnance Department stated: "Our lead was obtained chiefly, and in the last years of the war entirely, from the lead mines at Wytheville, Virginia. The mines were worked night and day - and the lead converted into bullets as fast as received"

In the years afterwards, though owners came and went, the Lead Mines at Austinville continued to operate, producing a continuous supply of lead for various commercial and sometimes military markets. Over time zinc also was added to their list of marketable products.

On December 31, 1981 the oldest continuously operating mines in the entire United States closed when New Jersey Zinc Company permanently shut down its lead and zinc works in southern Wythe County, Virginia (Weinberg, 1981) - ending the fascinating 225-year-long story of a mining complex whose history is intricately intertwined with that of southwestern Virginia.

The Commercial Manufacture and Transportation of "White Gold" - - - Salt

The natural salt deposits and ponds in and around present-day Saltville, Va. have attracted the attention of countless migratory birds and animals for eons of time, certainly to that of the wooly mammoths, mastodons, sloths, and similar large prehistoric mammals. Later other herd animals such as buffalo, elk, and deer continued to use the old pathways to the unique valley in search of the same resource.

Native American tribes followed from the time of Clovis to more modern tribes. There is also evidence that a large village existed in the Saltville valley during the Woodland Period sometime between 1,500 BC and 1,500 AD. Dr. Jim Glanville and other researchers note that the Spanish encountered such a tribe (probably Yuchi) living there and trading salt with other tribes during their expedition of the 1540's.

Early explorers into the region did not fail to notice the unique value of this secluded valley either. In 1748 Col. James Patton led an expedition for the Loyal Land Company that was exploring and mapping land for their land grant from the British Crown. Accompanying him was Dr. Thomas Walker, John Buchanan, James Woods, and Charles Campbell. Their survey plat showed the site as the "Buffalo Lick" and on October 23, 1753, 330 acres of land, making up the heart of the "Salt Lick", was granted to Charles Campbell for thirty-five shillings by Lord Robert Dinwiddie in the name of George II, the King of England. At that time more than one-third of the grant area was covered by water.

Following Charles Campbell's death in 1767 his widow, Margaret Campbell, moved to Aspenvale, located some eight miles west of Marion, Va., near Seven-Mile Ford with her son William and her four daughters. William inherited the Salt Lick from his father.

In 1775, when he was thirty years old, William was commissioned as Captain in the first regiment of regular troops raised in Virginia. When Lord Dunmore ordered the removal of the colonists' gun powder from the arsenal in Williamsburg Captain Campbell led a detachment of riflemen to respond to Patrick Henry's call for volunteers and there met Henry and his sister Elizabeth who was living with him. Their friendship grew and on April 21, 1776 they were married and the couple moved to Aspenvale where their two children were later born.

Captain Campbell led the American volunteers in their defeat of Col. Patrick Ferguson and his British Loyalist Army in 1780 at King's Mountain. He won much acclaim for his leadership there and at Guilford Court House and was promoted to the rank of Brigadier General. In 1781 he left Aspenvale for the last time to join Lafayette near Williamsburg. Shortly before the siege of Yorktown he became ill and died at the home of Elizabeth's half-brother. Following his death the Salt Lick passed to his daughter, Sarah Buchanan Campbell.

In 1793 at the age of 15, Sarah married Gen. Francis Preston, the second son of Col. William Preston, and "the Preston name became indelibly associated with the salt lick". (Blackwell) Soon afterwards Francis dug a well on the property and began the extraction of salt for commercial purposes. He also began to aggressively buy up other land in the valley. In 1799, William King secured land and built a salt furnace in the valley as well and two years later he leased the early salt production facility owned by Francis Preston. In 1802 King also bought land to create King's Boat-Yard at the mouth of the North Fork of the Holston River (present day Kingsport, TN) primarily to receive the salt produced at his operation in Saltville and to ship it down river. The port, consisting of a wharf, warehouse, boarding house, and the right to build flat-boats, soon became a busy commercial center. The Town that grew around it was known as Christianville – and later Kingsport, Tennessee.

The Legend of Milly Wheatley

The Rye Cove area of Scott County still wasn't populated enough for safe travel in 1819. A story is told that in that year William Wheatley and his wife rode some distance to a religious service at a neighbor's house. The family only had one gun and Wheatley took it in case they encountered wild animals or bandits along the way.

The Wheatley children remained at home. Milly was the oldest at 17. Her brothers, "Anter" and Jackie were younger. The family, like most of those living around them, was poor and owned only a single hog that they were feeding to slaughter when it got fat and the weather turned cold. The hog pen was a short distance from the main house.

Around bedtime they heard the pig begin to squeal. The children ran to the window but could not see what was bothering it. Milly suspected it was being attacked by some sort of predator but had no idea just what kind. Since their parents had taken the gun they had no weapon with which to face any dangerous wild animal and weren't sure what to do.

Milly begged her brothers to do something but they refused to leave the cabin. The pig kept squealing and Milly eventually couldn't stand it. She ran out on the porch to see what was out there but it was impossible to see through the darkness. Soon she heard deep vicious growls from what sounded like a large predator. She suspected it was a bear but wasn't sure.

She again begged her brothers to go with her to save the pig. It was all they had for the approaching winter and she knew they would be hungry if it was killed. Her brothers were afraid and still refused to leave the safety of the cabin. Finally she had all she could take of the pitiful squealing from the pig, grabbed a long-handled iron skillet from the stove, and ran into the darkness in the direction of the pig pen.

Her brothers shouted for her to come back but she ignored them and kept running. Soon the noise of the battle grew louder and they knew by now she must have reached the pig pen. Then the sounds of the fight suddenly stopped. In the silence they heard the iron skillet ring out once, almost like a bell. Then twice more. The clanging of the skillet continued for what seemed like a long time but was probably only a couple of minutes. Then complete silence returned once again. The pig was quiet too and there was no further growling from what ever had attacked it. But Milly was not responding to their frantic calls to her. Both of them were now on the porch terrified that something bad might have happened to her. Just then from the darkness they heard her familiar voice yelling to them. "You fraidy cats can come on out here now." In spite of their continuing uncertainty they quickly ran to the sound of her voice.

Milly had not only defended the family pig with her trusty skillet she'd taken out one of the largest bear ever seen in the area at that time. The brothers helped her drag it out of the pig pen into the yard. Her parents returned soon afterwards to hear the amazing story from the excited boys and the family celebrated Milly's bravery long into the night. As news spread the next day neighbors came by to see the bear and hear the story for themselves. Meat from the bear was shared with the entire community.

Milly eventually married Rafe Kilgore in 1820. They made their home on the Rocky Fork of the Guest River near the Big Laurel area in Wise County.

As far as we know she never had to use her iron skillet again – that is to hunt bears.

William Gray

In 1813 William Gray married Nancy Green Stallard and soon afterward the couple built a log house on a hill overlooking a bend of Clinch River, a short distance downriver from Dungannon, in Scott County, VA, His wife's two grandfathers had previously cleared a spot there for their cabins when the area was still plagued by hostile Indians. On that hill "through both ingenuity and hard work he built his plantation of several hundred acres into a self-sufficient and productive farm that eventually made him one of the wealthiest men of his day'.

About 1835 William added a mill which provided important meal for his table and animals, and those of his neighbors. The mill stood until 1957 when it was torn down by one of William's great-grand son, Otto Dingus. Mr. Dingus shared his memories of some of the unique and unusual construction methods used in the old log mill house. The mill flume started about three hundred feet upstream from the mill where there was a small dam of earth and limestone rocks about three feet deep. It carried water down a steep incline and onto the large overshot wheel that turned the machinery.

Mr. Dingus recalls that his grandfather Dingus and his great grandfather, Billy Gray, were great friends. Once when his grandfather Dingus was visiting Billy Gray removed a brick from the chimney inside the house and showed him where he had some money hidden, since there were no banks in those times. That night Mr. Dingus did not sleep and come morning he went to Gray and

advised him to move the money. He feared that if it was stolen, he knowing its whereabouts might look suspicious and perhaps damage their lifelong friendship.

Near where Billy Gray's L-shaped log house once stood is a brick spring house where the family water supply came from and where the milk and butter were kept cool on hot days. It is shaded by a large catalpa tree that must be well over a century old and has been a home for wild bees for many years. The mill and spring house creek have large catalpa trees spaced from the spring house to where the creek empties into Clinch River planted by loving hands many years ago.

Sometime in the 1890's a school was built on the Gray property. Otto Dingus attended school there in 1899. His father lived across Clinch River and the children were rowed across the river in a flat boat to and from school. It is not known when the last school was taught there but some of the teachers were Cowan Stallard, Clara Kidd, Mozell Cox, Laura Rhoten, Maggie Wolfe and Bascom Dingus.

Upon a limestone point a short distance from the old mill site stands a rapidly deteriorating but architecturally intriguing Free Will Baptist Church built by Billy Gray. The lumber in the building is first quality whipsawed yellow poplar. Inside the church is one of the few "Mourner's benches" to be found anywhere. On the lawn of the church stands the solitary tomb of the builder with this epitaph: *In Memory of William Gray. Born February 13th 1806. Died January 14th 1888 - Age 81 years, 11 months, and 1 day* This was his last request to sleep by the Free Will Baptist Church he built. His grave could not be dug deep enough in the hard limestone rock so it was built partially above ground with limestone and mortar. The top of the tomb is covered with two flat limestone slabs about four inches thick.

Around the hillside from the church is a low opening in the hillside that one can only crawl into but which opens up inside to form a fair size cave. During the Civil War the Gray family hid their hams and bacon in the cool darkness to prevent them being taken by the contending armies and "bushwhackers"

(The author of the above account was not noted and is unknown to me. It is included because of its historical value.)

The Lewis & Clark Expedition
(The Corps of Discovery)

With the Louisiana Purchase in 1803 the territory of the United States doubled overnight. Months before the $15 million deal was finalized, however, President Thomas Jefferson won approval from Congress to send a team of explorers to find a passable water route west to the Pacific Ocean.

Jefferson appointed his personal secretary, Meriwether Lewis, to lead the "Corps of Discovery." Once Lewis grasped the full scope and challenges of the expedition he called on his Army friend and fellow Virginian, William Clark, to be his equal in command.

"If therefore there is anything... in this enterprise, which would induce you to participate with me in it's fatiegues, it's dangers and it's honors," Lewis wrote to Clark, "believe me there is no man on earth with whom I should feel equal pleasure in sharing them as with yourself."

What follows is a brief overview of this incredible expedition:

Ed Vebell/Getty Images

May 14, 1804

The Corps of Discovery embarks from Camp Dubois outside of St. Louis, Missouri, in a 55-foot keelboat to begin the westward journey up the Missouri River. Among the 41-man crew of volunteers, soldiers and one African American slave, is Patrick Gass, a carpenter from Pennsylvania. Gass writes in his journal about the expected dangers ahead, including "warlike nations of savages of gigantic stature" and impassable mountain ranges.

"The determined and resolute character, however, of the corps, and the confidence which pervaded all ranks dispelled every emotion of fear, and anxiety for the present," writes Gass, "[and] seemed to insure to us ample support in our future toils, suffering and dangers."

August 20, 1804

Sergeant Charles Floyd, the youngest man on the expedition, dies of a suspected ruptured appendix near modern-day Sioux City, Iowa. Amazingly, Floyd is the only death the team experiences during the entire two-year expedition.

September 25, 1804

Of all Lewis and Clark's encounters with Native American tribes, the meeting with the Teton Sioux (Lakota) near modern-day Pierre, South Dakota, is among the most tense. Jefferson had charged the Corps with Indian diplomacy, which consisted mainly of announcing the Louisiana Purchase and presenting tribal chiefs with peace medals and American flags.

But communication difficulties are common during the expedition, given that Lewis and Clark often rely on three-way translation (native language to French to English and back) or sign language to converse with chiefs who often have their own political agendas.

On this day the Teton Sioux mistake the explorers for merchants and don't like the idea of the Americans selling weapons to rival tribes up the Missouri River. A young Teton Sioux chief, trying to insert himself into the confrontation, feigns drunkenness and stumbles into Clark, who rashly draws his sword. In an instant, Clark's soldiers raise their rifles and the Teton braves draw their bows and arrows.

After exchanging angry threats and boasts through nervous interpreters Black Buffalo, the elder Chief, breaks the tension and calls for peace. After three tense and restless days at the Teton Sioux village the upriver journey is allowed to proceed.

November 11, 1804

With winter fast approaching the Corps builds a shelter and spends the winter at Fort Mandan in North Dakota among the friendly Mandan and Hitatsa Indians. Clark records that the natives there appear to be more "European" than any tribe they encounter, with many having light skin and hair. He also mentions that their houses and social customs seem unique. George Catlin, the famous painter, would later spend several years with the Mandan and came to believe they were descendants of the lost Welsh Party led by Prince Madoc (because of their language, customs, and the blond hair and blue eyes shared by many of the tribe).

On November 11 Clark makes a hasty scribble in his journal about the arrival of "two Squars of the Rock Mountain, purchased from the Indians by...a frenchmen." One of those nameless squaws is the famous Sacagawea.

Bettmann Archive/Getty Images

At first the value of Sacagawea to the expedition is not apparent. She is the 17-year-old, pregnant wife of Toussaint Charbonneau, a French-Canadian trader. Charbonneau was hired by Lewis and Clark as a Hidatsa interpreter. But it would not be long before Sacagawea proved to be an invaluable member of the expedition.

"Sacagawea helped Lewis and Clark in a number of ways," says Jay Buckley, a history professor at Brigham Young University and author of several books about Western exploration. "Both in letting native tribes know that they came in peace, as well as helping the men with finding edible plants to improve their health."

June 2, 1805

Lewis and Clark rely largely on information gathered from Indians and white traders to chart the fastest and safest route westward toward the Pacific. But they are fully unprepared for a major fork in the Missouri River in north-central Montana. Only one fork is the true Missouri and they will know it by a series of majestic waterfalls upstream mentioned by the Mandan-Hidatsa.

Lewis and Clark call for a vote. Thirty-one people vote for the right fork and only two vote for the left—those two were Lewis and Clark. Not willing to defy their men, Lewis and Clark send exploring parties up each fork and have them report back. A second vote is taken with exactly the same result.

"But the men, to their credit, say, 'We're going to follow you,'" says Buckley.

June 13, 1805

Anxious to prove he's right, Lewis scouts ahead of the rest of the Corps and is overjoyed (at first) to find the Great Falls, describing them as a "truly magnificent and sublimely grand object, which has from the commencement of time been concealed from the view of civilized man."

But it soon becomes clear that the portage around the Great Falls is going to be far more difficult than he expected. To help with the challenge the men cut down trees and fashion crude wagons. They then drag the canoes and equipment across miles of unforgiving, cactus-strewn terrain.

"It takes them almost a month and a half to take all of their gear 18 miles," says Buckley. "It's probably one of the slowest parts of the whole trip."

August 8, 1805

Before she was kidnapped by the Hidatsa at age 12, Sacagawea lived among the Shoshone people along the border of modern-day Montana and Idaho. By August of 1805 Lewis and Clark believe the fate of the expedition is in jeopardy. They conclude that their success depends on them finding the Shoshone and buying horses from them, and soon. It's the only way the Corps can hope to cross the Rocky Mountains before winter.

Depending on memories of traveling through the area during her childhood, Sacagawea provides valuable clues that they are on the right path. On August 8, Lewis writes in his journal:

"The Indian woman recognized the point of a high plain to our right which she informed us was not very distant from the summer retreat of her nation on a river beyond the mountains. . . . this hill she says her nation calls the beaver's head from a conceived resemblance. . . . she assures us that we shall either find her people on this river on the river immediately west of it's source. . . . as it is now all important with us to meet with those people as soon as possible."

August 17, 1805

The expedition finally make contact with the Shoshone and Sacagawea is joyfully reunited with her brother Cameahwait, who is now the Shoshone chief. This relationship and her ability to communicate their desire to purchase horses from the tribe is crucial and further enables her to secure a guide for the route beyond their village.

September 11, 1805

Even with horses and a Shoshone guide named Old Toby, the crossing of the Bitterroot Mountains in Idaho proves to be the most grueling and life-threatening section of the entire journey.

It was only mid-September but the snow on the western flank of the Bitterroots is already deep and Old Toby gets lost. Traveling is treacherous and horses slip and tumble down the mountain. The men, who have grown accustomed to eating five to seven pounds of meat daily in the game-rich plains, begin to starve. They become so desperate they start eating the colts.

Eleven days later they stumble out of the forest snow-blind and weak with hunger, and are taken in by a village of Nez Perce Indians. Buckley says that the Nez Perce debate killing the half-dead intruders who are accompanied by a Shoshone woman, their bitter enemy. But a Nez Perce woman named Watkueis, who lived among white men as a captive, convinces them to spare the strangers and befriend them.

The Nez Perce hospitality has one drawback. Lewis and Clark's men make themselves sick from overindulging on piles of dried fish and boiled roots.

Clark writes in his journal, "I find myself very unwell all the evening from eating the fish & roots too freely." A week later, he adds, "Capt. Lewis & myself eat a Supper of roots boiled, which Swelled us in Such a manner that we were Scercely able to breath for Several hours."

November 7, 1805

After paddling dugout canoes down the treacherous Columbia River for weeks Clark believes the men have finally reached the Pacific. "Great joy in camp we are in View of the Ocian," writes Clark with his trademark creative spelling. "This great Pacific Octean which we been So long anxious to See. and the roreing or noise made by the waves brakeing on the rockey Shores (as I Suppose) may be heard disticly."

But to Clark's dismay they have only arrived at the edge of Gray's Bay, a storm-tossed brackish estuary 20 miles inland from the Pacific. Powerful waves and strong winds swamp and paralyze the canoes.

In a typical journal entry marked November 14, Clark writes, "rained all the last night without intermition, and this morning. wind blows verry hard but our Situation is Such that we Cannot tell from what point it comes—one of our Canoes is much broken by the waves dashing it against the rocks." The Corps finally crosses the estuary with the help of local Clatsop Indians and their large, ocean-going canoes.

Fort Clatsop in the Oregon Country near the mouth of the Columbia River.

Kean Collection/Archive Photos/Getty Images

November 24

After finally reaching the Pacific Coast, it is time for the Corps to hunker down in Winter quarters. Lewis and Clark put the decision to a vote as to where to build Fort Clatsop which would be their home for the next five months. A tally of the votes is recorded in Clark's journal, including historic votes from York, the African American slave, and Sacagawea, an Indian woman.

"Janey [one of Sacagawea's nicknames] is in favour of a place where there is plenty of Potas," wrote Clark, referring to Wapato, a type of native root vegetable.

December, 1805 - March, 1806

Conditions at Fort Clatsop are "horribly miserable," says Buckley. "From December to March, it rained all but 12 days. They were stuck in cramped, smoky quarters subsisting on lean elk meat. They were ready to start the return journey as soon as they thought possible, and they actually left too soon."

May, 1806

Returning to the Nez Perce, Lewis and Clark go against the natives' advice and try to cross the thickly forested Bitterroots before the snow fully melts. "It was their only retreat during the whole expedition," says Buckley.

June 8, 1806

The month spent with the Nez Perce waiting for the snow to melt is one of the most enjoyable and leisurely of the entire two-year journey. By day, Lewis and Clark's men and the Indians compete in foot races and boyhood games like "prison base," a type of tag. And by night, they stay up late dancing and playing the fiddle around the fire.

"Last evening the indians entertained us with seting the fir trees on fire," writes Lewis, describing one of their last nights among the Nez Perce. "This exhibition reminded me of a display of fireworks. The natives told us that their object in seting those trees on fire was to bring fair weather for our journey."

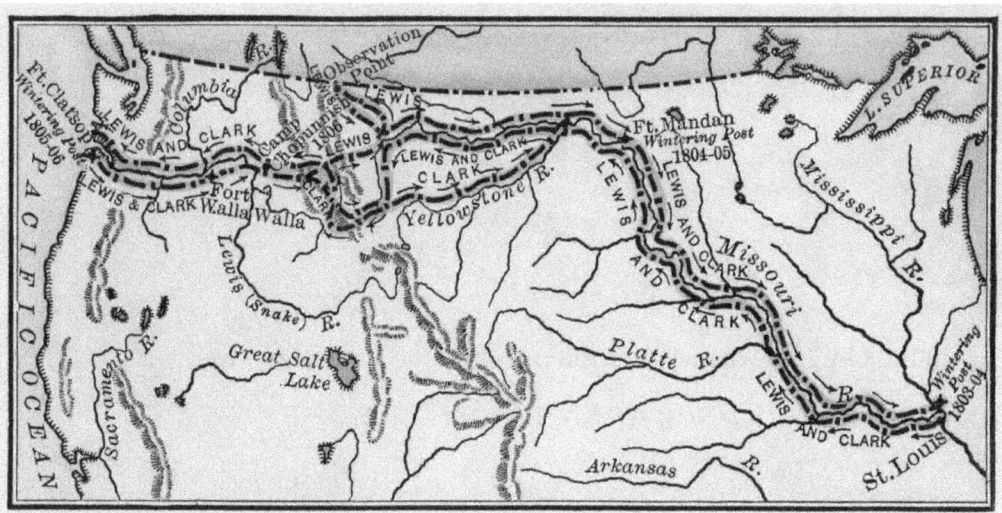

A map depicting the route taken by Lewis and Clark on their first expedition from the Missouri River (near St. Louis, Missouri) to the mouth of the Columbia River (at the Pacific Ocean in Oregon), and their return trip, 1804 - 1806.

Stock Montage/Getty Images

July 3, 1806

After easily crossing the Bitterroots with the help of Nez Perce guides, the Corps splits into four different groups for the next leg of the journey. Clark leads a group to explore the Yellowstone River. Lewis takes another up the Marias River, which includes the northernmost edge of the Louisiana Territory. Without any way to communicate with each other, they plan to reunite at Fort Mandan.

July 25, 1806

Clark etches his name and the date into a sandstone outcropping near modern-day Billings, Montana that he names Pompy's Tower after Sacagawea's son. It remains the only physical evidence of Lewis and Clark's expedition that survives today.

July 26, 1806

Lewis's group is met by a small band of Blackfeet warriors in Montana. After camping with them overnight Lewis catches the Blackfeet trying to steal their guns and horses, and kills a young brave.

"That was the only native death on the whole expedition," says Buckley. "And Lewis was so concerned that the Blackfeet would come after him, he and his men jump on their horses and ride for almost 24 hours straight to get down to the Missouri River and meet up with the rest of the party."

September 23, 1806

A month after Lewis and Clark reunite at the confluence of the Missouri and Yellowstone Rivers, and weeks after saying goodbye to Sacagawea at Fort Mandan, the Corps of Discovery arrive back in St. Louis. The exhausted explorers are greeted as heroes.

"Even though there were all these difficulties with mountains and rivers and climates and natives, they all live—they all come back," says Buckley. "And the Lewis and Clark expedition becomes America's odyssey."

Explorer, William Clark

Bettmann Archive/Getty Images

Explorer, Meriwether Lewis

(Where journals were directly quoted, original spellings were used, including spelling errors.)

Members of the Voyage of Discovery:

Meriwether Lewis   (Expedition Leader)

William Clark   (Expedition Leader)

John Boley

William Bratton

Toussaint Charbonneau   (French Guide)

John Collins

John Colter

Colter the Mountain Man

Pierre Cruzatte   (pilot of the boats)

John Dame

Drouillard/Drewyer

Reubin Field

Charles Floyd

Robert Frazer

Thomas Proctor Howard

John Ordway

Nathaniel Hale Pryor

Sacagawea   (Native American Lady Guide)

George Shannon

John B. Thompson

Ebenezer Tuttle

Isaac White

Richard Windsor

York (Clark's servant)

Other Explorations Into the Uncharted Western Lands:

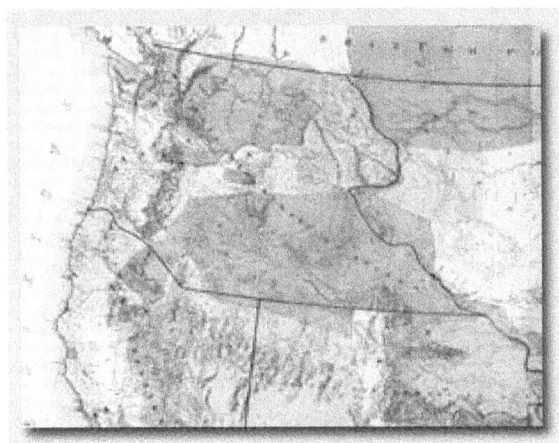

During the first decade of the nineteenth century the geographic image of western North America began to change dramatically. Based on the observations of Lewis and Clark information gathered from native people, and Clark's own crudely drawn maps, this image evolved from an almost empty interior with a single mountain range serving as a western continental divide, to one showing a tangle of mountains and rivers. A continent that had once seemed empty and simple because of what was unknown was now becoming filled in and much more complex.

It would take another fifty years after Lewis and Clark to completely fill in the empty unknown parts of the map and accurately depict the West we know today. Other explorers and map makers would be required, each discovering and documenting new geographic and scientific details about specific parts of the western landscape.

Many of these important expeditions are little known but certainly contributed valuable information that deserves remembering and celebrating.

Freeman's Survey of the Red River
Sometimes Called the 2nd Corps of Discovery

Planning for the expedition Jefferson called his "Grand Excursion" to the Southwest began in 1804 and was headed by William Dunbar. In 1806 despite the threat of Spanish opposition surveyor and astronomer Thomas Freeman and naturalist, Peter Custis, and a Team consisting of Capt. Richard Sparks, a forty-five-man military contingent, and French and Indian guides set out to explore the Red River, the southern boundary of the Louisiana Purchase. It was the first major scientific probe into the American West to be led by civilian scientists.

As part of his master plan for the exploration of the West President Thomas Jefferson considered the Red River expedition second in importance only to Lewis and Clark's investigation of the Missouri and Columbia Rivers. Though it was billed as a scientific survey the Red River expedition had strong commercial and diplomatic overtones as well and became an important element in the boundary dispute with Spain. By sending an American force up the Red River Jefferson hoped to accomplish several important objectives: to confirm reports that the Red might provide a commercially viable watercourse to Santa Fe, to identify and pacify the Indians of the region, and to more clearly identify and understand the Louisiana Purchase's disputed western border with

New Spain. The dream of tracing a water route to the southern Rockies and winning the Indians to the American side was cut short by political maneuvering and espionage closer home that culminated in armed Spanish intervention.

Hoping to provoke an international confrontation for personal gain, Gov. James Wilkinson had informed Spanish officials of the American plans for the expedition. While the Team poled their way up the river two Spanish military detachments marched to intercept them. Freeman and Custis entered the Red River on May 2, 1806 and left Natchitoches on June 2. They were 615 miles up the river on July 28 at a spot now known as Spanish Bluff. There they met a Spanish force under the command of Francisco Viana who ordered them to turn back. By August 1 the Americans were heading back down the river. The area explored by Freeman, in present-day Louisiana, Arkansas, Oklahoma, and Texas, was later incorporated into Zebulon Pike's official report and map published in 1810.

Though the expedition's failure caused political embarrassment for the Jefferson administration, the bloodless confrontation between American explorers and Spanish troops failed to trigger the war that Wilkinson and Aaron Burr had hoped for. The diplomatic uproar caused Spain to pursue a less confrontational policy, which effectively opened up the Red River country to American traders. Diplomatic tensions resulting from the Red River episode persuaded Jefferson to abandon an excursion up the Arkansas River that had been planned for 1807.

The scientific achievement of the Red River expedition was overshadowed by the more dramatic discoveries of Lewis and Clark and obscured in the controversy over the expedition's premature termination. The principal lasting contributions of the Red River expedition were the documents left by its leaders. As records of nineteenth-century scientific exploration Freeman's journal and Custis's natural history catalogues provide valuable information on the Indian life and ecology of the Red River.

The Journeys of Zebulon Montgomery Pike

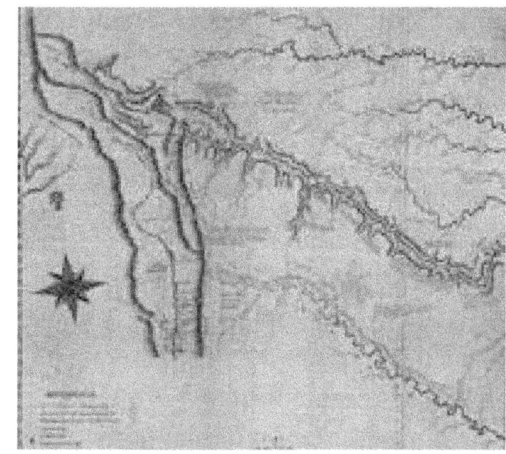

In mid-July 1806 Lewis and Clark were on their way back from the Pacific. At the same time young army Lieutenant Zebulon Montgomery Pike left St. Louis with twenty-three men to explore the Spanish borderlands. Unlike several other expeditions, Pike did not travel by the command of the President. Instead, he took his orders from General James Wilkinson, governor of the Louisiana Territory and sometime secret agent for the Spanish. Pike carried out two expeditions for Wilkinson. The first (August 1805–April 1806) took him up the Mississippi River into present-day Minnesota. Although instructed to chart the river and observe its natural resources and places suitable for military and commercial establishments, Pike also attempted to locate the river's headwaters. Leaving St. Louis in August 1805 he ascended the river as far as

Leech Lake in Minnesota, missing its source by only 50 miles or so. After spending the winter in present-day Minnesota, Pike and his party returned to St. Louis in April 1806 with a hand-drawn map of the upper Mississippi.

The second expedition began in July 1806 and drew to a close in late June 1807. Pike's instructions from Wilkinson took the explorer across a wide area of Western Land including territory that was part of the Spanish Empire. Pike was instructed to seek out the headwaters of the Arkansas and Red Rivers and to investigate Spanish Settlements in New Mexico.

Pike and his men left Missouri and traveled through the present-day states of Kansas and Nebraska eventually reaching Colorado, where he spotted the famous mountain peak later named in his honor. After exploring the region adjacent to the peak Pike traced the north fork of the Arkansas and searched for the Red River's source. Ill-prepared for harsh winter weather, Pike and his men built a small stockade on the upper Rio Grande. On February 1807, near present-day Alamosa, Colorado, Spanish forces took Pike and his men into custody for illegally entering Spanish Territory. His party was escorted to Santa Fe, then down to Chihuahua, back up through Texas, and finally to the border of the Louisiana Territory, where they were released.

Soon after returning to the east Pike was implicated in a plot with former Vice President Aaron Burr to seize territory in the Southwest for mysterious ends. However after an investigation, Secretary of State James Madison fully exonerated him. That he was a spy has been fairly well established by later Historians but just who he was spying for is still not completely clear.

The information he provided about the U.S. territory in Kansas and Colorado was of great help to U.S. Officials and did much to encourage future U.S. settlement there. Perhaps of even greater value were his reports about the weakness of Spanish settlements in the Southwest which stirred plans of future U.S. annexation. Pike later served as a brigadier general during the War of 1812 and he was killed by a British gunpowder bomb after leading a successful attack on York, Canada in April 1813

Long's Expedition To The Central and Southern Plains

Major Stephen H. Long's Scientific Expedition (1819-1820) was also technically a military exploration of the central and southern Great Plains and the Front Range of the Rockies. However, it contained a very strong scientific investigatory element as well. For the first time an American exploring party included professional scientists (a zoologist and a botanist) and two skilled artists. While not every future American expedition took along such skilled observers the pattern was set for increasingly scientific exploration.

Despite its valuable published reports, important and accurate maps, and impressive visual records, the Long expedition continues to suffer from a misconception about its impact on the American settlement of the Great Plains. In his "General Description of the Country" Long declared that portions of the central plains were "almost wholly unfit for cultivation, and, of course, uninhabitable by a people depending on agriculture." Most telling, he labeled part of the high plains on his 1821 map as "the Great American Desert." Some historical writers have felt that the idea of the "Great American Desert" may have deterred Americans from initially settling on the plains. Although a handful of maps and textbooks picked up this phrase, most Americans appear to have given it little attention and continued to think about the West as Jefferson envisioned it—"as a garden of the world, an Eden in the West".

The Trial of Aaron Burr

In the summer of 1807 the city of Richmond, Virginia was the scene of one of the most remarkable trials in early American history. The case involved and showcased several important historical characters but the defendant, 51-year-old Aaron Burr, was clearly the most recognizable figure. The New Jersey native had only recently served as Thomas Jefferson's Vice President but since leaving that office his reputation had been marred by political intrigue and his participation in a duel that had left Alexander Hamilton dead. Burr was accused of one of the gravest crimes in American law: treason. According to one account, he had been at the heart of a "deep, dark, and wicked conspiracy" against the young United States.

The nature and extent of the plot that resulted in the charges against Burr remain hazy even to this day. "Too many people told too many different stories and too many people had things to hide," historian Buckner F. Melton has written. What was known at the time was that he worked to raise a small army on the American frontier. He may have hoped to lead an independent campaign against Spanish-held territories in Texas and Mexico, but it's also possible that he planned to wrest a portion of the newly acquired frontier from Spain or perhaps the United States. According to some contemporaries Burr had designs on founding a new western nation with himself as its emperor.

What came out in the trial indicated that Burr's conspiracy appeared to have originated in 1804—the same year that he shot Alexander Hamilton dead in Weehawken, New Jersey. At the time Burr's career was in shambles. Political parties had shunned him, Thomas Jefferson had dropped him as vice president, and the Hamilton duel had left him with potential murder indictments hanging over his head. Desperate to remake his name the former Continental Army colonel began plotting a grand military enterprise on the American frontier. After making contact with a British foreign minister named Anthony Merry, Burr floated the idea that Louisiana and other territories west of the Appalachians might be persuaded to secede from the United States. That August Merry sent a dispatch to London in which he reported that Burr had offered "to lend his assistance to His Majesty's Government in any manner in which they may think fit to employ him, particularly in endeavoring to effect a separation of the Western part of the United States from that which lies between the Atlantic and the mountains."

Britain never took Burr up on his offer and Merry's letter wouldn't resurface for decades—but the former vice president continued to plot. In early 1805 he journeyed west and spent several months traveling the Ohio and Mississippi Rivers scouting the territory and recruiting supporters. At one point he met with Harman Blennerhassett, a wealthy Irish immigrant who owned an island in the Ohio River. Upon reaching New Orleans he made contact with a group of businessmen who, among other things, favored the annexation of Mexico. Burr eventually was able to put together an impressive group of allies which included dozens of frontier politicians and shady characters. His most important co-conspirator, General James Wilkinson, was the highest-ranking officer in the U.S. Army. Wilkinson had a reputation for espionage and grand schemes —it would later come to light that he was a paid agent for the Spanish—and he also had vast resources at his disposal. With his frontier troops he could serve as official cover for any military operations in Mexico or the West.

Burr was careful not to reveal the full extent of his plans to any of his potential recruits but his movements didn't go unnoticed. He had attracted attention wherever he traveled on the frontier and by the time he returned to the East Coast in late 1805 the media was abuzz with rumors. One Philadelphia paper speculated that Burr would soon be "at the head of a revolution party." It also referenced reports that he planned to "engage in the reduction of Mexico" with the aid of "British ships and forces."

Despite the controversy beginning to swirl around him Burr forged ahead with his plans. In August 1806 he struck out for the frontier a second time and made his way to Blennerhassett's island, which he intended to use as a rallying point for his forces. Around that same time he allegedly sent a coded letter to General Wilkinson. "I have at length obtained funds," it read, "and have actually commenced."

Wilkinson received the letter that October but unfortunately for Burr the general had lost his nerve. Convinced the scheme would fail Wilkinson betrayed the plot and sent warning to President Thomas Jefferson that a vast conspiracy was brewing in the West. Jefferson was left fuming. He immediately issued a proclamation instructing government officials to take actions to block the frontier plot and arrest its ringleaders.

By December 1806 the authorities began to close in on Burr. Militia groups raided his outpost at Blennerhassett's Island while he was away on business and many of his supporters began to abandon the scheme. Burr had hoped to raise a large army of volunteers but when he finally rendezvoused with his force it numbered fewer than 100 men. Undeterred the former vice president packed the "army" into flatboats and set out down the Mississippi. He intended to reach New Orleans but as he neared the city in early 1807 he learned of Wilkinson betrayal and Jefferson's calls for his arrest. Following a desperate attempt to flee Burr was captured in February near present day Mobile, Alabama. By late March the authorities had brought him back to Virginia to face trial.

Almost no one in 1807 knew for sure what Burr had been up to on the frontier but President Jefferson demanded that he be charged with treason—a crime punishable by death. The case of United States v. Aaron Burr began that summer in Richmond. With Supreme Court Chief Justice John Marshall presiding prosecutors spent several months presenting witnesses against the former vice president. The accounts were often muddled and contradictory but the prosecution maintained that Burr had been the mastermind behind an attempt to wage war against the United States. "He was the Alpha and Omega of this treasonable scheme," lawyer Alexander MacRae proclaimed during one speech, "the very body and soul, the very life of this treason."

Burr and his team of lawyers—which included two former U.S. attorneys general—mounted a strong defense against the charges. Not only did they prove that Wilkinson had doctored the cipher letter he allegedly received from Burr they argued that the definition of treason outlined in the Constitution required evidence of an "overt act" from the accused. When Chief Justice Marshall ruled in favor of this interpretation of the law the prosecution's case crumbled. Burr had repeatedly spoken about various illegal schemes, but since he had been absent when his troops gathered on Blennerhassett's Island—the only "overt act" that could be proven—there was no evidence that he had taken up arms against the government. With this in mind the jury found him not guilty of treason.

Burr was cleared of the charges on October 1807 but the debate surrounding his actions in the West has continued ever since. Some historians believe he was planning to mount some sort of expedition against Mexico and Texas while others contend that he had more sinister hopes of starting a revolution on the frontier. And still others believe Oregon, which was disputed territory, may have been his ultimate goal. Burr's own claim at trial was that he was planning to colonize a tract of land in Louisiana. Given his intense secrecy his true motives may never be known for certain. "Reaching a final judgment on Burr is difficult," author David O. Stewart has written. "The confusion has persisted because he had several alternative goals, and because he said so many different things to so many different people."

Despite his victory in court Burr was branded a villain in the United States and hanged in effigy in several cities. The disgraced political titan later spent a few years in self-imposed exile in Europe but returned home in 1812 and established a legal practice in New York, where he lived until his death in 1836. To this day he remains one of the few major American politicians to have been tried for treason.

(History.com - Updated AUG 22, 2018 Original MAY 31, 2017)

Aaron Burr's Notorious Treason Case by Evan Andrews

The Mysterious Death of Meriwether Lewis

On October 11th, 1809 Meriwether Lewis died of gunshot wounds at Grinder's Stand, a log-cabin inn on the Natchez Trace some seventy miles southwest of Nashville. He was thirty-five years old. He was on his way to Washington to meet with President Jefferson. The next day servants found Lewis shot dead outside the Inn. A companion, James Neely, wrote a letter to Jefferson: "Sir: It is with extreme pain that I have to inform you of the death of his Excellency Meriwether Lewis, governor of upper Louisiana, who died on the morning of the 11th, and I am sorry to say, by suicide." This much of the story is known for certain. The rest of the story remains one of the great mysteries of the early United States. Whether it was suicide or murder has remained the topic of much debate and the central theme of several books since that day.

Scholars have reconstructed lunar cycles to prove that the innkeeper's wife couldn't have seen what she said she saw that moonless night. Black powder pistols have been test-fired, forgeries claimed and mitochondrial DNA extracted from living relatives. Yet even now precious little is known about the events of October 10, 1809, after Lewis – armed with several pistols, a rifle and a tomahawk – stopped at Grinder's Stand.

Captain Meriwether Lewis was President Thomas Jefferson's Aide and chosen leader for the Corps of Discovery Expedition into the expansive territory of Louisiana acquired from France in 1803. Lewis picked his friend, William Clark, as his co-commander. The journey from St. Louis to the Pacific and back again, lasting from May 1804 to September 1806, is better known by the names of its two principal officers, Lewis and Clark.

At the time of his death the expedition had been over for three years. Lewis had been appointed the second Governor of Louisiana Territory in 1807. He seems to have had significant challenges in this role. In the fall of 1809 he was making his way to Washington, D.C. to press his case for reimbursement for expenditures and to defend himself against his Territorial Secretary, Frederick Bates, who persistently complained about Lewis to officials there. And to meet with President Jefferson.

By some accounts, Lewis arrived at the inn with servants; by others, he arrived alone. That night Mrs. Grinder, the innkeeper's wife, heard several shots. She later said she saw a wounded Lewis crawling around begging for water but was too afraid to help him. He died, apparently of bullet wounds to the head and abdomen, shortly before sunrise the next day. One of his traveling companions who arrived later buried him nearby.

At this point theories of what actually took place differ widely. Some believe he died by his own hand, others suspect he was the victim of bandits, and still others feel something far darker and more conspiratorial was going on that resulted in his death.

Those believing the suicide theory point to the fact that Lewis was subject to emotional instability and periods of anxiety and depression. Lewis had reportedly attempted to take his own life several times a few weeks earlier and was known to suffer from what Jefferson called "sensible depressions of mind." Clark had also observed his companion's melancholy states. "I fear the weight of his mind has overcome him," he wrote after receiving word of Lewis's fate. At the time of his death Lewis's depressive tendencies were compounded by other problems as well. He was having financial troubles and likely suffered from alcoholism and other illnesses, possibly syphilis or malaria, both of which are known to sometimes cause bouts of dementia. And he appeared to be having trouble readjusting to his celebrity status, his desk-job, and life in general – even to the point of not being able to complete his journals of the trip. Collectively, many historians feel, these issues resulted in him taking his life on that night in Tennessee.

Opponents of this theory however remind us of the fact that he had just completed the most exciting trip of his day and was enjoying much deserved recognition for their accomplishments. They say he was much less depressed than many historians believe and that there are copies of very coherent letters from him to governmental officials written only days before his death. They point out that he had been promoted to a very important and powerful position as Governor of the Louisiana Territory and had much more of the sort of work he had always enjoyed before him. As to whether he had an alcohol problem, they wonder why his chronically whining Lieutenant never mentioned this in his many letters of complaint. And they end by submitting the fact that he was an excellent shot and wondered why he would have to shoot himself twice and still lay wounded and suffering for hours before dying, if he had really tried to kill himself. To many this theory is full of a lot of holes filled with little more than suppositions.

Other historians point to the fact that the Natchez Trace, which ran between Nashville, Tn and Natchez, Mississippi (440 miles) was a rugged and notoriously dangerous route. They state that it was frequented by unscrupulous and dangerous bandits who often preyed on travelers. They believe it was some of these bandits that followed Meriwether Lewis to his resting place for the night and then robbed and killed him as they did many others.

Following the same train of thought other murder theories point more at the Inn keeper herself, Mrs. Grinder, whose recollection of events that night was always vague and changeable. They feel he may have not been the first or last traveler that she conspired with others to rob, and then kill to cover her tracks.

Though Lewis's mother is said to have believed he was murdered that idea didn't have much traction until the 1840s. In that year a commission of Tennesseans set out to honor Lewis by erecting a marker over his grave. While examining the remains, committee members wrote that "it was more probable that he died at the hands of an assassin." Unfortunately, they failed to say why.

And still other equally sincere and well-informed historians, hold to another more conspiratorial theory about how and why Meriwether Lewis' life came to such an untimely end. They point to other events going on at the time and Lewis' connection to them. As a result of the Louisiana Purchase the United States became dramatically larger literally overnight. Boundaries were not yet clear and there was much more land in the West that belonged either to Spain or that was still no-man's land or disputed territory. In short a wise and enterprising individual might well be able to capitalize on the situation to carve out a private empire for himself.

We now know that powerful people, some in high governmental offices, were working to do just this. Former Vice President Aaron Burr was found to be one of them and was eventually tried for

Treason (in 1807). He was acquitted of the charges because his plans were discovered before he personally committed an "overt act" against his Country, which the statute required for a verdict of treason. But the trial revealed many lurid details of conspiracy and espionage Burr and others were involved in.

One of the "other" co-conspirators with Aaron Burr was General George Wilkinson. No doubt, Wilkinson was a traitor and a double agent, corrupt right up to his eyebrows. We now know beyond doubt that he was a paid spy of the Spanish colonial empire all of his life, while at the same time he was the highest-ranking officer of the United States Army in the West. We know that Wilkinson encouraged the Spanish Colonial Authorities to send out at least four military intercept parties to arrest or turn back the Lewis and Clark Expedition as it traveled to the Pacific Ocean, and at least one on its return trip. Did he also send out someone (perhaps James Neeley) to intercept and kill Meriwether Lewis on that fateful night? Those that think so must ask themselves why. He probably did want Lewis dead from all the bad blood between them but enough to act on it? That is still not clear.

Time has also revealed another bit of curious information – that Meriwether Lewis himself was involved in subterfuge. Documents have surfaced that reveal he and President Jefferson were up to more during the Corps of Discovery than even William Clark knew. In secret diaries that Lewis kept and was to share only with the President he recorded information he learned about Spanish settlements and strength in the West, desirable fort locations, safe river crossings, Native American tribes that might be enticed to become allies, etc. And most importantly, when he instructed his men to build Fort Clatsop in Oregon Territory, he was actually formally establishing a "settlement" that President Jefferson planned to use as an argument to annex the contested Territory as part of the United States. No wonder the Spanish sought to interrupt the expedition and no wonder General Wilkinson (and perhaps Aaron Burr, and other conspirators) were upset as it now appears they had plans of their own to claim part of Oregon as their own private empire.

As can easily be seen those who accept either of the theories discussed have considerable information to support their conclusion, but are any of them correct? We will likely never know for sure.

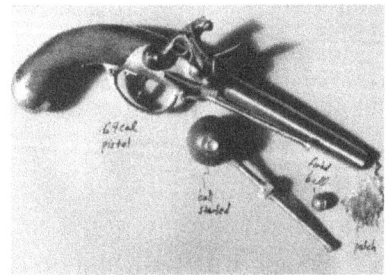

The Natchez Trace

For thousands of years people have been using the Natchez Trace that winds its way through the states of Mississippi, Alabama, and Tennessee, connecting Nashville, Tenn. with Natchez, Missippi. The earliest known people to utilize the forested road, called a trace, were the Mississippi Mound builders whose culture flourished from about 800 A.D. to 1500 A.D. These hunters and gatherers followed the early footpaths created by the foraging bison, elk, deer and other large game that made paths through the dense undergrowth. These early people also built roads, cultural centers, and numerous earthen monuments which were used as burial sites and temples. Several of these sites can still be seen along the Natchez Trace Parkway, and throughout the Eastern portion of America.

Later, the trace was frequented by the Choctaw, Chickasaw, and Natchez tribes who called the region home and traveled the trail on hunting and trading expeditions. By the 1540's when the first European explorer, Hernando de Soto, came to the region, the path was well worn and the Mississippi Mound builders were essentially gone. Later more explorers would use this "wilderness road," followed by frontiersmen and pioneers.

Some of the most regular travelers of the Natchez Trace were farmers and boatmen from the up-stream regions of Pennsylvania, Ohio, Kentucky, Tennessee, and Southwest Virginia who floated supplies, timber, and other goods down-stream to ports in Natchez, Mississippi and New Orleans, Louisiana during the 1800's. Regardless of where they came from they were usually collectively known as "Kaintucks."

Other famous figures traveled the Natchez Trace including Meriwether Lewis, who had previously led the Lewis and Clark Expedition. While making his way from Missouri to Washington D.C. in 1809 he died under mysterious circumstances at a small cabin in Tennessee. He was buried there where his body remains today.

U.S. Troops began to improve the Natchez Trace beginning in 1801 but it wasn't until the War of 1812 that the military began to make regular use of it. The popular path through Choctaw and Chickasaw lands became a vital thoroughfare when it was believed British ships threatened the

Gulf Coast. Having traveled the Trace repeatedly on other business General Andrew Jackson relied on the Trace several times for the transportation of his troops.

His cavalry traveled to Washington, Mississippi just north of Natchez on it in 1813. And when the troops were released without participating in battle the entire 2nd Division Tennessee Regiment slogged their way back along the Trace. Though the road was the best choice at the time the troops still had to contend with knee-deep mud, oxen dying from the heat, an occasional rattlesnake, and a "heavy a shower of hail and rain that ever fell upon poor soldiers in the world," according to soldier A.J. Edmundson. It was during this trip that Andrew Jackson earned his nickname "Old Hickory."

Travelers in the region relied heavily on the Trace that meandered through a diverse terrain of swamps, rivers, and rolling hills. The Trace was a road home, a path of exploration, and a link to the growing population of the Old Southwest.

Over time new roads and population centers were developed, steamships carried people and supplies upstream, and the Old Trace fell out of use. Though the trace was no longer regularly used it was not forgotten. Its' centuries of history, legends, and lore from the many occupants and travelers along the trail continue to "haunt" those who live and travel through the area.

The Great New-Madrid Earthquake of 1811

At 2:15 a.m. on December 16, 1811 residents of the frontier town of New Madrid, in what is now Missouri, were jolted from their beds by a violent earthquake. The ground heaved and pitched hurling furniture, snapping trees, and destroying barns and homesteads. The shaking rang church bells in Charleston, South Carolina, and toppled chimneys as far as Cincinnati, Ohio.

"The screams of the affrighted inhabitants running to and fro, not knowing where to go or what to do—the cries of the fowls and beasts of every species—the cracking of trees falling...formed a scene truly horrible," wrote one resident. The devastation was terrible and its effects were everywhere.

As people were starting to rebuild that winter two more major quakes struck, on January 23 and February 7. In the known history of the world no other earthquakes have lasted so long or produced so much evidence of damage as the New Madrid earthquakes. Three of the earthquakes are on the list of America's top earthquakes: the first one on December 16, 1811 a magnitude of 8.1 on the Richter scale; the second on January 23, 1812 at 7.8; and the third on February 7, 1812 at 8.8 magnitude.

Tremors were felt as far away as New York City, Boston, Montreal, and Washington D.C. President James Madison and his wife Dolly felt them in the White House. Church bells rang in Boston. From December 16, 1811 through March of 1812 there were over 2,000 earthquakes in the central Midwest, and between 6,000-10,000 earthquakes in the New Madrid area, near the junction of the Ohio and Mississippi Rivers.

The Midwest was sparsely populated and deaths were few but 8-year-old Godfrey Lesieur saw the ground "rolling in waves." Michael Braunm observed the river suddenly rise up "like a great loaf of bread to the height of many feet." Sections of riverbed below the Mississippi rose so high that part of the river ran backward. Thousands of cracks, some five miles long, ripped open fields and geysers burst from the earth spewing sand, water, mud and coal high into the air.

After the February 7 earthquake boatmen reported that the Mississippi River actually ran backwards for several hours. The force of the land upheaval 15 miles south of New Madrid created Reelfoot Lake, drowned the inhabitants of an Indian village, devastated thousands of acres of virgin forest, and created two temporary waterfalls in the Mississippi. Many Boatmen on flatboats along the river actually survived this experience and lived to tell the harrowing tale.

The First Steamboat on The Western Waters

The first steamboat travel on the Ohio and Mississippi Rivers took place during the New Madrid earthquakes. The New Orleans set out from Pittsburgh on October 20, 1811 bound for New Orleans. Captain Nicholas Roosevelt had brought along his young wife, their two year old daughter, and a Labrador dog. Ten days after leaving Pittsburgh his wife, Lydia, gave birth to a son in Louisville, Kentucky. They waited a while for her to recover and for the water to rise prior to crossing the dangerous waters and reef at the Falls of the Ohio (Louisville, Ky.). On the night before the day of the earthquake, December 16, the steamboat was anchored near Owensboro, Kentucky about 200 miles east of New Madrid, Missouri. Their dog insisted on staying in the cabin with them instead of sleeping on the deck as he usually did.

Without realizing it they were heading straight towards the epicenter of the greatest earthquake in American history. Their steamboat, which was intended to be an advertisement for steam travel, was thought instead to be the cause of the earthquake by many who saw it. At Henderson, Kentucky where no chimneys were left standing after the quake, they stopped to visit their friends, the painter John James Audubon and his wife Lucy. Floating in the middle of the Ohio River they were protected from the worst of the earthquake tremors shaking the land but not from the hazards of falling trees, disappearing islands, and collapsing river banks.

After entering Indian Territory on December 18th, they were chased by Indians who believed the "fire canoe" had caused the earthquake but they managed to escape capture by outrunning them. They even had a small cabin fire that night which they managed to put out.

Thousands of trees were floating on the waters of the Mississippi as they approached New Madrid on December 19th, three days after the earthquake. They found that the entire town of New Madrid had been destroyed. They didn't dare to stop and pick up a few survivors for fear of being overrun as they were without supplies. Most alarming was the fact that they had not seen a boat ascending the river in three days. They did however see many boats that were wrecked and abandoned. It was undoubtedly a miracle that they survived and kept on going.

RAFTS OF TREES ON THE MISSOURI.

They tied up at one island and it sank during the night. Their dog, Tiger, alerted them to oncoming tremors. On December 22 they encountered the British naturalist, John Bradbury, on a boat at the mouth of the St. Francis River who told them the town of Big Prairie was gone.

They arrived at Natchez, Mississippi on December 30 and celebrated the first marriage aboard a steamboat on the 31st, when the steamboat engineer married Lydia's maid. Amazingly they arrived at New Orleans on January 10, 1812, safe and sound, after traveling 1,900 miles from Pittsburgh on the first steamboat to travel the western waters.

Chief Sitting Bull

Sitting Bull, who was perhaps the most powerful and best known Native American Chief, was born in 1831 near Grand River, Dakota Territory in what is today South Dakota. He was the son of Returns-Again, a renowned Sioux warrior who named his son "Jumping Badger" at birth. The young boy killed his first buffalo at age 10 and by 14 joined his father and uncle on a raid of a Crow camp. After the raid his father renamed him Tatanka Yotanka, or Sitting Bull, for his bravery.

Sitting Bull soon joined the Strong Heart warrior society and the Silent Eaters, a group that ensured the welfare of the tribe. He led the expansion of Sioux hunting grounds into westward territories previously inhabited by the Assiniboine, Crow and Shoshone, among others.

Sitting Bull first battled the U.S. Army in June of 1863 when they came after the Santee Sioux (not the Dakota) in retaliation for what was called the Minnesota Uprising. This conflict was sparked when federal agents withheld food from the Sioux living on reservations along the Minnesota River. Over 300 Sioux were arrested in the uprising but President Abraham Lincoln commuted the sentences of all but 39 of the accused.

Sitting Bull faced the U.S. military again at the Battle of Killdeer Mountain on July 28, 1864 when U.S. forces under General Alfred Sully surrounded an Indian trading village, eventually forcing the Sioux to retreat. These face-offs convinced Sitting Bull to never sign a treaty that would force his people onto a reservation.

In 1868 Red Cloud, chief of the Oglala Teton Dakota Sioux, signed the Fort Laramie Treaty with 24 other tribal leaders and representatives of the U.S. government including Lieutenant

General William Tecumseh Sherman. The treaty created the Great Sioux Reservation and earmarked additional land for the Sioux in parts of South Dakota, Wyoming, and Nebraska.

Sitting Bull's anti-treaty stance won him many followers and around 1869 he was made supreme leader of the autonomous bands of Lakota Sioux—the first person to ever hold such a title. Members of the Arapaho and Cheyenne tribes soon joined him.

Confrontation with American soldiers escalated in the mid-1870s after gold was discovered in the Black Hills, a sacred area to Native Americans that the American government had recognized as their land following the 1868 Fort Laramie Treaty.

As white prospectors rushed into the Sioux lands the American government set aside the treaty and declared war on any native tribes that prevented it from taking over the contested land. When Sitting Bull refused to abide by these new conditions the stage was set for confrontation.

In June 1876 the chief led a successful battle against American forces in the Battle of the Rosebud. A week later he was engaged in another battle, this time against General George Armstrong Custer in the now famous Battle at Little Bighorn. There Sitting Bull and Crazy Horse led thousands of Sioux and Cheyenne warriors against Custer's undermanned force wiping out the American general and his roughly 300 men.

For the U.S. government the defeat was an embarrassment and the Army increased its efforts to wrest control of the territory from Native American tribes. To protect his people Sitting Bull led his people into Canada where they remained for four years.

In 1881 Sitting Bull returned to the Dakota territory where he was held prisoner until 1883. In 1885 after befriending Annie Oakley he joined Buffalo Bill Cody's Wild West Show. The pay was more than good—$50 a week to ride once around the arena—but Sitting Bull quickly grew tired of the performances and life on the road and decided to return to his people. "[I] would rather die an Indian than live a white man," he famously declared.

Upon his return to his home Sitting Bull continued to live the uncompromising life that had characterized his earlier year, and to attract many loyal followers. But everything had changed. The once proud Sioux found their free-roaming life destroyed, the buffalo gone, themselves confined to reservations dependent on Indian Agents for their existence.

In a desperate attempt to return to the days of their glory many embraced a new mysticism preached by a Paiute shaman called Wovoka. Wovoka called himself the Messiah and prophesied that the dead would soon join the living in a world in which the Indians could live in the old way surrounded by plentiful game. A tidal wave of new soil would cover the earth, bury the whites, and restore the prairie. To hasten the event the Indians were to dance the Ghost Dance. Many dancers wore brightly colored shirts emblazoned with images of eagles and buffaloes. These "Ghost Shirts" they believed would protect them from the bluecoats' bullets.

During the fall of 1890 the Ghost Dance spread through the Sioux villages of the Dakota reservations revitalizing the Indians and bringing fear to the whites. A desperate Indian Agent at Pine Ridge wired his superiors in Washington, "Indians are dancing in the snow and are wild and crazy. We need protection and we need it now. The leaders should be arrested and confined at some military post until the matter is quieted, and this should be done now."

While there is no evidence that Sitting Bull was a practitioner of the Dance, U.S. President Benjamin Harrison feared he would join the popular movement and ordered the Army to forcibly suppress the Ghost Dance. The Indian police — personally hostile to Sitting Bull's clan and now authorized under military orders — were sent to capture him. During the arrest the proud Chief was killed – some say executed.

In his inaugural address a year earlier President Harrison famously declared that as a Christian nation the United States would require Indians to convert to Christianity and that all Native religions would be actively suppressed.

After Sitting Bull was killed a chief named Big Foot, who in fact was a practitioner of the Ghost Dance, and next on the army's list to be arrested, fled with 300 followers toward the Pine Ridge reservation in present day South Dakota. Pursuant to the presidential order General Nelson A. Miles dispatched 5,000 troops in below-zero weather to capture them.

On December 28, 1890 a reorganized band of General George Armstrong Custer's 7th Cavalry, still smarting from defeat at the Little Big Horn 14 years earlier, caught up with Big Foot and some 350 of his followers camped on the banks of Wounded Knee creek. The army charged with the responsibility of arresting Big Foot and disarming his warriors surrounded their camp. The confrontation was tense. Trouble had been brewing for months.

On the morning of December 29, Chief Big Foot, racked with pneumonia and dying, sat among his warriors and powwowed with the army officers. Suddenly the sound of a shot pierced the early morning mist. Within seconds the entire camp erupted into a flurry of gun-fire, smoke, and terror. Indian braves raced to retrieve their discarded rifles and federal troopers fired volley after volley into the Sioux camp. From the heights above the army's Hotchkiss guns raked the Indian teepees with grapeshot. Clouds of gun smoke filled the air as men, women and children scrambled for their lives. Many ran for a ravine next to the camp only to be cut down in a deadly cross fire.

When the smoke cleared and the shooting stopped, approximately 300 Sioux men, women, and children were dead, Big Foot among them. Twenty-five soldiers lost their lives as well. As the remaining troopers began the grim task of removing the dead a blizzard swept in from the North. A few days later they returned to complete the job. Scattered fighting broke out again but the massacre at Wounded Knee put an end to the Ghost Dance movement and any hope that Native Americans may have still had of the land ever returning to them. The Indian Wars were now over.

Hauling off the dead at the Massacre of Wounded Knee

https://www.history.com/topics/native-american-history/sitting-bull

https://www.biography.com/political-figure/sitting-bull

https://www.history.com/topics/native-american-history/wounded-knee

http://www.eyewitnesstohistory.com/knee.htm

The Little-Known War of 1812

The tensions and conflicts that caused the War of 1812 arose from the nearly constant conflict between France and Britain resulting in American interests being caught in the middle and often damaged as the two countries attempted to undermine the economies of the other. American shipping initially prospered from free trade with the British, French, and Spanish empires but conflicting national laws soon surfaced to create conflict as Britain and France took measures to block the United States from trading with the other. By enforcing maritime laws going back to 1756 and enacting new regulations the two countries placed the United States in the untenable situation that American ships that obeyed Britain faced capture by the French in European ports, and if they complied with Napoleon's Continental System, they could fall prey to the Royal Navy. Although the U.S. complained loudly their protests were largely ignored.

After Thomas Jefferson (who was pro-French) became president (in 1801) relations with Britain slowly deteriorated as they began to more forcibly enforce their restrictive laws. The decisive British naval victory at the **Battle of Trafalgar** (October 21, 1805) and subsequent efforts by the British to **blockade** French ports prompted the French Emperor, **Napoleon,** to cut off Britain from European and American trade. Napoleon countered with laws that basically designated all neutral ships who visited British ports as enemy vessels. Soon British made a similar decree requiring neutral ships to obtain licenses at English ports before trading with France or their colonies. Back and forth these laws and decrees went, each more restrictive and burdensome than the former – and the United States was heavily impacted by them all.

The Royal Navy's use of impressment to keep its ships fully crewed also provoked Americans. The British accosted American merchant ships to seize alleged Royal Navy deserters, carrying off thousands of U.S. citizens into the British navy. In 1807 the frigate H.M.S. Leopard fired on the U.S. Navy frigate *Chesapeake* and seized four sailors, three of them U.S. citizens. London eventually apologized for this incident, but it came close to causing war at the time. Jefferson, chose to responded through bringing economic pressure against Britain and France by pushing Congress (in December 1807) to pass the Embargo Act. This Act forbade all export shipping from U.S. ports and most imports from Britain. Unfortunately, the Embargo Act hurt Americans more than the British or French and plunged the American economy into a depression. Many Americans simply chose to defy it. Just before Jefferson left office in 1809 Congress replaced the Embargo Act with the Non-Intercourse Act which exclusively forbade trade with Great Britain and France. This measure also proved ineffective and it was eventually replaced as well.

Britain's refusal to yield on the issue of neutral rights originated from more than the emergency created by the European war. British manufacturing and shipping interests demanded that the Royal Navy promote and sustain British trade against Yankee competitors. The policy born of that attitude convinced many Americans that they were being treated again as a mere colony. Britons, on the other hand denounced American trading with France labeling the United States a participant in Napoleon's Continental System.

Events on the U.S. northwestern frontier caused additional friction between the two countries. The Shawnee brothers, Tecumseh and Tenskwatawa, attempted to form an Indian confederation to halt further American expansion into their land. Although Maj. Gen. Isaac Brock, the British commander of Upper Canada (modern Ontario), had orders to avoid worsening American frontier problems American settlers blamed British intrigue for the growing tensions with Indians in the Northwest Territory. As concerns about war grew Brock sought to supplement his regular troops and Canadian militia forces with Indian allies which was enough to confirm the worst fears of American settlers.

Brock's efforts to recruit Indian to his side were aided in the fall of 1811when Indiana territorial governor, William Henry Harrison, fought the Battle of Tippecanoe and destroyed the Indian settlement at Prophet's Town, near modern Battle Ground, Indiana. Harrison's victory convinced most Indians in the Northwest Territory that their only hope of preventing further encroachments by American settlers lay with the British. American settlers in turn believed that Britain's removal from Canada would end their Indian problems. And many Canadians suspected that American expansionists were using Indian unrest as an excuse for a war of conquest against them.

When James Madison was elected to the presidency in 1808 he instructed Congress to prepare for war with Britain. On June 18, 1812, buoyed by the arrival of "war hawk" representatives the United States formally declared war for the first time in the nation's history. Citizens in the Northeast opposed the idea but many others were enthusiastic about the nation's "Second War of Independence" from British oppression. Ironically the British Parliament was already planning to repeal their trade restrictions. By the time the ship carrying news of the declaration of war reached Great Britain, almost a month and a half after war had been declared, the restrictions had been repealed. Hearing of the declaration the British chose to wait and see how the Americans would react to the repeal. The Americans after hearing of the repeal were still unsure how Great Britain would react to the declaration of war. Thus, although one of the main causes for war had vanished, fighting began anyway. The poorly trained U.S. army numbered roughly 6,700 men and now faced an experienced adversary with over 240,000 soldiers spread across the globe. The America's military fleet was large but Britain's was much larger and more experienced. The United States entered the war seeking to secure commercial trading rights and uphold its national honor. The American strategy was to quickly bring Great Britain to the negotiating table on these issues by invading Canada. Captured Canadian territory, they felt, could be used as a powerful bargaining chip against the crown.

The invasion of Canada which began in the summer of 1812, ended in disaster. By the end of the year American forces had been routed at the Battle of Queenston Heights on the Niagara River. A thrust into modern day Québec had been turned back after advancing fewer than a dozen miles. And Detroit had been surrendered to the Canadians. Meanwhile British-allied Native Americans continued their raids in Indiana and Illinois where they massacred many settlers.

The Americans enjoyed more success at sea. Although the British were able to set a semi-successful blockade along the Atlantic seaboard the American Navy won several battles against British warships and were able to capture a number of British trade vessels. Throughout the war the American Navy continued to ably combat the formidable Royal Navy. American fortunes improved little through most of 1813. An attempt to retake Detroit failed near **Frenchtown**, Michigan. The resulting massacre of American prisoners at the hands of Native Americans on January 23, 1813 inspired Kentucky soldiers to enlist in large numbers. American attempts to take Canada resulted in only temporary footholds at York and Fort George along the Niagara front. The Battles of Chateuaguay and Chrysler's Farm again prevented American forces from advancing on Montréal. The only considerable American successes occurred in September with Oliver

Hazard Perry winning a major naval battle on Lake Erie, and in October when the Tecumseh's Confederacy of northwestern Native American tribes was crushed at the Battle of the Thames.

Towards the end of 1813 a war among the Creek nations erupted in the Southeast between factions influenced by Tecumseh's nativism and those who sought to adopt white culture. The opposition faction known as the Red Sticks, attacked American outposts including Fort Mims, Alabama. Andrew Jackson organized a force of militia over the winter of 1813-1814 and, with the help of Cherokee Warriors, defeated the Red Sticks at the Battle of Horseshoe Bend on May 24, 1814. Through the Treaty of Fort Jackson he forced both sides of the Creek Nation, even those allied to him, to cede nearly 23 million acres of what would become Alabama and portions of Georgia.

In April a brief peace broke out in Europe as Napoleon was forced into his first exile. Great Britain consequently was able to shift more resources to the North American theater. The tone of the war changed as Secretary of the Treasury Albert Gallatin described, "We should have to fight hereafter not for 'free Trade and sailors rights,' not for the Conquest of the Canadas, but for our national existence." At the same time however the British began the process of repealing their policies of impressment and trade strangulation.

On July 5, 1814 newly promoted Brigadier General Winfield Scott led a force into Upper Canada and scored a decisive victory at the Battle of Chippawa but was forced to withdraw weeks later after the bloody Battle of Lundy's Lane near Niagara Falls.

On August 19, 1814 an expeditionary force of 4,500 battle hardened British veterans under the command of General Robert Ross landed at Benedict, Maryland and began a lightning campaign. After routing Maryland militia at the Battle of Bladensburg, Ross's men captured and burned the public buildings in Washington, D.C., including the White House. That month peace negotiations began in the European city of Ghent.

On September 12, Ross and his force attempted to take Baltimore with the support of the Royal Navy. The Maryland militia held off the land assault at the Battle of North Point, killing Ross. Fort McHenry withstood the British bombardment in a 25-hour battle that inspired the American national anthem. The British abandoned their designs on Baltimore but soon launched another invasion of the Gulf Coast.

On December 24, 1814 the Treaty of Ghent was signed and peace was agreed upon. Word was again slow to travel across the Atlantic and on January 8, 1815 Andrew Jackson engaged a British force outside of New Orleans resulting in a stunning but ultimately pointless victory. On February 18, 1815 the Treaty of Ghent was officially ratified by President Madison and the nation ended the War of 1812 with "less a shout of triumph than a sigh of relief." 15,000 Americans died during the war. The terms of the peace were *status quo ante bellum*, "the way things were before the war." All land reverted back to its original owners. British agents stopped supporting Native American raiders. The British trade restrictions and impressment policies had already been repealed. America had fought its old master to an honorable draw and Britain had avoided disaster in North America while defeating the French in Europe. Canada gained a proud military heritage. Surprisingly relations between the warring factions generally improved after the war. The Native Americans however were the real losers of the war. Many of them had fought in the hopes that

Great Britain would insist upon a recognized Native nation in North America as part of the peace but the British quickly abandoned this issue during the peace negotiations. Without British money and weapons the Native Americans lost the ability to defend their lands and attack U.S. settlements. The result was an increasing rate of U.S. expansion into what remained of Indian Land.

Treaties and the Indian Removal Act of 1830

(Andrew Jackson)

As the 19th century began land-hungry Americans poured into the backcountry of the coastal South and began moving toward and into what would later become the states of Alabama and Mississippi. Since Indian tribes living there appeared to be the main obstacle to westward expansion white settlers petitioned the federal government to remove them. Although Presidents Thomas Jefferson and James Monroe argued that the Indian tribes in the Southeast should exchange their land for lands west of the Mississippi River they did not take steps to make this happen.

In 1814 Major General Andrew Jackson led an expedition against the Creek Indians climaxing in the Battle of Horse Shoe Bend (in present day Alabama near the Georgia border). There Jackson's force (which included several hundred Cherokee Braves) soundly defeated the Creeks and destroyed their military power. He then forced upon the Indians a treaty whereby they surrendered to the United States over twenty-million acres of their traditional land—about one-half of present day Alabama and one-fifth of Georgia. Over the next decade Jackson led the way in the Indian removal campaign helping to negotiate nine of the eleven major treaties to remove Indians.

(Depiction of William Weatherford surrendering to Andrew Jackson after the Battle of Horseshoe Bend)

Under this kind of pressure Native American tribes—specifically the Creek, Cherokee, Chickasaw, and Choctaw—realized that they could not defeat the Americans in war. The appetite of the settlers for land seemed to be unending so the Indians adopted a strategy of appeasement. They hoped that if they gave up a good deal of their land they could keep at least a part of it. The Seminole tribe in Florida resisted in the Second Seminole War (1835-1842) and the Third Seminole War (1855-1858) but neither appeasement nor resistance worked.

From a legal standpoint the United States Constitution empowered Congress to "regulate commerce with foreign nations, and among the several States, and with the Indian tribes." In early treaties negotiated between the federal government and the Indian tribes the latter typically acknowledged themselves "to be under the protection of the United States of America and of no other sovereign whosoever." When Andrew Jackson became president (1829-1837) he decided to build a systematic approach to Indian removal on the basis of these legal precedents.

To achieve his purpose Jackson encouraged Congress to adopt the Removal Act of 1830. The Act established a process whereby the President could grant land west of the Mississippi River to Indian tribes that agreed to give up their homelands. As incentives the law allowed the Indians financial and material assistance to travel to their new locations and start new lives and guaranteed that the Indians would live on their new property under the protection of the United States Government forever. With the Act in place Jackson and his followers were free to persuade, bribe, and threaten tribes into signing removal treaties and leaving the Southeast.

In general terms Jackson's government succeeded. By the end of his presidency he had signed into law almost seventy removal treaties, the result of which was to move nearly 50,000 eastern Indians to land owned by the United States west of the Mississippi River but excluding the states of Missouri and Iowa as well as the Territory of Arkansas. In the process it opened millions of acres of rich land east of the Mississippi to white settlers. Despite the vastness of the Indian Territory, the government intended that the Indians' destination would be a more confined area—in what later became eastern Oklahoma.

The Trail of Tears (Robert Lindneux, 1942)

The Cherokee Nation resisted the removal challenging in court the Georgia laws that restricted their freedoms on tribal lands. In his 1831 ruling on Cherokee Nation v. the State of Georgia, Chief Justice John Marshall declared that "the Indian territory is admitted to compose a part of the United States," and affirmed that the tribes were "domestic dependent nations" and "their relation to the United States resembles that of a ward to his guardian." However, the following year the Supreme Court reversed itself and ruled that Indian tribes were indeed sovereign and immune from Georgia laws. President Jackson nonetheless refused to heed the Court's decision. He obtained the signature of a Cherokee chief agreeing to relocation in the Treaty of New Echota, which Congress ratified against the protests of Daniel Webster and Henry Clay in 1835. The Cherokee signing party represented only a faction of the Cherokee, and the majority followed Principal Chief John Ross in a desperate attempt to hold onto their land. This attempt faltered in 1838 when under the guns of federal troops and Georgia state militia, the Cherokee tribe were forced to the dry plains across the Mississippi. The best evidence indicates that between three and four thousand out of the fifteen to sixteen thousand Cherokees died along the way from the brutal conditions of the "Trail of Tears."

By the 1840's, with the exception of a small number of Seminoles still resisting removal in Florida, no Indian tribes resided in the American South. Through a combination of coerced treaties and judicial decisions the United States Government succeeded in paving the way for the westward expansion and the incorporation of new territories as part of the United States.

Gen. Winfield Scott's Orders Concerning the Cherokee Removal

ORDERS. No. 25.
Head Quarters, Eastern Division.
Cherokee Agency, Ten. May 17, 1838.

MAJOR GENERAL SCOTT, of the United States' Army, announces to the troops assembled and assembling in this country, that, with them, he has been charged by the President to cause the Cherokee Indians yet remaining in North Carolina, Georgia, Tennessee and Alabama, to remove to the West, according to the terms of the Treaty of 1835. His Staff will be as follows:

LIEUTENANT COLONEL W. J. WORTH, acting Adjutant General, Chief of the Staff.
MAJOR M. M. PAYNE, acting Inspector General.
LIEUTENANT R. ANDERSON, & E. D. KEYES, regular Aids-de-camp.
COLONEL A. H. KENAN & LIEUTENANT H. B. SHAW, volunteer Aids-de-camp.

Any order given orally, or in writing, by either of those officers, in the name of the Major General. will be respected and obeyed as if given by himself.

The Chiefs of Ordnance, of the Quarter-Master's Department and of the Commissariat, as also the Medical Director of this Army, will, as soon as they can be ascertained, be announced in orders.

To carry out the general object with the greatest promptitude and certainty, and with the least possible distress to the Indians, the country they are to evacuate is divided into three principal Military Districts, under as many officers of high rank, to command the troops serving therein, subject to the instructions of the Major General.

Eastern District, to be commanded by BRIGADIER GENERAL EUSTIS, of the United States' Army, or the highest officer in rank, serving therein: - North Carolina, the part of Tennessee lying north of Gilmer county, Georgia, and the counties of Gilmer, Union, and Lumpkin, in Georgia. Head Quarters, in the first instance, say, at Fort Butler.

Western District, to be commanded by COLONEL LINDSAY, of the United States' Army, or the highest officer in rank serving therein: -- Alabama, the residue of Tennessee and Dade county, in Georgia. Head quarters, in the first instance, say, at Ross' Landing.

Middle District, to be commanded by BRIGADIER GENERAL ARMISTEAD of the United States' Army, or the highest officer in rank, serving therein: -- All that part of the Cherokee country, lying within the State of Georgia, and which is not comprised in the two other districts. Head Quarters, in the first instance, say, at new Echota.

It is not intended that the foregoing boundaries between the principal commanders shall be strictly observed. Either, when carried near the district of another, will not hesitate to extend his operations, according to the necessities of the case, but with all practicable harmony, into the adjoining district. And, among his principal objects, in case of actual or apprehended hostilities, will be that of affording adequate protection to our white people in and around the Cherokee country.

The senior officer actually present in each district will receive instructions from the Major General as to the time of commencing the removal, and everything that may occur interesting to the service, in the district, will be promptly [promptly] reported to the same source. The Major General will endeavor to visit in a short time all parts of the Cherokee country occupied by the troops.

The duties devolved on the army, through the orders of the Major General & those of the commanders of districts, under him, are of a highly important and critical nature.

The Cherokees, by the advances which they have made in christianity and civilization, are by far the most interesting tribes of Indians in the territorial limits of the United States. Of the 15,000 of those people who are now to be removed -- (and the time within which a voluntary emigration was stipulated, will expire on the 23rd instant --) it is understood that about four fifths are opposed, or have become averse to a distant emigration; and altho' [although] none are in actual hostilities with the United States, or threaten a resistance by arms, yet the troops will probably be obliged to cover the whole country they inhabit, in order to make prisoners and to march or to transport the prisoners, by families, either to this place, to Ross' Landing or Gunter's Landing, where they are to be finally delivered over to the Superintendent of Cherokee Emigration.

Considering the number and temper of the mass to be removed, together with the extent and [unclear: fastnesses] of the country occupied, it will readily occur, that simple indiscretions -- acts of harshness and cruelty, on the part of our troops, may lead, step by step, to delays, to impatience and exasperation, and in the end, to a general war and carnage -- a result, in the case to those particular Indians, utterly abhorrent to the generous sympathies of the whole American people. Every possible kindness, compatible with the necessity of removal, must, therefore, be shown by the troops, and, if, in the ranks, a despicable individual should be found, capable of inflicting a wanton injury or insult on any Cherokee man, woman or child, it is hereby made the special duty of the nearest good officer or man, instantly to interpose, and to seize and consign the guilty wretch to the severest penalty of the laws. The Major General is fully persuaded that this injunction will not be neglected by the brave men under his command, who cannot be otherwise than jealous of their own honor and that of their country.

By early and persevering acts of kindness and humanity, it is impossible to doubt that the Indians may soon be induced to confide in the Army, and instead of fleeing to mountains and forests, flock to us for food and clothing. If, however, through false apprehensions, individuals, or a party, here and there, should seek to hide themselves, they must be pursued and invited to surrender, but not fired upon unless they should make a stand to resist. Even in such cases, mild remedies may sometimes better succeed than violence; and it cannot be doubted that if we get possession of the women and children first, or first capture the men, that, in either case, the outstanding members of the same families will readily come in on the assurance of forgiveness and kind treatment.

Every captured man, as well as all who surrender themselves, must be disarmed, with the assurance that their weapons will be carefully preserved and restored at, or beyond the Mississippi. In either case, the men will be guarded and escorted, except it may be, where their women and children are safely secured as hostages; but, in general, families, in our possession, will not be separated, unless it be to send men, as runners, to invite others to come in.

It may happen that Indians will be found too sick, in the opinion of the nearest Surgeon, to be removed to one of the depots indicated above. In every such case, one or more of the family, or the friends of the sick person, will be left in attendance, with ample subsistence and remedies, and the remainder of the family removed by the troops. Infants, superannuated persons, lunatics and women in a helpless condition, will all, in the removal, require peculiar attention, which the brave and humane will seek to adapt to the necessities of the several cases.

All strong men, women, boys & girls, will be made to march under proper escorts. For the feeble, Indian horses and ponies will furnish a ready resource, as well as for bedding and light cooking utensils – all of which, as intimated in the Treaty, will be necessary to the emigrants both in going to, and after arrival at, their new homes. Such, and all other light articles of property, the Indians will be allowed to collect and to take, with them, as also their slaves, who will be treated in like manner with the Indians themselves.

If the horses and ponies be not adequate to the above purposes, wagons must be supplied.

Corn, oats, fodder and other forage, also beef cattle, belonging to the Indians to be removed, will be taken possession of by the proper departments of the Staff, as wanted, for the regular consumption of the Army, and certificates given to the owners, specifying in every case, the amount of forage and the weight of beef, so taken, in order that the owners may be paid for the same on their arrival at one of the depots mentioned above.

All other movable or personal property, left or abandoned by the Indians, will be collected by agents appointed for the purpose, by the Superintendent of Cherokee Emigration, under a system of accountability, for the benefit of the Indian owners, which he will devise. The Army will give to those agents, in their operations, all reasonable countenance, aid and support.

White men and widows, citizens of the United States, who are, or have been intermarried with Indians, and thence commonly termed, *Indian countrymen*; also such Indians as have been made denizens of particular States, by special legislation, together with the families and property of all such persons, will not be molested or removed by the troops until a decision on the principles involved can be obtained from the War Department.

A like indulgence, but only for a limited time, and until further orders, is extended to the families and property of certain Chiefs and head-men of the two great Indian parties, (on the subject of emigration) now understood to be absent in the direction of Washington on the business of their respective parties.

This order will be carefully read at the head of every company in the Army.

[Signed] Winfield Scott. *By Command:*

General Winfield Scott's Address to the Cherokee At Their Removal

From the Cherokee Agency, Maj. Gen. Winfield Scott delivered an ultimatum to the Cherokees remaining in northern Georgia -- they had to go west, and they had to go now:

"Cherokees! The President of the United States has sent me with a powerful army, to cause you, in obedience to the treaty of 1835 [Treaty of New Echota], to join that part of your people who have already established in prosperity on the other side of the Mississippi. Unhappily, the two years which were allowed for the purpose, you have suffered to pass away without following, and without making any preparation to follow; and now, or by the time that this solemn address shall reach your distant settlements, the emigration must be commenced in haste, but I hope without disorder. I have no power, by granting a farther delay, to correct the error that you have committed. The full moon of May is already on the wane; and before another shall have passed away, every Cherokee man, woman and child in those states must be in motion to join their brethren in the far West.

My friends! This is no sudden determination on the part of the President, whom you and I must now obey. By the treaty, the emigration was to have been completed on or before the 23rd of this month; and the President has constantly kept you warned, during the two years allowed, through all his officers and agents in this country, that the treaty would be enforced.

I am come to carry out that determination. My troops already occupy many positions in the country that you are to abandon, and thousands and thousands are approaching from every quarter, to render resistance and escape alike hopeless. All those troops, regular and militia, are your friends. Receive them and confide in them as such. Obey them when they tell you that your can remain no longer in this country. Soldiers are as kind-hearted as brave, and the desire of every one of us is to execute our painful duty in mercy. We are commanded by the President to act towards you in that spirit, and much is also the wish of the whole people of America.

Chiefs, head-men and warriors! Will you then, by resistance, compel us to resort to arms? God forbid! Or will you, by flight, seek to hid yourselves in mountains and forests, and thus oblige us to hunt you down? Remember that, in pursuit, it may be impossible to avoid conflicts. The blood of the white man or the blood of the red man may be spilt, and, if spilt, however accidentally, it may be impossible for the discreet and humane among you, or among us, to prevent a general war and carnage. Think of this, my Cherokee brethren! I am an old warrior, and have been present at many a scene of slaughter, but spare me, I beseech you, the horror of witnessing the destruction of the Cherokees.

Do not, I invite you, even wait for the close approach of the troops; but make such preparations for emigration as you can and hasten to this place, to Ross's Landing or to Gunter's Landing, where you all will be received in kindness by officers selected for the purpose. You will find food for all and clothing for the destitute at either of those places, and thence at your ease and in comfort be transported to your new homes, according to the terms of the treaty.

This is the address of a warrior to warriors. May his entreaties by kindly received and may the God of both prosper the Americans and Cherokees and preserve them long in peace and friendship with each other!

John G. Burnett's Story of the Removal of the Cherokees

Copied by permission from the Cherokee Messenger, a publication of the Cherokee Cultural Society of Houston

Birthday Story of Private John G. Burnett, Captain Abraham McClellan's Company, 2nd Regiment, 2nd Brigade, Mounted Infantry, Cherokee Indian Removal, 1838-39.

Children:
This is my birthday, December 11, 1890, I am eighty years old today. I was born at Kings Iron Works in Sulllivan County, Tennessee, December the 11th, 1810. I grew into manhood fishing in Beaver Creek and roaming through the forest hunting the deer and the wild boar and the timber wolf. Often spending weeks at a time in the solitary wilderness with no companions but my rifle, hunting knife, and a small hatchet that I carried in my belt in all of my wilderness wanderings.

On these long hunting trips I met and became acquainted with many of the Cherokee Indians, hunting with them by day and sleeping around their camp fires by night. I learned to speak their language, and they taught me the arts of trailing and building traps and snares. On one of my long hunts in the fall of 1829, I found a young Cherokee who had been shot by a roving band of hunters and who had eluded his pursuers and concealed himself under a shelving rock. Weak from loss of blood, the poor creature was unable to walk and almost famished for water. I carried him to a spring, bathed and bandaged the bullet wound, and built a shelter out of bark peeled from a dead chestnut tree. I nursed and protected him feeding him on chestnuts and toasted deer meat. When he was able to travel I accompanied him to the home of his people and remained so long that I was given up for lost. By this time I had become an expert rifleman and fairly good archer and a good trapper and spent most of my time in the forest in quest of game.

The removal of Cherokee Indians from their life long homes in the year of 1838 found me a young man in the prime of life and a Private soldier in the American Army. Being acquainted with many of the Indians and able to fluently speak their language, I was sent as interpreter into the Smoky Mountain Country in May, 1838, and witnessed the execution of the most brutal order in the History of American Warfare. I saw the helpless Cherokees arrested and dragged from their homes, and driven at the bayonet point into the stockades. And in the chill of a drizzling rain on an October morning I saw them loaded like cattle or sheep into six hundred and forty-five wagons and started toward the west.

One can never forget the sadness and solemnity of that morning. Chief John Ross led in prayer and when the bugle sounded and the wagons started rolling many of the children rose to their feet and waved their little hands good-by to their mountain homes, knowing they were leaving them forever. Many of these helpless people did not have blankets and many of them had been driven from home barefooted.

On the morning of November the 17th we encountered a terrific sleet and snow storm with freezing temperatures and from that day until we reached the end of the fateful journey on March the 26th, 1839, the sufferings of the Cherokees were awful. The trail of the exiles was a trail of death. They had to sleep in the wagons and on the ground without fire. And I have known as many as twenty-two of them to die in one night of pneumonia due to ill treatment, cold, and exposure. Among this number was the beautiful Christian wife of Chief John Ross. This noble hearted woman died a martyr to childhood, giving her only blanket for the protection of a sick child. She rode thinly clad through a blinding sleet and snow storm, developed pneumonia and died in the still hours of a bleak winter night, with her head resting on Lieutenant Greggs saddle blanket.

I made the long journey to the west with the Cherokees and did all that a Private soldier could do to alleviate their sufferings. When on guard duty at night I have many times walked my beat in my blouse in order that some sick child might have the warmth of my overcoat. I was on guard duty the night Mrs. Ross died. When relieved at midnight I did not retire, but remained around the wagon out of sympathy for Chief Ross, and at daylight was detailed by Captain McClellan to assist in the burial like the other unfortunates who died on the way. Her unconfined body was buried in a shallow grave by the roadside far from her native home, and the sorrowing Cavalcade moved on.

Being a young man, I mingled freely with the young women and girls. I have spent many pleasant hours with them when I was supposed to be under my blanket, and they have many times sung their mountain songs for me, this being all that they could do to repay my kindness. And with all my association with Indian girls from October 1829 to March 26th 1839, I did not meet one who was a moral prostitute. They are kind and tender hearted and many of them are beautiful.

The only trouble that I had with anybody on the entire journey to the west was a brutal teamster by the name of Ben McDonal, who was using his whip on an old feeble Cherokee to hasten him into the wagon. The sight of that old and nearly blind creature quivering under the lashes of a bull whip was too much for me. I attempted to stop McDonal and it ended in a personal encounter. He lashed me across the face, the wire tip on his whip cutting a bad gash in my cheek. The little hatchet that I had carried in my hunting days was in my belt and McDonal was carried unconscious from the scene.

I was placed under guard but Ensign Henry Bullock and Private Elkanah Millard had both witnessed the encounter. They gave Captain McClellan the facts and I was never brought to trial. Years later I met 2nd Lieutenant Riley and Ensign Bullock at Bristol at John Roberson's show, and Bullock jokingly reminded me that there was a case still pending against me before a court martial and wanted to know how much longer I was going to have the trial put off?

McDonal finally recovered, and in the year 1851, was running a boat out of Memphis, Tennessee.

The long painful journey to the west ended March 26th, 1839, with four-thousand silent graves reaching from the foothills of the Smoky Mountains to what is known as Indian territory in the West. And covetousness on the part of the white race was the cause of all that the Cherokees had to suffer. Ever since Ferdinand DeSoto made his journey through the Indian country in the year 1540, there had been a tradition of a rich gold mine somewhere in the Smoky Mountain Country, and I think the tradition was true. At a festival at Echota on Christmas night 1829, I danced and played with Indian girls who were wearing ornaments around their neck that looked like gold.

In the year 1828, a little Indian boy living on Ward creek had sold a gold nugget to a white trader, and that nugget sealed the doom of the Cherokees. In a short time the country was overrun with armed brigands claiming to be government agents, who paid no attention to the rights of the Indians who were the legal possessors of the country. Crimes were committed that were a disgrace to civilization. Men were shot in cold blood, lands were confiscated. Homes were burned and the inhabitants driven out by the gold-hungry brigands.

Chief Junaluska was personally acquainted with President Andrew Jackson. Junaluska had taken 500 of the flower of his Cherokee scouts and helped Jackson to win the battle of the Horse Shoe, leaving 33 of them dead on the field. And in that battle Junaluska had drove his tomahawk through the skull of a Creek warrior, when the Creek had Jackson at his mercy.

Chief John Ross sent Junaluska as an envoy to plead with President Jackson for protection for his people, but Jackson's manner was cold and indifferent toward the rugged son of the forest who had saved his life. He met Junaluska, heard his plea but curtly said, "Sir, your audience is ended. There is nothing I can do for you." The doom of the Cherokee was sealed. Washington, D.C., had decreed that they must be driven West and their lands given to the white man, and in May 1838, an army of 4000 regulars, and 3000 volunteer soldiers under command of General Winfield Scott, marched into the Indian country and wrote the blackest chapter on the pages of American history.

Men working in the fields were arrested and driven to the stockades. Women were dragged from their homes by soldiers whose language they could not understand. Children were often separated from their parents and driven into the stockades with the sky for a blanket and the earth for a pillow. And often the old and infirm were prodded with bayonets to hasten them to the stockades.

In one home death had come during the night. A little sad-faced child had died and was lying on a bear skin couch and some women were preparing the little body for burial. All were arrested and driven out leaving the child in the cabin. I don't know who buried the body.

In another home was a frail mother, apparently a widow and three small children, one just a baby. When told that she must go, the mother gathered the children at her feet, prayed a humble prayer in her native tongue, patted the old family dog on the head, told the faithful creature good-by, with a baby strapped on her back and leading a child with each hand started on her exile. But the task was too great for that frail mother. A stroke of heart failure relieved her sufferings. She sunk and died with her baby on her back, and her other two children clinging to her hands.

Chief Junaluska who had saved President Jackson's life at the battle of Horse Shoe witnessed this scene, the tears gushing down his cheeks and lifting his cap he turned his face toward the heavens and said, "Oh my God, if I had known at the battle of the Horse Shoe what I know now, American history would have been differently written."

At this time, 1890, we are too near the removal of the Cherokees for our young people to fully understand the enormity of the crime that was committed against a helpless race. Truth is, the facts are being concealed from the young people of today. School children of today do not know that we are living on lands that were taken from a helpless race at the bayonet point to satisfy the white man's greed.

Future generations will read and condemn the act and I do hope posterity will remember that private soldiers like myself, and like the four Cherokees who were forced by General Scott to shoot an Indian Chief and his children, had to execute the orders of our superiors. We had no choice in the matter.

Twenty-five years after the removal it was my privilege to meet a large company of the Cherokees in uniform of the Confederate Army under command of Colonel Thomas. They were encamped at Zollicoffer and I went to see them. Most of them were just boys at the time of the removal but they instantly recognized me as "the soldier that was good to us". Being able to talk to them in their native language I had an enjoyable day with them. From them I learned that Chief John Ross was still ruler in the nation in 1863. And I wonder if he is still living? He was a noble-hearted fellow and suffered a lot for his race.

At one time, he was arrested and thrown into a dirty jail in an effort to break his spirit, but he remained true to his people and led them in prayer when they started on their exile. And his Christian wife sacrificed her life for a little girl who had pneumonia. The Anglo-Saxon race would build a towering monument to perpetuate her noble act in giving her only blanket for comfort of a sick child. Incidentally the child recovered, but Mrs. Ross is sleeping in a unmarked grave far from her native Smoky Mountain home.

When Scott invaded the Indian country some of the Cherokees fled to caves and dens in the mountains and were never captured and they are there today. I have long intended going there and trying to find them but I have put off going from year to year and now I am too feeble to ride that far. The fleeing years have come and gone and old age has overtaken me. I can truthfully say that neither my rifle nor my knife were stained with Cherokee blood.

I can truthfully say that I did my best for them when they certainly did need a friend. Twenty-five years after the removal I still lived in their memory as "the soldier that was good to us".

However, murder is murder whether committed by the villain skulking in the dark or by uniformed men stepping to the strains of martial music.

Murder is murder, and somebody must answer. Somebody must explain the streams of blood that flowed in the Indian country in the summer of 1838. Somebody must explain the 4000 silent graves that mark the trail of the Cherokees to their exile. I wish I could forget it all, but the picture of 645 wagons lumbering over the frozen ground with their cargo of suffering humanity still lingers in my memory.

Let the historian of a future day tell the sad story with its sighs, its tears and dying groans. Let the great Judge of all the earth weigh our actions and reward us according to our work.

Children - Thus ends my promised birthday story. This December the 11th 1890.

Copied by permission from the Cherokee Messenger, a publication of the Cherokee Cultural Society of Houston

DRAYTON S. HALE

Although there is some inconsistency in the records according to his marriage record and his enlistment record into the Union Army, Drayton Hale was born in Russell Co., VA on January 25, 1839. Soon after his birth his Mother became very ill and spent the rest of her life in an institution. He was reared by an Uncle, Jim Vermillion, who was known to many by his nick-name "Captain". Curiously this nick-name seems to have been passed on to Drayton causing many people to mistakenly conclude that he was a Captain in the Army, which is untrue. He moved to Scott Co., Va in 1845.

Ruth Dougherty, Drayton's Aunt was a teacher in Russell County. She was persuaded by a Dr. Sallings to come to Scott County to teach his children and a school was established and held in his home. Drayton attended this school and was a very bright and enthusiastic student, often requesting and receiving extra instruction. Later the school was moved to the home of his Aunt Ruth and was held at night to better accommodate students who had to work on the farm during the day. Drayton was an avid reader and enjoyed books on a wide variety of topics. He also spent much time reading the Bible and was said to have developed a good understanding of the scriptures at an early age.

One of his favorite subjects was history and he enjoyed studying the Constitution and reading the debates of the great statesmen. He was particularly impressed with the writings of Daniel Webster who believed in, "Liberty and union now and forever more, one and inseparable." These patriotic sentiments seem to have a strong impact on Drayton and would influence later choices he would make.

He was married to Ruth C. Frazier in 1859 by Rev. Charles C. Addington in the vicinity of Estillville, (now Gate City, Va.), and the couple had 8 children. (1)

In 1860 a momentous and very divisive Presidential Election was held with far-reaching consequences. It was the first such election that Drayton was old enough to participate in. By that time Drayton was a strong Union man and believed the Southern States should not be allowed to secede. He had carefully followed the speeches and writings of Candidate Lincoln and adamantly proclaimed his decision to cast his first vote for him even though most of his neighbors felt otherwise.

His designated polling place, at Peter's Precinct in Scott Co., had no ballots available for the Republican Party so Drayton proudly wrote his choice on a piece of paper and signed his name. There was no such thing as a secret ballot in those days and a vote was cited by the election officials "Drayton S. Hale for Abraham Lincoln and Hannibal Hamlin." As might be expected this created quite a stir in the community and later on that evening a friend came to warn him that several men from the area were planning to form a "neck-tie party" for him. He managed to elude them and escape into Kentucky that night before they could carry out their threats.

Soon after arriving in Kentucky Drayton began making preparations to bring his family to join him. He mentioned in a letter to his cousin, C. D. Vermillion, dated May 27, 1861 that "his sentiment about his politics had in no way cooled. If anything it had been brooded upon by his absence". He managed to return to his home and bring his family back with him to Kentucky but his departure was said to be punctuated by rifle balls.

In his personal recollections Drayton states, "On my return to Kentucky I resumed working a crop of corn. As soon as the corn was laid by I got up a school on the Kentucky river some two miles from Whitesburg. The term of the school was three months. I taught the school about half out. When the political atmosphere got so high in the area I soon determined to join the Union Army and assist in my humble way to settle the trouble."

He was sworn in at Camp Burns in Estill County, Kentucky for three years. After drilling with the Eighth Kentucky Infantry he came down with the measles. After his recovery he was sent to Harrodsburg and assigned to Company D, 19th Kentucky Infantry.

He served with the Union forces over three years, from November 1, 1861, to January 1, 1865. He participated in the capture of Cumberland Gap, and in the retreat of General Morgan from Cumberland Gap in 1862. He served under Sherman during his seven days fighting before Vicksburg, and in the following month, January, 1863, was in the battle of Arkansas Post. At the second battle of Vicksburg he was carried off the battlefield with typhoid fever and sent in a hospital boat to Jefferson Barracks, St. Louis, MO.

After he was discharged from the Army he and his family moved to Minnesota, where he acquired a tract of 160 acres of land. There Drayton became quite active in civic affairs and was instrumental in organizing Todd County, where he served as a Commissioner of Revenue and Land Assessment. (2)

The terrible Civil War finally came to an end but the nation was left scarred and even more divided than before. The assassination of President Lincoln served to punctuate the feelings of many Americans, on both sides of the issues. Drayton wrote about his feelings in a letter to his cousin, C. D. Vermillion, from Minnesota in May 1865.

"The infernal devils killed our President. It will do them no good. I never felt so bad about it in my life. Some have rejoiced at him being shot down. I know one thing, if any person abuses him before me I will hit him with an axe or anything else I can find. Any other man would do the same thing that has served in the Union Army. Poor old Abe, I feel so bad about this, Abraham Lincoln stands side by side with George Washington."

"I have an honorable discharge from the United States Army and would not give it for their whole Confederacy. I want to tell those rebels if there was but ten acres left of the United States I would claim my part and help to defend it."

"I can't forget some of those Hell Hounds of secession. I intend to go to Virginia some day, and some of the people who waylaid me on the road to shoot me four years ago the 27th of this month, had better look out. They had the advantage then but Providence and time brings things on my side." (3)

In 1871 Drayton did return from Minnesota to Scott County. Thankfully over the years, much of the bitterness and hatred had settled down. No one in the community seemed to bear him any ill will and the "Hell Hounds" he wrote about from Minnesota never showed up. He was left to live in peace and to carry on his business as a farmer and later as a miller.

He bought a farm on Copper Creek and built his first mill. This mill did not meet his needs so he set about to look for a farm with a better water supply and mill site.

After a period of time he found what he was seeking and bought a farm with a very large spring near Copper Creek, in Scott County, Va, that came to be known as the "Hale Spring". The spring produced a very large volume of water and, having a steep fall, resulted in tremendous water power. A dam was constructed and a mill was soon built for grinding corn and bolted wheat flour. To this day some of the foundation stones still stand and part of the route of the mill race is still visible. (4)

His farming and milling operations were very successful and he built a large home with a stone foundation and two stone chimneys cut from limestone found on the farm. Stone was also cut and laid around the huge spring to a height of about four and one-half feet. The house and stone were torn down in the late thirties, moved to Kingsport, Tennessee, and rebuilt there.

As time went by it became evident that the mill needed to be expanded and that even the large spring branch could not supply enough water to meet his expected needs. In 1897 he devised an ingenious way to remedy his situation. To increase his supply of water he would tap into the near-by creek. Soon work began on a tunnel through the narrow part of a ridge that separated a bend in Copper Creek, known as the "dog's tail," because of its shape. It was a tremendous undertaking.

This tunnel was dug by hand by men using only picks, shovels, and occasionally dynamite. The soil and rock were wheel barrowed to the outside. The tunnel was approximately three-hundred-thirty feet long, six and one-half to seven feet high, and six to seven feet wide.

It took about seven years to dig the tunnel and build the dam. While this was being done carpenters worked on the mill house and workmen installed the mills, which included a corn mill, a roller mill, and a saw mill. Everything was ready for service when the tunnel was completed and the mills were in use up until about the time of Drayton's death. Afterwards the farm was divided and the mills were sold. (1)

Drayton was instrumental in getting a post office established in his community in the 1800's and it was named Hale's Mill in honor of him. This post office was in use until 1916 when it was discontinued and moved to Nickelsville. (4)

Throughout his life he took an active interest in politics, especially Presidential campaigns, speaking at schools and churches in behalf of Garfield in 1880, Harrison in 1888, and in the election of McKinley in 1896. (5) He also did some writing on various subjects which he contributed to the local paper. One of these that merits mentioning is an obituary which he titled "A Tardy Obituary of Rev. John Strong." Rev. Strong died in 1852, but he did not write the obituary until 1910. He must have made a great impression on Mr. Hale for in the obituary he says "as a boy of 12, I loved him, being so often in his home. His fine collection of books I had free access to, and I borrowed and returned." As further evidence of the deep impression left on him by the Rev. Strong he mentions the last sermon he heard him preach, and the text he used. (6)

Drayton Hale's life came to an end on January 22, 1916 and he was interred in the family cemetery on his farm. His wife, Ruth Frazier Hale, died in 1921 and was interred in the Mt. Pleasant Church cemetery. His body and those of other members of his family were exhumed and reinterred with her there.

Perhaps an appropriate close to this narrative would be this quote from the obituary of Rev. Strong by Mr. Hale:

"It is a matter of regret that in our country here, no records are kept and few epitaphs written above the sleeping dust of our ancestors. Who, if true as I have often thought, we need never be ashamed of. Thoughts of those examples of citizenship and Christian examples could see us as I view them in memory's hall. It seems they would weep, even in that land where weeping is unknown. May they all rest in peace till the time comes when all that knew them will be gathered with them." "Don't, don't let the pride of ancestry die out. It is a noble thing." (6)

Footnotes:
(1) Interview with I. D. Vermillion, March 12, 1977; (Omer Addington)
(2) Hale, Nathan Cabot: Gate City, Virginia Sesquicential Speech, August 17, 1965;
(3) Letter written to C. D. Vermillion from Minnesota, May 6, 1865;
(4) General Service Administration National Archives and Records Service;
(5) Interview with Ezra Addington, March 12, 1977 (Omer Addington)
(6) Hale, D. S.: A Tardy Obituary of Rev. John Strong (Clipping from Gate City Herald, 1910).

Orlean Puckett: The Life of a Mountain Midwife, 1844-1939

THE HOLLOW – The babies sleep eternally in one long row beneath dry dying grass shaded by enormous pokeweed growing over a split-rail fence. Most of their resting places are marked by simple field stones, one at the head, one at the foot, barely three feet apart.

These are 20 of Orlean Puckett's children, the ones you read about on the sign outside the Puckett cabin on the Blue Ridge Parkway. The ones who died when they were babies or were stillborn. Four more are buried on top of the mountain where Orlean and John Puckett lived after they took leave of their Patrick County home "below the mountain," as locals refer to the foothills and flatlands.

The Pucketts lost 24 babies between 1862 and 1881. How a woman could bear perennial tragedy such as this (she lost two in one year) and live to be almost 100 years old is unfathomable today.

The story could have ended there, just another mountain tragedy from the days of primitive science, homegrown medicine, and hard luck. As it turned out, Orlean Puckett's story was just beginning.

Unable to have a child of her own, Orlean Puckett discovered another way to bring babies into the world. When she was almost 50 years of age she became a midwife. Not just any midwife either. She would become the most famous of all the mountain midwives and "granny women" who helped numerous women through the ordeals of childbirth.

She is believed to have brought more than 1,000 babies into the lush, green hills of Patrick, Carroll and Floyd counties in Virginia. She helped bring Bob Childress, the "man who moved a mountain" and who built the famed stone churches along the parkway, into the world. She worked with the early country doctors, including the redoubtable Arthur C. Gates, who brought modern medicine into The Hollow in the 20th century.

Orlean Puckett lost 24 babies but gained a thousand children.

"And they all loved her," said Karen Cecil Smith, a North Carolina writer who wrote a book about Puckett. "She rose above the tragedy of her life. She could have been jealous of other women, but she never was. She loved their babies and they loved her. Her story needed to be told."

In 2012 Puckett was posthumously honored as one of the Library of Virginia's "Virginia Women in History".

The Beautiful Resort at Holston Springs on the Holston River

The ultimate in elegance: The Rufus Ayers home on Holston River. Fire destroyed the beautiful dwelling.

Mineral springs were once thought to have many medicinal benefits and spas and resorts sometimes developed around them. Such was the case with the beautiful resort called "Holston Springs" (between Weber City and Yuma, Virginia), beside the North Fork of the Holston River. The resort which was developed sometime before 1855 was on a beautiful 2,500 acre estate and featured both alkali and white sulphur water from the 4 springs on the property. The elegant lodge that housed guests included 24 rooms and was situated on a 20-acre lawn with a large fish pond well stocked with native fish. Additional guest cabins were also provided on the grounds near the main lodge. Guests could also enjoy a leisurely horse-back ride along the foothills of the mountain or boating on the river. The farm surrounding the home extended to the base of Clinch Mountain.

By 1863 the beautiful lodge was used by the Confederates as a hospital. On February 11 of that year Captain Edward O. Guerrant (Adjutant) to General Humphrey Marshall records in his journal that has been preserved in the book entitled "Bluegrass Confederate" a trip to the resort/hospital that would serve as his headquarters for some time. "General (Humphrey Marshall) gone to Holston Springs three miles below. Rode down after dinner. Crowded. A section of Pegram's artillery here – on the road to Kentucky, I guess. Secured a room for myself and Jeff Davis (his horse). Holston Springs are situated at the southern foot of Clinch Mountain – 3 miles from Estillville (now Gate City) in Scott County, Va. and 2 miles below "Moccasin Gap"- where Moccasin Creek passes through the mountain and flows to the Holston River. It is just over the mountain from Estillville and beautifully situated on the banks of the beautiful, blue Holston – which is here about the size of Licking near its mouth, and very clear. The stream runs along by the yard. The main building built of brick, large and commodious - faces the river – and a long row of neat white cottages stretches off to the right. Half way between the house and the river (50 yards from each), are the springs, 4 in number, all coming out in 10 feet of each other, a warm spring, a cold spring, chalybeate, and sulphur. The grounds are plotted with grass and set with trees. Sick men from the Batteries and Jessee's Companies occupy the Cottages. My room was in the 2d story – rt. corner – fronting the river. A long porch extended the who length of the house – both above and below."

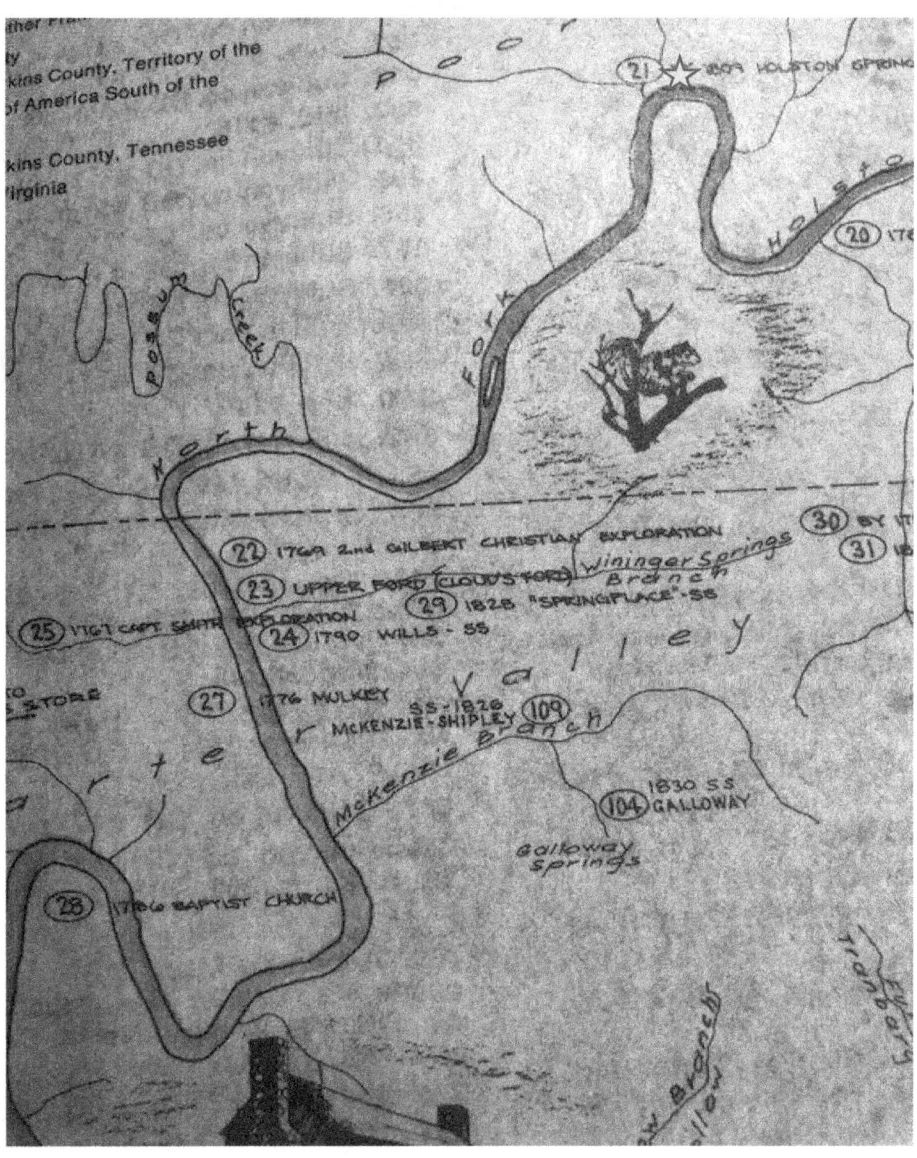

The Hospital at Holston Springs was a busy place with many soldiers being treated for various illnesses and wounds. Unfortunately many did not survive to return to their families. Several were buried nearby or were left in the care of compassionate families in other areas where some of them still remain in the small cemeteries there.

<u>Wolfe Cemetery near Holston Springs</u> where 55 Confederate Soldiers are buried near Holston Springs (the Old Confederate Hospital).

The ultimate in elegance: The Rufus Ayers home on Holston River. Fire destroyed the beautiful dwelling.

The Rufus Ayers Mansion on the North Fork of the Holston

Rufus Ayers was born on May 20, 1849 in Bedford County, Virginia. He was the eldest child of Maston J. and Susan Lewis Wingfield Ayers. His ancestry included General Andrew Lewis, commander of the American forces at the Battle of Point Pleasant, and John Lewis, first settler of Augusta County. After living there for a few years he and his family decided to set out for Texas to make a new home. They stopped off in Goodson (now Bristol Va/Tn) to visit relatives and liked the area so much they decided to stay.

His family moved to Goodson in 1855 where he attended Goodson Academy. In 1858 his father died leaving his mother with six small children. The Academy closed at the start of the Civil War and at age 15 Rufus ran away and joined the Confederate Army. He served with a detached command of scouts in East Tennessee.

After the war he came back and settled at Estillville, now Gate City, VA where he engaged in farming. He gave this up after a few years and went into the mercantile business. He spent a few rather unsuccessful years in this business before finally deciding to devote his time to the study of law in the office of Henry S. Kane, one of the most distinguished lawyers of Southwest Virginia.

In 1872 he was admitted to the bar. About two years later he became Commonwealth's Attorney of Scott Co. It was in his role as a lawyer that Ayers won deep respect from people all across Virginia and was praised by people all over the nation. The most famous case in which he was involved was the Virginia Stage Debt Question. This case involved grievances that certain bondholders had against the state of Virginia. Bitter legal battles raged between Virginia and her bondholders. Ayers fought the case to the Federal Courts and was finally arrested for contempt of court by Judge Bond of Maryland. He was sent to jail but was freed by a writ of "habeas corpus". The people of Virginia praised Ayers highly for the way he upheld the law of Virginia in this case. This case probably had more to do with Ayers' success as a lawyer than any other one thing throughout his law career. He set up law offices in both Gate City and Big Stone Gap where he and his son, Harry J. Ayers, were in joint practice. They had an outstanding firm and were often called into many important area cases, such as the Shoemaker Will Case.

General Ayers was prominent in politics, serving a term as attorney-general of Virginia. It was at this time that people began calling him "General" Ayers. Contrary to what many people probably think he was not given this name because of his being a military man but because of his being attorney-general. After his term as attorney-general Ayers was persuaded to run for governor of Virginia. He was nominated and accepted on the Democratic ticket but after a few weeks he dropped out of the race and decided to devote his time to the development of Southwest Virginia

General Ayers purchased a beautiful 2,500 acre estate on the banks of the North Fork of the Holston River, known as Holston Springs. He remodeled the once resort and Confederate hospital, containing 24 rooms, into an elegant mansion. The grounds consisted of a 20 acre lawn, a large fish pond well stocked with native fish, while the farm surrounding the home at the base of Clinch Mountain nurtured more than 100 purebred registered Jersey cows and a large herd of hogs of various breeds. Among the prominent persons who availed themselves of his hospitality were the Duke and Duchess of Marlborough.

By 1876 he had become one of the state's foremost industrial leaders. He was instrumental in obtaining a charter for a railroad from Bristol to Big Stone Gap, the founding of the Virginia Coal and Iron Company (serving on its board of directors for many years), the Appalachia Steel and Iron Company, and the Virginia, Tennessee, and Carolina Steel and Iron Company. Ayers also made many contributions to the town of Big Stone Gap through the Big Stone Gap Improvement Committee of which he was the organizer and president. This committee was instrumental in the development of all industry in and around Big Stone Gap. It is said to have fathered the coke furnaces, electric lights, and water works and to have heartily supported the railway, interstate tunnel, Mountain Park Association, planning mills, and brick plants in and around the Town.

In the 1880's General Ayers built a large stone mansion in Big Stone Gap, Va. that serves today as the Southwest Virginia Museum.

In 1891 Ayers tried to put into effect an outdoor recreation program on both a state and national level. This idea took the form of an organization known as the Mountain Park Association. James F. Fox, president of the Mountain Park Association wrote: "I was put in this position without my knowledge and General Ayers, who is the father of the Association will, after the annual meeting next May, be the president in name as he has been in reality, having acquired the land for us on the most favorable terms from Mr. (Patrick) Hagan at a time when the Norfolk and Western Railway people were bidding high for it for a summer resort, directed the survey and made all other necessary arrangements."

Rufus Ayers also played a part in the financial affairs of other areas of Southwest Virginia. He established the bank of Gate City, then the only bank between Bristol and Cumberland Gap. He also established and ran the R. A. Ayers and Company Bank at Big Stone Gap and had dealings in practically all of Big Stone Gap's financial affairs.

On May 14, 1926, after many years of hard work as a promoter of Southwest Virginia, General Rufus A. Ayers died at the age of seventy-seven, in the hospital in Radford, VA. His death was greatly mourned by people all across Virginian.

Grave site of the late Rufus A. Ayers located in historic Estill Cemetery, Gate City.

Educational Opportunities in the Appalachian Counties of Virginia and Kentucky:

Information concerning educational opportunities on the Appalachian Frontier during much of the 1800's is often sketchy and difficult to completely rely on. In general it is fair to say that while the education of young people was recognized as important by most families opportunities to participate in formal schooling varied considerably from county to county and was often dependent upon where students lived.

At first only the most densely populated areas of the region were fortunate enough to have a school but over the years more and more small rural schools were added to serve the growing population. Students almost always had to either walk or ride a horse to and from school consequently schools had to be located every 3 to 5 miles to be accessible to those they served. Occasionally students who lived too far away would board with families near the school during the week.

Saratoga School, Scott County, Va.

The following chart provides a snapshot of the central Appalachian region in 1850 and illustrates both interesting educational demographics and population distribution data.

County:	Population:	Colleges:	Public Schools:	Enrollment of Public Schools:	Pupils per School:
Breathitt, Ky.	3,785	0	4	80	20.0
Clay, Ky.	5,421	0	15	300	20.0
Estill, Ky.	5,985	0	10	215	21.5
Floyd, Ky.	5,715	0	12	302	25.17
Harlan, Ky.	4,268	0	15	330	22.0
Johnson, Ky.	3,873	0	11	305	27.73
Knox, Ky.	7,050	0	39	975	25.00
Laurel, Ky.	4,143	0	6	180	30
Lee, Va.	10,267	0	45	550	12.22
Letcher, Ky.	2,512	0	15	298	19.87
Owsley, Ky.	3,774	0	0	0	NA
Perry, Ky.	3,092	0	0	0	NA
Pike, Ky.	5,365	0	6	180	30.00
Russell, Va.	11,919	0	27	537	20.63
Scott, Va.	9,829	0	50	1,000	20.00
Smyth, Va.	8,162	0	22	600	27.27
Tazewell, Va.	9,942	0	36	654	18.17
Washington, Va.	14,612	1	36	1,512	42.00
Whitley, Ky.	7,447	0	47	1,197	25.47
U.S. Bureau of the Census of 1850					

The Issue of Secession:

Was secession legal?

No, although it was not ruled illegal until after the war. This was a complex question at the time with able legal minds to be found arguing both sides of the issue. The United States Supreme Court, in Texas v. White, 74 U.S. 700 (1868), determined that secession was unconstitutional. Chief Justice Salmon Chase wrote in his majority opinion that, "The ordinance of secession...and all the acts of legislature intended to give effect to that ordinance, were absolutely null. They were utterly without operation in law."

However:

The issue was more than a Judicial one and its answer could not be completely settled in the usual legal fashion. Following the successful outcome of the War for Independence many American Colonies were reluctant to completely give up their individual rights in order to join together as the United States of America. As a result crafting an acceptable system of government proved a major sticking point for many, particularly those who most feared the possibility of creating a Federal Government that would potentially become as oppressive as the monarchy they had just fought and died to overthrow.

Representatives were chosen from each state and they tirelessly worked to put together a Constitution that would address the concerns of all and that could garner enough votes to be ratified. Virginia was one of the stronger states and many very outspoken patriots from there were involved in crafting and arguing for the passage of the Constitution - men like George Washington, Thomas Jefferson, John Adams, Patrick Henry, Ben Franklin, etc. Some states could not be pacified until they were assured that should there ever come a time that their fears were a reality, that they could secede from the Union.

After what seemed and eternity the members of the Constitutional Convention came to an agreement and signed the United States Constitution on September 17, 1787 in Philadelphia, Pennsylvania.

So at least in the minds of many of the states, when the Federal Government began to enact laws that benefited some states but seriously penalized others (particularly in the South), their worst fears had come true. And then when President Lincoln was elected in 1860 with the pledge to keep Slavery out of the free states and an expressed intent to do away with it in all states, if at all possible, several southern states began the process of seceding from the Union - feeling they were exercising rights promised them by the Founding Fathers.

When did the Southern states secede from the Union?

South Carolina - December 20, 1860
Mississippi - January 9, 1861
Florida - January 10, 1861
Alabama - January 11, 1861
Georgia - January 19, 1861
Louisiana - January 26, 1861
Texas - February 1, 1861
Virginia - April 17, 1861
Arkansas - May 6, 1861
North Carolina - May 20, 1861
Tennessee - June 8, 1861

Virginia was a good example of the sort of struggles this issue wrought in many of the states.

Describing the 1861 convention in which Virginians finally voted for secession, Lincoln declared to the U.S. Congress, "¹ The course taken in Virginia was the most remarkable-perhaps the most important." This simple statement expresses Virginia's exceptional place in the history of the secession movement and the eventual coming of civil war in America.

At the opening of the Civil War Virginia was important for two major reasons. First because of the especially prominent and distinguished role it played in early American history and second its strategic location. For these reasons Virginians were truly torn over the decision of whether to secede. Because Virginia was not only sandwiched geographically but also economically, socially, and culturally between the North and the South her decision to leave the Union was a long-fought battle. Although several other southern states followed the lead of South Carolina and seceded shortly after Lincoln's election to the presidency, and several more left after his inauguration, Virginia did not break its ties with the Union until the North took military action against the South. Virginia could not accept the reality that if she stayed in the Union she would be forced to both support the war effort financially and send troops against her southern neighbors.

The Right of States to determine their own destiny was more than a slogan to many – it was a reason to secede from the Union and join the Confederacy.

Causes of the Civil War?

THE BATTLE OF GETTYSBURG, Pa JULY 3d 1863.

One of the surest ways of creating an argument - or worse, is to prompt a debate about the cause of the American Civil War. It seems that people interested in the event have varying opinions about this issue that they cling to tenaciously.

A common assumption held by many to explain the cause of the American Civil War was that the North was no longer willing to tolerate slavery as being part of the fabric of US society and that the political power brokers in Washington were planning to abolish slavery throughout the Union. Therefore, for many people slavery is the key issue to explain the causes of the American Civil War. However, it is not as simple as this and slavery, while a major issue, was not the only issue that pushed the Nation into the 'Great American Tragedy'. To better understand the larger picture it is necessary to look at what else was going on in the years before the war – in particular economic conditions and actions by the U.S. Congress.

In 1816 Congress passed its first Tariff (known as the Dallas tariff) with an explicit function of protecting U.S. manufactured items from overseas competition. Prior to the War of 1812 tariffs had primarily served to raise revenues to operate the national government. The bill was conceived as part of a solution to help avoid a projected federal deficit. Northern States generally supported the move as it also benefited business in that area.

In 1824 the Northern dominated Congress passed a series of protective tariffs on imported manufactured goods averaging 35%. The goal of these tariffs was to protect the young manufacturing industry of New England. The result was an economic boom in the North which made them very popular there. However, in Southern States it was a far different result as they caused exports in the South to drop 25% in just 2 years.

Although Southern States argued strongly to the contrary in 1828 Congress voted to impose additional protective tariffs which raised taxes on imported manufactured goods from Europe. The result was that goods from Europe were much more expensive. Because England could not sell as many goods to America they could not purchase as much of the agricultural products of the south.

The South was hurt badly by these tariffs. They could not sell as much of their products and they had to pay more for the manufactured goods they needed and had to import. They were forced to purchase necessary manufactured goods from northern factories because of the shortage of imports, regardless of the costs.

The South called the tariffs of 1828 the Tariffs of Abominations. They clearly hated these laws which many felt were designed to help the North at the expense of the South. John C. Calhoun, of South Carolina, called for the nullification of the laws claiming States Rights over Federal Law, which would later be echoed in the calls for secession from the Union.

Then in 1832 again Congress raised the average tariff level to 50%. Southern States once again rose in opposition to the move. South Carolina called a state convention and voted to nullify the 1828 and 1832 tariffs. Despite their efforts the tariffs still remained near 15% until 1860.

In the 1860 Presidential Election the issue of tariffs was one of the major issues debated with Lincoln generally being in favor of them as a legitimate means of protecting American industrial interests and raising revenue for the Federal Treasury. In their 1859-60 session the U.S. House of Representatives passed the Morris Tariff Bill which once again had the effect of raising the tax on southern goods - this time from 15% to 37%, with scheduled increases to 47 % within 3 years. This tariff like all the others was very popular in the North, as it protected their industrial interests, but further damaged the Southern economy.

When Abraham Lincoln won election in 1860 on a platform supporting tariffs and pledging to keep slavery out of the territories, seven slave states in the deep South seceded and formed a new nation, the Confederate States of America. The incoming Lincoln administration and most of the Northern people refused to recognize the legitimacy of their secession. They feared that it would discredit the Republic and create a fatal precedent that would eventually fragment the no-longer United States into several small, squabbling countries.

By April 1861 slavery had become inextricably entwined with States' Rights, the power of the federal government over the states, the South's 'way of life' etc. – all of which made a major contribution to the causes of the American Civil War. (The History Learning Site). Indeed this point of view has much validity as well, and was a rallying cry for many Confederate Volunteers from different states where slavery was not a common occurrence - particularly among independent minded people from the Appalachian Mountain Regions of these states.

Regardless of your position on this controversial issue you will certainly find many who agree with you and others that place the major emphasis on other factors. However, it is historically more accurate to realize that there were many issues about which the Northern and Southern States disagreed and that eventually entered into the decision of some states to secede from the Union and form the Confederacy - and that eventually led to the American Civil War.

Slavery In the Appalachian Region:

While slavery was perhaps the single most unresolvable political issue facing America in the years immediately before the Civil War, it was certainly not the only one, and not always the primary one. In fact for the counties comprising the Appalachian Region of Virginia and Kentucky the low number of slaves would suggest that decisions about the loyalty of many individuals from southwestern Virginia and eastern Kentucky during the conflict were often made for a variety of other reasons.

County:	Total Population:	Slave Population:	Percentage Slave:
Breathitt, Ky	3785	170	4.49%
Clay, Ky	5421	515	9.50%
Estill, Ky	5985	411	6.87%
Floyd, Ky	5714	149	2.61%
Harlan, Ky	4268	123	2.88%
Johnson, Ky	3873	30	0.77%
Knox, Ky	7050	612	8.68%
Laurel, Ky	4145	192	4.63%
Lee, Va	10267	787	7.67%
Letcher Ky	2510	62	2.47%
Owsley Ky	3774	136	3.60%
Perry Ky	3092	117	3.78%
Pike Ky	5365	98	1.83%
Russell, Va	11919	982	8.24%
Scott, Va	9829	473	4.81%
Smyth, Va	8162	1064	13.04%
Tazewell, Va	9942	1060	10.66%
Washington, Va	14612	2131	14.58%
Whitley, Ky	7447	201	2.70%
Total	127,162	9313	7.32%
Totals for 1860:	160157	9968	6.22%

From the U.S. Bureau of Census, Seventh Census of the United States, 1850.

Of this region the upper valley counties of Russell, Tazewell, Smyth, and Washington (all in Virginia), had by far the largest numbers of slaves. This was largely because the land there enabled larger farming operations and they had easy access to the Virginia & Tennessee Railroad to get their crops to market. Factoring out these four counties drops the regional percentage of slaves to 4.94 in 1850 and 3.58 in 1860.

In many parts of the region slaves were much more heavily involved in work other than agriculture. The Salt-Works at Saltville, Va. and Goose Creek, Ky. employed hundreds of slaves. Other large employers were iron furnaces, coal mines, and the timbering industry. Transporting goods produced also utilized large numbers of slaves. Others worked as flat-boat guides, wagon-drivers, etc.

Dr. Mary Walker – Civil War Surgeon

Dr. Mary Walker was born in 1832 in Oswego Town near Oswego, New York. As a child she was known for her strength of character and her tendency to speak her mind. As she grew up she became a very energetic and independent young woman who was determined to live a life that made a difference in the world. In her early years she wore bloomers, the pantaloon style garb of the radical feminists of the age. When she graduated from Syracuse Medical College in 1855, the only female in her class, she became one of the few women physicians in the country.

At the outbreak of the Civil War in 1861 Dr. Walker, then 29, travelled to Washington D.C. and applied for an appointment as an Army surgeon. The Medical Department summarily rejected her application with considerable negative comments.

Not one to be discouraged she stayed in Washington serving as an unpaid volunteer in various camps. When the patent office was converted into a hospital she served without pay as assistant surgeon. During that time she was instrumental in establishing an organization that aided needy women who came to Washington to visit wounded relatives.

Dr. Walker met with considerable abuse over her persistent demands to be made a surgeon but also earned considerable respect for her many good works. Meanwhile she abandoned bloomers and adopted a modified version of male attire with a calf length skirt worn over trousers, keeping her hair relatively long and curled so that anyone would know she was a woman.

In November of 1862 Dr. Walker took her request to the Virginia headquarters of Major General

Ambrose Burnside and was taken on as a field surgeon, although still on a volunteer basis. She treated the wounded at the Battles of Warrenton and in Fredericksburg in December of that year.

About a year later she was in Chattanooga tending the casualties of the battle of Chickamauga. After the battle she again requested a commission as an Army doctor, this time to Major General George H. Thomas. After some deliberation he appointed her an assistant surgeon in the Army of the Cumberland, assigning her to the 52d Ohio Regiment. She soon received many accolades for her bravery under fire.

In April 1864 she was captured by Confederate troops, having remained behind to tend wounded after a Union retreat. Primarily because of her male attire she was charged and convicted of being a spy. She spent four months in various prisons, suffering much abuse for her unladylike occupation and attire. She was eventually exchanged for a Confederate surgeon in August of 1864.

In October of the same year the Medical Department granted Dr. Walker a contract as an acting assistant surgeon. Despite her requests for battlefield duty she was again not sent into the field. She spent the rest of the war as superintendent at a Louisville, Ky. female prison hospital and a Clarksville, Tenn., orphanage.

Released from government contract at the end of the war Dr. Walker lobbied for a brevet promotion to major for her services. Secretary of War Stanton would not grant the request. Wishing to honor her, President Andrew Johnson asked for another way to recognize her service. A Medal of Honor was presented to Dr. Walker in January 1866 which she proudly wore every day for the rest of her life.

Following the war Dr. Walker remained active in the women's rights movement and crusaded against immorality, alcohol and tobacco and for clothing and election reform. One of her more unusual positions was that there was no need for a women's suffrage act as women already had the vote as result of being American citizens.

Her taste in clothes caused frequent arrests on such charges as impersonating a man. At one trial she asserted her right to, "Dress as I please in free America on whose tented fields I have served for four years in the cause of human freedom." The judge dismissed the case and ordered the police never to arrest Dr. Walker on that charge again. She left the courtroom to hearty applause.

In 1916 Congress revised the Medal of Honor standards to include only those with actual combat experience against an enemy. Several months later the Board of Medal Awards which was reviewing the merits of the awardees during the Civil War ruled that Dr. Walker's medal, as well as those of 910 other recipients, were unwarranted and revoked.

She died on February 21, 1919 at the age of 86. However Dr. Walker was not forgotten. Nearly 60 years after her death, at the urging of a descendent, the Army Board for Correction of Military

Records reviewed her case. On June 19, 1977 Army Secretary Clifford L. Alexander approved the recommendation by the board to restore the Medal of Honor to Dr. Mary E. Walker, surgeon.

She remains the sole female recipient of the Medal of Honor.

The Bush Mill

Before 1859 Joshua and Sarah Addington owned approximately 350 acres of land on Amos Branch and Copper Creek in Scott County, VA. On January 18, 1859 they sold property on Amos Branch, about a mile northwest of Nickelsville, to John Dickenson of Russell County, Virginia. Sometime later he built a log grist mill there. His mill served Nickelsville and the larger community for several years,

On November 12, 1870 John Dickenson and his wife Fanny sold the mill and property to Valentine Bush for $6,000.00. It is likely that Valentine Bush was actually operating the mill before purchasing it from John Dickenson. This is suspected for in 1866 Valentine's son, George G. Bush, "was sitting astride his horse while it was drinking from Amos's branch, next to the grist mill, and was ambushed by an unknown assassin. The shot killed him instantly and Valentine found [him] lying in the water". George is buried in the Nickelsville First Baptist Church Cemetery in the older, smaller section on the East side of the Church. His headstone reads: *"Felled by the hand of an assassin."*

Valentine Bush and his wife, Nancy Gose Bush and family, including W.T. Frazier, his son-in-law, were definitely operating the mill in 1870. W.T Frazier married Bush's daughter, Elisa A. (Bush) Frazier.

The original log mill was eventually destroyed by fire. The exact date of the fire is unknown and the surrounding circumstances supported only by local legends. According to these legends the fire occurred on April 1 sometime in the late 1800's. Because it was "April Fool's Day" farmers in nearby fields saw the smoke but initially thought the cries for help were some kind of joke. By the time they realized that the mill was actually on fire and responded it was too late to save it.

It is likely that the fire that destroyed the original log mill occurred in 1895 as work began on the new Bush Mill in 1896. They would surely have used the limestone foundation stones, taken from Copper Ridge, that supported both the old log mill and the fifteen hundred (1,500) foot mill race from the limestone dam downstream to the mill. The new mill was framed with oak beams and covered with yellow poplar boards.

"The first bushel of wheat was poured into the mill at 5 p.m., September 24, 1897, by W.T. Frazier and Frank Stewart. Jim Stewart, the first mill[w]right was responsible for building the spouts, troughs, boxes, and assembling the machinery. Machinery was supplied by Tyler and Tate of Knoxville, Tenn. Jim Stewart also built the first wheel for the mill which was made of wood. Later, the second wheel was hauled by wagon from Gate City by Harve Castle and Will Elam."

The Bush Mill was the center of community life and a very busy place. People brought bushels of wheat and corn by horse-drawn wagons. Some carried their "turn of corn" [sack full] to the mill by horseback. They waited in line for millers to grind their grain, and while they waited they visited, shared stories, and caught up on community news.

Millers charged a grinding toll. "For one bushel of wheat [60 lbs.] one would receive 37 lbs. of flour and 12 lbs. of bran. The price for grinding one bushel of corn was one toll dish (1 gal.) full." At harvest time, the mill operated around the clock. The night miller or millers hung oil lamps from the ceiling to illuminate the milling operation. W.T Frazier provided overnight lodging nearby for those who needed it. His wife, Eliza A., cooked for the guests and mill workers.

Five years later Valentine Bush, now 94 years old, deeded about sixty-three acres of land, including the Bush Mill, to his grandchildren. (R.S. Richmond, Nellie Carrico, Lizzie Richmond, Maud Richmond and Allie Horn).

Valentine Bush died in 1904. On September 23, 1909 his heirs sold the mill and about 16½ acres to J.H. Darter. J.H. Darter and J.M. Darter were brothers and partners in the Bush Mill property. About two years later J.M. sold his half interest to his brother for $1,500.00. William Washington (W.W.) "Bee" Bond ran the mill for J.H. and J.M Darter and he and his family are pictured at the mill below.

W.W. Bond, his family and others are shown in this 1909 picture. Note that W.W. Bond's left arm is missing. It was amputated above his elbow because of cancer. His wife, Nannie E. (McConnell) Bond, is standing between two unidentified ladies. The three young men on the timbered pier above the others are young Samuel Henry Bond and his brothers, George and Pat.

Samuel H. (S.H.) Bond married Dona E. (Frazier) Bond on June 17, 1911 and they began housekeeping at the little house on the small lot beside the mill. At the time Sam helped his father, W.W., operate the mill for J.H. and J.M. Darter. Sam and W.W. Bond bought the mill from J.H. Darter on February 18, 1920. W.W. and Sam Bond renamed the Bush Mill the "Bond Roller Mill," and it operated under that name for thirty-two (32) years.

In the mid1940's Sam Bond was stricken with cancer and his son in law, James Howard Dixon, and their family moved back to the area and ran the mill until 1952 when it was sold to Lonnie Hartsock.

Lonnie Hartsock operated the mill for a while, mostly grinding corn. He also opened a small store on the smokehouse floor of the small dairy building which was on the property. He died before he could pay off the Negotiable Promissory Notes on the two tracts of land. Dona Bond, widowed by then, took the property back on September 22, 1958.

On September 26, 1959, Dona Bond sold the property to the Nickelsville Chapter of the Future Farmers of America. The Bush Mill is now owned by the Scott County, Virginia School Board and is on long-term lease to the Nickelsville Ruritan Club, who maintain it and sponsor special commemorative festivals there.

On these special days Bush Mill once again becomes the center of the community and warm conversation and laughter mingle with the rushing of Amos Branch in the little valley, as it has for over 150 years.

(Special Acknowledgement is given to my cousin, Jay (James H.) Dixon, Ph.D., for his extensive and well-researched manuscript – "Bush Mill History" copyright April 19, 2008, from which most of the information in this article was taken).

The 48th Virginia Infantry Regiment (C.S.A.)

The Regiment was organized at Big Spring, near Abingdon, Va. in September of 1861, and was composed of volunteers from Lee, Russell, Scott, Smyth, and Washington Counties. Virginia's Governor Fletcher recommended John Arthur Campbell of Washington County for the position of Colonel of the 48th and Thomas Stuart Garnett of Westmoreland County for the position of Lieutenant Colonel. Both were graduates of the VMI Class of 1844 and were approved by the legislature.

The following local militia companies were organized and became part of the 48th Virginia Infantry Regiment:

The Smyth Rifle Greys was the first to organize, May 18, 1861, and was composed of 97 men from in and around Seven Mile Ford. Led by Captain James Scott Greever, they were designated Company D in April of 1862.

The Osborne Ford Independents from Scott County were the second company to organize, enrolling 89 men at Osborne Ford (now Dungannon) on the Clinch River, on May 25. They elected Henry W. Osborne their Captain and were designated Company C.

The Holston Foresters registered 75 men on June 15 in Washington County electing David A. P. Campbell their Captain and were designated Company F.

The Mountain Marksmen enrolled 92 men in Washington County on June 18 and elected Cummings Campbell their Captain and were designated Company I.

The Campbell Greys of Washington County registered 95 men in Abingdon on June 20 and elected Milton White their Captain, becoming Company B.

The Russell Guards of Russell County enlisted 84 men on June 25 and became Company K, commanded by Captain John H. Candler.

The Clinch Mountain Boomers enrolled 67 men in Scott County on June 26 and became Company H with William James Smith as their Captain.

The Stock Creek Greys enlisted 75 men on July 1 in Scott County and was commanded by Captain John Matlock Vermillion. They were designated Company A.

The Nickelsville Spartan Band enrolled 74 men at Nickelsville in Scott County on July 2. With Henry M. McConnell as their Captain. They were designated Company E.

The Lee County Guards enlisted 69 men at Jonesville in Lee County on July 15, commanded by Captain Elbert S. Martin and designated Company G.

The Nickelsville Spartan Band

The Nickelsville Spartan Band was formed July 2, 1862 and enrolled 74 men from in and around the Town of Nickelsville, Va. The group elected a local farmer, Henry M. McConnell, as their Captain. The women of the Town supplied the volunteers with shoulder bags made of heavy cloth or leather and provisions for two days. After a few days the group marched 35 miles to Abingdon, Va. and on July 13, 1861 they were mustered into the Virginia Army of Volunteers as Company H of the 48th Regiment. Company H became part of Gen. Stonewall Jackson's army and fought in several engagements. Company H was then placed in Company E of the 48th Virginia Regiment.

The soldier of the 48th were recruited from five southwestern Virginia counties including Lee, Russell, Smyth, Scott, and Washington. They first joined Generals Loring and Lee in their fruitless expedition in the western Virginia mountain. In the rain and damp of this campaign many found that death was as likely to come by disease as a Northern bullet. They spent a miserable winter around Romney, WV. The spring found them in the Shenandoah Valley where they took part in the actions that were to immortalize General Thomas J. "Stonewall" Jackson. They were engaged at McDowell, Winchester, Cross Keys, and Port Republic.

They marched out of the mountains to help in the defense of Richmond at Gaines Mill and Malvern Hill. In the Second Bull Run campaign they fought at Groveton, Bull Run, and Ox Hill (Chantilly). They were at Sharpsburg and Fredericksburg. Chancellorsville was glorious and deadly. The 48th was with Jackson when he marched around Hooker's army and rolled up the Federal XI Corps. Sadly later that day "Stonewall" received the wound that would kill him. The next morning Lt. Col. Thomas W. Garnett, commander of the 48th, was mortally wounded in the throat. One third of the regiment was killed, wounded, or captured at Chancellorsville.

Gettysburg was equally horrific. On the evening of July 2, 1863 the 48th crossed Rock Creek and charged up Culp's Hill - "a rugged and rocky mountain, heavily timbered and difficult of ascent; a natural fortification, rendered more formidable by deep entrenchments and thick abatis,. They managed to push to within 10 paces of the Union line. Five men were killed or wounded carrying the regimental colors. Over 36% of the men of the regiment were killed or wounded July 2 & 3, 1863.

On May 5, 1864, the 48th was one of the first units engaged in the Battle of the Wilderness. Their regimental commander, Brig. Gen. John Marshal Jones, was wounded in one of the first Federal volleys. He was surrounded by men of the Federal V Corps. It is said that he was then killed because he refused to surrender to enlisted men and an officer was not present.

In the early hours of May 12, 1864, while most of the regiment were going out on picket duty in front of the Mule Shoe salient at Spotsylvania, "Gen. Hancock's II Corps came out of the fog, rolled over the 48th, and into the salient".

The division of Edward "Old Allegheny" Johnson was virtually destroyed. Many of the division, including 104 from the 48th and General Johnson, were captured. The 48th left the trenches of Petersburg later that summer to join Jubal Early's march up the Shenandoah to the defenses of Wahsington, DC. They fought at Monocracy and Fort Stevens before the disasters of Fisher's Hill and Cedar Creek destroyed Early's command.

They returned to the siege at Petersburg and took part in the futile assault on Fort Stedman. What remained of the regiment joined Lee in the final campaign to Appomattox Court House. Of the 1,312 men who served in the regiment, only 5 officers and 40 enlisted men received their paroles at the surrender and only one member of the Nickelsville Spartan Band was able to attend.

The regiment had the following higher command assignments:

May 20, 1862, 2nd Brigade, Stonewall Jackson Division, Army of the Northern Division Famous Battles/Engagements: Shenandoah Valley, May 15-June 17 1862; Harper's Ferry, WV-May 24-30,1862; 2nd Bull Run Campaign/Battle-Aug 16-Sept 2, 1862; Battle Antietam (Sharpsburg), MD-Sept 16 & 17,1862; Battle ;of Chancellorville, VA-April 27-May 5, 1863; Battle of Gettysburg, PA Campaign May 1-August 1863,Battle July 1-3, 1863; Retreat to Manassas Gap, VA July 5-24, 1863; Sheridan's Campaign, Shenandoah Valley-Aug 7-Nov 28, 1864; Assault, Ft. Stedman, VA March 25, 1865; Appomattox Campaign, Mar.28-April 9,

1865 Surrender-Under Gen. Robert E. Lee, Appomattox Courthouse, Va. April 9, 1865.

(*Information from Appalachian Quarterly June 2002 Issue).

The 64th Virginia Mounted Infantry Regiment

The 64th Virginia Mounted Infantry Regiment was formed from troops raised in Lee, Scott, Wise and Buchanan counties in Virginia for service in the Confederate States Army during the American Civil War. It served as an infantry regiment, a cavalry regiment, and a mounted infantry (dragoon) unit, and had a mixed reputation.

Its troops originally were recruited in 1861 as the 21st Virginia Infantry Battalion, or the "Pound Gap Battalion", with assurances that they would be fighting mostly near home in western Virginia, and eastern Tennessee and Kentucky. Many failed to re-enlist after their year of service ended in 1862. Morale was a problem in part because of the poor clothing and provisions they were issued, as well as their initial duties of arresting and guarding Unionists in the tri-state region. The 64th Virginia also gained a reputation for their lack of discipline.

The 64th Regiment Virginia Mounted Infantry was organized in December 1862 in Abingdon by consolidating the 21st and 29th Virginia Infantry Battalions. The 21st had been raised by Confederate Brigadier General Felix K. Zollicoffer and Major John B. Thompson after the 1861 harvest, with soldiers volunteering for a year's service. It was supposed to defend Southwest Virginia from Pike County, Kentucky and the watershed of the Tug River to the Saltville, Virginia saltworks, including the Cumberland Gap. Its commander, Brigadier General Humphrey Marshall, (a former Kentucky congressman) wanted these troops sent to Nashville, TN, but the 5th Kentucky was sent instead.

They were consolidated with the newly recruited 29th Virginia Infantry as 1861 ended. However, General Zollifoffer died in the Battle of Mill Springs in Kentucky on January 18, 1862 and so had limited association with the unit, and General Marshall would also resign in the late spring (he later withdrew his resignation but was assigned elsewhere).

On September 9, 1862 Confederate brevet General John W. Frazer surrendered most of this dismounted unit at the Cumberland Gap to Union General Ambrose Burnside. Col. Campbell Slemp of the 64th Virginia and Major Byron G. McDowell of the 62nd North Carolina however, slipped out into the mountains with about 600 men rather than surrender, and re-formed their unit at Zollicoffer, Tennessee (now Bluff City, Tennessee).

Captain William R. Boles of the 64th Virginia angrily attacked Col. Frazer when he heard the order, but was pulled off by Union officers. Many of the 1,026 Confederate prisoners (425 of them members of this unit, plus troops from Georgia, North Carolina, Kentucky, and Tennessee) were sent to Louisville, Kentucky then to Camp Douglas (Chicago). There, about 150 died in the unsanitary conditions and 43 men enlisted in the Union Army or Navy to escape the horrible prison camp. Col. Frazer wrote his official account of the Battle of the Cumberland Gap while a Union prisoner at another camp.[2]

The surrender necessitated a late 1862 reorganization. The new unit was sometimes known as the 64th Virginia Mounted Infantry or the 64th Virginia Infantry. After September 1, 1863, it was also called the 64th Virginia Cavalry because another reorganization in October 1863 briefly placed the 64th Virginia in Brig. John Stuart Williams' Cavalry Brigade. However, that brigade drew ill will in the Lee County area by its methods of confiscating provisions, especially horses to replace mounts.

On October 20, 1863 a federal raiding party sent by Union General Wilcox surprised Col. Slemp's encamped 64th Infantry near Jonesville and managed to destroy much of their equipment and supplies. On November 5, 1863, Williams' brigade managed to intercept the federal raiders but the 64th Virginia basically tagged along.

In January 1864 Col. Slemp was court-martialed by Brig. Gen. "Grumble" Jones for dereliction of duty based on events of November 7, 1863, when Slemp ordered 10 or 15 wagons captured from the enemy moved, endangering the column while on the road from Rogersville to Blountville. Although many Virginians tried to get the charges dropped and Lt. Col. Auburn L. Pridemore tried to press charges against Gen. Jones for leapfrogging past Col. Giltner's 4th Kentucky Cavalry and crossing the Holston River behind enemy forces on that specified date, Capt. H. Brown of the 8th Virginia Cavalry and Major Rhea of Tennessee continued to press the dereliction and ill-discipline charges. Col. Slemp hurt his cause by slipping house arrest in Abingdon prior to trial and instead returning home to Lee County. He was convicted, relieved of command, and dismissed from the Confederate army.[3]

Later the 64th Virginia continued to confront the Federals in various conflicts in East Tennessee, Western Virginia, and North Carolina until the war's end. However its equipment and manpower problems continued. During April 1864 it totaled 268 effectives, but in April 1865, fewer than 50 when it was disbanded.

The major field officers (all future U.S. congressmen) were Colonels Campbell Slemp of Company A, Auburn L. Pridemore of Company C, and Lieutenant Colonel James B. Richmond (after January 1863); as well as Major Harvey Gray (of Company E and F, especially after February 1864).

The Blackwell Letters From the Civil War

Actual letters to and from soldiers who were far away from their families during the Civil War give us a rare glimpse into this time and the situations faced by those who lived through it. The following letters are representative of many that have survived to provide us this unique opportunity. (The letters are not edited and contain their original spelling.)

Dear Brother,

dear brother will drop you a few lines I go your letter and _____ 100 and a half of 1 dollar for 1 box fifty cents a _____ in the big _____ You said nothing about the little _____ in your letter and I not know what to think about it but I paid for 2 boxes one box in the big box and one box marked to me I want you to write to me about it and if I send you 10 dollars _____ money 2 $5 dollars bills and I sent for 1 pair of boots 5 gallons of Whisky if you can for its from 15-20 dollars a gallon. I want you to send me a bill of everything you send me. I don't know wether I will get the things you sent me or not but I think I will. _____ brother you don't know the trouble that I see in this army for they are so many sorts of people where if I could jest be at your house and rest one week how glad I would be. With Riba and David and Liza an you all. Dear Mother I will have to be in a hurry for my candle is getting very near burnt out an it is bed time. Well dear mother sisters and brothers I would like to be with you all but distance keeps me from you all but if alive when my time is out I am coming home to see you. If I could be with you all how glad I would be but if I dont never more see you on earth I hope to meet you in heaven to where worry and trouble is no more. Tell Brother William to try and do the things that is right to shun all _____ company and do all he can for mother. _____ _____ _____ _____ _____ _____ _____ will try to bring my letter to a close and god bless you all _____ this troublesome world and (if lord?) when they come to die save them in they kingdom for your sake my friends.

B M Blackwell to mother sisters and Brothers _____ _____ _____ good by brother

Chimbaraso Hospital #1
Ward 1
Richmond Virginia

September the 5 1863

Dear Brother,

I once more take my pen in hand to inform you that I am still nocking about as _____ and I hope when this comes to hand it will find you still well and your family. Mat I have been a looking for a letter from you for 2 or 3 days, tho I have not got it yet. Dear brother, I havt no news to rite this morning of any importants. Mat, I heard that the yankis had Knoxville, Teenessee and was marching for Saltville, and I want you to let me no if it is so or not and Mat I want you to let me no what you intend to doo if they doo come. Mat if I was you I wod stay with my famly and dy with them for I dont think that you nor me ought to fight for we did not have no hand in making it I don't intend to do any fighting if I can help it for hear is those swell headed upshots that owns all the property and has keep out of the armmy all the while that I can hear them saying that we have done this and we have done that, and we have whipped the yankis hard and all this kind of thing and you no what they are up to all the time If you don't I do They ar speculating and making more of this rebelion money than they no what to do with and now they are giving 20 dollars of it for one dollar of gold or silver How can they afford to do this Why very easy for they have made so much that they dont no what to do with it And how have they made all this money Why they have mad it off the soldiers that is the field fiting for their (slaves) And how have they made it off them? They have made it by selling what the soldiers ought to of had. They would go and press whatever they wanted, and pay the government price for it, and then sell it for 20 prices, and the government paid for these things and these speculators sell it and put the money in their pockets, and to ask them what we are fighting fro, they will say, "for our liberty that our forefathers gained for us." I say it is a lie. It is true they fought and gained our independence, and established a union and constitution, which was called the United States of America, and we have rebelled against the Union, and if you was to say you was a Union man you would be shot or put under arrest right short, and I say they are fighting against what our forefathers fought for, and anybody else that can see. And the soldiers get eleven dollars a month, and how can a man that has a family support them? It would not pay for more than one meal vituals for a small family, and what encouragement does a soldier have to fight under such a government as they have got in the Confederate States? I tell you the poor soldiers gets poor encouragement to fight for.

Mat...everything looks like it is going on wrong since Jackson was killed, and I believe that we will at last have to come back in the Union at last, and I am sorry to think that all our hardships and fighting will do no good, for I was in hopes that we could gain our independence, tho I have lost all hopes, I don't think we will ever gain our independence as long as we fight or turned against my country for I am not, tho if they evacuate Virginia they will leave me unless they are very smart, and have plenty of guards and chains to keep in in the cars.

Mat...I want you to write as soon as this comes to hand, and give me all the news, and let me know if you got that letter that had another one in it, and if you gave it to them. Give my love and best respects to all my inquiring friends, and stay at home as long as you can get the chance. So I will bring my badly composed letter to a close, so nothing more., I hope this cruel war will soon end. So goodbye dear Brother for this time.

Only remain your affectionate Brother until death, (From B. M. Blackwell to Mathew R. Blackwell)

Sept the 29 1863
                         Dear brother

After respects I drop you a few lines which leaves me jest tolerable well her hoping they may find you enjoying the same Gods blessing I received yours of the 13 of this month, and have never had the chance to anser until now I have no news this morning Everything is still this morning, tho we have our marching orders We have to keep two days rashings at hand It is supposed that we will go to Port Royal, about sixty miles down the river from where we were in camp last winter, tho it is uncertain where we will go when we start I never make any calculations when we are throwing up breast works day and night, and have been for two weeks We will soon be fortified to Chancelorsville works where we fought last spring We have been looking for a big fight here for some time, tho I hope we will not have to fight here anymore Mat I heard that the Yankees were between Bristol and Abingdon, and I am afraid they will come to the Salt Works yet We have a heap of guard duty to do now We have to go on guard every other night Mat I will have to close James Holly is well and sends his "Howdy" to you Matt Tell N.M. that I would like to see her, and write to me and let me know where she is and what she is doing for herself I want to see you all very badly at this time I would like to see the children, and would like to see my "Pink" too, so I will close for the present Mat I want you to tell Mother to pay Dr. Henry what is coming to him It is not more than two or three dollars, I don't think Give my love and respects to J.D.B. So, will bring my few badly composed lines to a close. Write soon – nothing more, only

        I remain your affectionate Brother until death
        Benjamin M. Blackwell

To: Mr. Mathew R. Blackwell
Tell the children "Howdy" for me - So farewell for this time

May 6th, 1864

In line of battle between Love Grove and Chancelorsville about 16 miles below Average (Orange?) C.H., Va.

Matthew R. Blackwell, I am sorry to inform you that your brother Ben was killed yesterday evening. He was buried today. I fixed a board to put to his grave so his remains can be found at any time, if you wish to come after him. You can come to the 48 and some of us will go with you to his grave. Our loss yesterday was 80 killed, wounded and missing. Me, James and David Venable is yet unhurt, tho we are now under fire and has been all day. There is the hardest fight going on now that ever has been known, I think. Excuse me dear friend for not writing no more. I will write again as soon as this fight is over. Tell my folks we are well. Thompson McHerry was mortally wounded. I guess he is dead by this time. Thomas Dutton was killed. Dave Thomas and William Harden out of our company Wm. H. McNew is well as yet. They changed (charged?) us this morning with 6 lines of battle. We had but one line tho, we were in breast work. Our loss was about 8 this morning. There was about 16 hundred Yankees killed in front of our breast works and this place and report is that we are whiping them all around the line about 15 miles. All the rest of the boys is yet alive of that neighborhood as far as I have heard. Write soon. I will have to close if I get out alive. I will write all about it. The Yankee prisoners say they have 2 hundred thousand men on this side of the river. I would be surprised and this fight last 8 or 10 days. I will close hoping to hear from you soon. I yet remain your loving cousin till death,

        John S. Colley (Holley)

Wrote by the hands of a friend, I.M.T. Murdock. (Mr. Blackwell please let my folks know that I am alive and well. They are charging now and I have to close.)

        Your friend , I.M.T. Murdock

Hard Times and Deep Division Among The People of Southwest Virginia

By the autumn of 1864 families of Southwest Virginia were suffering terribly from hunger and the need of clothing and shoes. Many of the men had joined either the Confederate or Union Armies leaving women and those men either too young or old to serve to tend to the needs of the family and farms.

Communities and even families were often bitterly divided over the War and opinions were deeply and firmly held. Everyone, regardless of their loyalty, was suffering from the shortages and hardships created. Both armies were guilty of taking advantage of the people and making their plight worse.

The Confederate Congress passed a law that required people to give a percentage of their meager provisions to the Confederate Government to help feed the army. This embittered many people against the Confederacy and often led to people hiding their meat and vegetables in caves and other places where they hoped it couldn't be found by either Confederate or Union Troops who came through.

To make matters worse Marauders, who were little more than outlaw gangs, sometimes showed up stealing what little they had left. The people were tense and bitter and weary of the hardships they lived with.

Many courts, schools, and other community and civic activities were suspended. There was no association meeting held in the Stoney Creek district that year (1864) because *"there are no provisions to feed the people"*. The deep divisions in the communities extended to the Churches as well and in 1865 the Stoney Creek Association sent letters to its churches which read: *We advise our churches that if any of their members shall aid or assist the Federal Government in any way contrary to the laws of the Confederate States of America, that they be dealt with for disorder, unless full satisfaction be given, and that the same be excluded from the church.*

The Copper Creek Church sent the following reply to the Stoney Creek Association: *To be loyal to the Federal Government and the Union of the United states is just and right, that to support and defend the Federal Government against foreign enemies and domestic traitors is a moral obligation binding upon all good citizens, and it has received sanctions of the only true God of heaven and earth by bringing the so-called Southern Confederate Government to nothingness. Therefore, to be loyal to the Federal Government does not bring any member of our churches into disorder.*

The Copper Creek Church passed the following resolution: *that no minister of the Gospel of our faith and order be allowed to preach in this church without consent of the church who has aided in the rebellion against the United States.*

Other Churches held equally strong and divergent views about the War and everyone longed for the terrible War to be over. At times it seemed like it never would be.

Marauders in the Big Moccasin Valley

As the American Civil War dragged on people all across America began to increasingly suffer. There were shortages of almost all the goods they had come to depend on. In many homes only the women, children, and old men remained to tend the garden, farm animals and to all the necessities of life. This was particularly true in the South and was made considerably worse when the tide begun to turn against the Confederacy. With their defeat at the Battle of Gettysburg (July 1-3, 1863) and Vicksburg one day later, the problem was made much worse.

The fall of Vicksburg deprived the Confederacy of the use of the Mississippi River. The trans-Mississippi Department had come to be the principal sources from which horses, cattle, hogs and other supplies were obtained for the Southern armies. On July 9, 1863 the South lost the Port of Hudson, Louisiana and from this date communication between the states east and west of the Mississippi River were cut.

President Lincoln had proclaimed a blockade of the Confederate States on April 19, 1861 which eventually reached from Virginia to Texas, thus stopping the export of farm products from the Southern States and the import of foreign goods.

In response the Confederate Congress on March 26, 1863 passed the Impressments Tax which was a tax on goods and services. This included the tithe tax on agricultural products and livestock, in essence an income tax on the farmers and planters, which was paid in produce and live or slaughtered animals. It was by this tax that the Confederate armies were, to a large extent, supplied during the last year or so of the war.

As the spring of 1864 approached supplies in the South became very scarce and the people began to suffer from hunger and for the want of clothing and shoes.

Marauders had also begun to roam the South. Some of them under the pretense of collecting supplies for the Confederacy. Many such groups were nothing more than outlaws, preying on helpless citizens and stealing what little they had. There was little most people could do to stop them.

Like all rural communities Scott County had it's share of these marauders and in the Spring of 1864 a group of them began to raid and pillage in the Big Moccasin Valley. Their victims were mostly women and old men, as the Confederate Congress had passed the Conscription Act, Feb. 17, 1864 which required all men, 17 to 50, to serve in the Army.

The last week in April 1864 was a typical warm and beautiful time. The grass had turned green, spring flowers were blooming, the birds were nesting, and the people in Moccasin Valley had begun to get their land ready for planting.

One day in mid-afternoon a band of marauders came up the valley. Meeting no resistance they took everything they could carry away. Word spread and people worried who would be their next target. Most people hid what little they had left to live on, hoping it wouldn't be found. But others had suffered enough and began to consider another plan.

The outlaws crossed Big Moccasin Creek late in the afternoon and made camp on the east side. There they laughed and celebrated their successful raids. Later they cooked their supper of stolen provisions and rested in the shade of the trees along the bank of the creek as the sun sunk low on the horizon. As evening came and nightfall approached they opened their bedrolls and spread them in the thick grass, preparing to retire for the night. Feeling safe and secure they did not post a guard. Shortly after dark a heavy fog formed in the valley along the creek and all that could be heard that night was the croaking of the bullfrogs and shrill piping of the spring peepers. Their soothing songs made for a restful sleep.

Little did the gang of marauders anticipate what was about to befall them. As the last quarter of the moon began to rise over Clinch Mountain, women from the valley began to make their move. They went some distance down the creek and crossed to the east side and very quietly slipped up the creek to where the marauders were sleeping, being careful where they stepped as they drew near the camp. Silently they began to execute their plan of attack. The women worked in pairs. Each woman carried a large hickory maul. Choosing their targets they slipped into position. At the signal they each began to beat the men in the head with their mauls and continued to beat them until they were dead.

After the attack the women recovered their stolen property and that of others including food, guns, knives, jewelry and other valuable items. They also took the horses of the marauders which they would need for farm work.

The next day a common grave was dug and the women, with the help of the old men, carried and dragged each of them to their grave in the Osborne Cemetery, a short distance from where they met their doom. Who these men were is uncertain? Were they part of some Union Army company dressed in civilian clothes, perhaps members of Rowen Rogues who had infested Southwest Virginia, or maybe just common outlaws working only for themselves? A number of theories have been offered, but the mystery remains.

What became very clear is that pushing ordinary people too far often results in an extraordinary responses from them, as the women from the Big Moccasin Valley demonstrated that Spring night.

Excerpts From "The Bluegrass Confederate"

Eduard O. Guerrant was a young Kentuckian who served the Confederate cause from January 1862 through the end of the war as a secretary and adjutant in Kentucky forces, mainly for General Humphrey Marshall in Southwestern Virginia and Kentucky. Throughout this time he kept an extensive diary that gives us a rare, first-hand glimpse into this important time in our history.

Friday 9th May, 1862:

Surpassingly lovely day. Finished some writing for Gov. Hawes today. Became acquainted with Miss Ella Fry of Bristol. Quite a nice and clever girl. Supremely innocent. Escorted her to the R.R. Depot as she left on the evening train. Her ma invited me to stop if ever I passed thro Bristol. Would like to do so!

Saturday 10th May, 1862:

About 11 a.m. I paid my bill for 5 days & ½ $13.50 and started with a dispatch to Gen'l Williams who is encamped at Saltville – to move at daylight tomorrow morning towards Tazewell C.H. I overtook Dr. Rabbe of Carter Co. Ky on the road and finished the journey with him. We dined most excellently at Mr. Morell's – from a kind lady I purchased a fine cheese for the General. The road from Abingdon to Saltville or the Salt Works of Smythe leads through a valley as do all these S.W. Virginia roads. This is rather poorer than most of them, the land rough and rocky and the pastures almost primeval forests, with very little grass beneath.

Saltville is a dirty, smoky looking set of huge salt works and houses for the hands. Not more than 10 or 15 houses: here is the greatest salt manufacturing in the Southern Confederacy. I met Sam Crooks at the Saltworks and he went with me to Gen'l Williams encampment about a mile and 1/3 from town, on the banks of Holston, a beautiful, crystal, mountain streamlet somewhat larger than Old Slate.

Sunday 23d Novr., 1862:

Chilly, wintry morning. Sun rose bright and clear, and far away towards North Carolina revealed the snow covered Clinch Mountains, grandly lifting up their huge white backs like Northern Polar bears. All other snow gone.

Wednesday 31st Dec., 1862:

Waked up this morning in Tennessee! Yesterday evening the enemy destroyed the R.R. bridges across the Holston and Watauga thereby entailing inestimable trouble, expense, and injury to the country. Last night he encamped between the two rivers near their confluence. Today various reports from citizens, scouts, & etc. arrived, reporting him at Halls near Blountville. People of

Bristol and country around foolishly impatient for an advance. Col. Giltners reg't arrived from Lebanon about noon. Late in the evening Giltner's, Clays, & Johnson's Cavalry were all moved towards Moccasin Gap via Blountville. Hawkins & Slemps Infantry & 2 sections of artillery followed hard after. Reports from Baldwin announce the enemy moving off towards Kingsport.

Saturday 25th March, 1865:

Somewhat more pleasant today. Moved the whole command early this morning across Clinch River to Nickelsville, thence across to Big Moccasin. Hd. Qtrs. At Mr. Sutton's tonight. Dismt'd Battn went via Osborne's Ford & Old C. H. to Hansons. 4th K'y stayed near Nickelsville.

Nickelsville is hardly big enough to be named - an old blacksmith shop, grocery, ("played out") & two or three old shanty looking houses. The area called Nickelsville is situated in a big level blackjack swamp. Scott Co. is the poorest and meanest County almost in Western Va. (maybe except Wise & Buchanan).

The 10th K'y Cav. Is at Osborne's Ford and has been "righting" this country, which of late has gotten very wrong. Somewhat Lincolnized. Tired of war & doing without coffee and calico & c.

Wednesday 23d. Nov., 1864:

Stayed in camp all day, trying to keep warm & couldn't., and wrote a few orders, passes, etc. and am sitting tonight, the last one up (as usual) in my cold tent by a warming pine log heap nearly frozen writing this little memorandum for you, dear gentle reader, who may never read a line of it, or give me credit for it if you do, who may never see it, or believe it if you do. But so I write, as the "sower sows" in hope and faith.

Edited by: Davis, William C. and Swentor, Meredith L. (Editors), "Bluegrass Confederate" (The Headquarters Diary of Edward O. Guerrant), Louisiana State University Press, Baton Rouge, L.A., 1999, print

Civil War Graves in the Nickelsville Community Cemetery

One of the things I enjoyed most about growing up in the Small Town of Nickelsville, Virginia was listening to the older folks tell stories and share legends about times past. Somewhere along the way I heard that there were unknown Civil War Soldiers buried in the old Cemetery that now surrounds the 1st Baptist Church. Exploring the area it was easy to see graves with only a field stone and no inscription or only a depression to mark what was clearly a very old grave. Who could be buried there I always wondered. Was it possible that they were unknown Civil War Soldiers? If so who might they be and why were they buried in Nickelsville? These and other questions would often cross my mind but remain unanswered for many years.

Over the years my interest in local history continued and grew, as did my collection of information and primary source material. Among the documents I eventually acquired was an article by Wayne G. McConnell that was published in the Historical Sketches of Southwest Virginia (Publication No. 38 – 2004), which referenced a listing of Confederate Veterans that were buried in our old Community Cemetery. This list was kept by Robert L. McConnell, an older gentleman from our area and given to his sister-in-law, Mrs. Mildred Fleenor McConnell. Excitedly I read what was at least a partial answer to this intriguing question that I had pondered so long. According to Mr. McConnell the following Confederate Veterans were buried there:

Aaron Hartsock, Co. E 64th Va. Mtd. Infantry – on the East side of the Church. The grave has an old marble Confederate marker with no dates.

John Dunlap Gaye, 1833 - 1862, Clarke County, Kentucky - buried on the East side of the Church. The grave has a large, but aging family marker with birth and death years only.

Robert C. (Dugan) Kilgore, - buried on the West side of the Church. A monument was erected by his sister, Mrs. B. F. Curtis but Wayne McConnell did not find the stone.

James M. Quillen, Jan. 30, 1823 - Aug. 22, 1895 – buried on the West side of the Church.

Dr. James Wallace – buried on the West side of the Church, no stone found.

William Bush – Nov. 27, 1840 - Jan. 7, 1902. – buried on the West side of the Church.

Captain. Jas. B. Jackson – (not found), found James Wyly Jackson, Dec. 25, 1831 - Sept. 24, 1902 – buried on the West side of the Church (could this be the same person?)

Jacob Kilgore, July 20, 1844 – Feb. 28, 1920 – buried on the West side of the Church.

Robert H. Dickerson, June 9, 1837 – Feb. 28, 1920 – buried on the West side of the Church.

John H. Darter, Nov. 18, 1848 – Apr. 31, 1937 – buried on the West side of the Church.

John T. Smith, no stone found – buried on the East side of the Church.

George T. Smith, no stone found – buried on the East side of the Church.

Peter H. Kilgore (son of Dugan), no stone found – buried on the West side of the Church.

George G. Bush, October 16, 1838 – Aug. 4, 1866 – buried on the East side of the Church. Has an aging family stone with dates. (Son of Valentine Bush. He was shot by an unknown assassin upstream above the Bush Mill.)

In August of 2011, The Sons of Confederate Veterans out of Eastern Kentucky identified the location and placed markers on the following additional Confederate graves in the Nickelsville Community Cemetery:

Private Harvey H. Archer, 1828 – June 25, 1862. A resident of Nicholas Co., Kentucky. He enlisted in Company D of the 1st Battalion Kentucky Mounted Rifles at Prestonsburg, Ky. on Oct. 22, 1861. No other family information found – Died near Nicholsville, Va. and was buried on the East side of the Church.

Private John H. Archer, 1830 – May 4, 1862. A resident of Nicholas Co., Kentucky. It is suspected but not verified that he is the brother of Harvey Archer. He married Mary Berry in 1856 and enlisted in Company D of the 1st Kentucky Mounted Rifles at Prestonsburg, Ky. on Oct. 22, 1861. He died near Nicholsville, Va. and was buried on the East side of the Church.

* Private John Dunlap Gay, 1833 – April 24, 1862. He was the son of John Dunlap and Catherine Gay. In 1860 he was single and living in Winchester, Kentucky (Clark Co.). He enlisted in Company C of the 1st Battalion Kentucky Mounted Rifles at Prestonsburg, Ky. on Oct. 21, 1861. Sick of the fever and left with a McConnel family near Nicholsville, where he later died. Buried on the East side of the Church.

Private Harvey Owens, 1844 – June 20, 1863. He was born in Perry Co. Kentucky. In 1860 he was single and living in Maggofin Co., Ky. He enlisted in Company D of the 5th Kentucky Infantry on Sept. 3, 1862 at Licking Station (in Maggofin County, Ky.). He was left in a Private Hospital in Cassellwood, Va. and died there. Buried on the East side of the Church.

Private Martin Taylor, 1835 – April 20, 1862, He was the son of Thomas and Sealy Taylor and was married to Millie Taylor. They had two sons and a daughter. Before the war he lived at Lusby's Mill, Kentucky. On October 19, 1861, he enlisted in Company B of the 1st Battalion Kentucky Mounted Rifles in Owen County, Ky. He was sick of the fever near Nicholsville on April 15 and died 5 days later. Buried on the East side of the Church.

* John Dunlap Gay contracted the fever and was left with a McConnel Family near Nicholsville, Va to care for him. The family did what they could for him but he did not recover and was buried in the cemetery as described above. Mr. McConnel was a traveling salesman and on one of his trips to Eastern Kentucky he sought out John's family to let them know what had happened to him and where he was buried. Perhaps this was fulfillment of a promise he made to John or just a feeling of responsibility he had for a young man who had died far from his family. He managed to find the family and share the sad news they had so dreaded to hear. John's sister arranged for a tombstone to be placed on his grave, and it remains today on the East side of the Church with the stones placed by the Sons of Confederate Veterans (SCV) on his and the graves of the other four Confederate soldiers buried beside him.

Each of the others had a story that has thus far eluded me. When and where they were born, when they enlisted and with which battalion, and when and where they died was documented, but this scant information and little more, is all that either the SCV or I have been able to discover. I wish I knew more and perhaps one day I will stumble upon some record or bit of information that will help me better understand who these young men were and how they came to the little Town of Nickelsville to live for a short time and then to die and be buried here.

I am sure that there are other unknown Confederate War Veterans buried in our old Community Cemetery as there are clearly several other graves sites with no marker to identify who is buried there. There may also be Union Veterans buried there as Southwest Virginia was quite divided in its opinion about the Civil War.

It is also important to note that there are many other old cemeteries across the region several of which may also contain the graves of Civil War Veterans, both known and unknown.

And so the mystery of the Civil War Veterans buried in our Community Cemetery continues. A few questions have been partially answered, but, as is often the case in historical research, we are left with even more new questions to wonder about.

Kate Warne, Private Investigator

In 1856 an attractive young widow came into the offices of Allan Pinkerton. At the time he was well on his way to fame as the founder of America's first detective agency. At the time he had no idea that his visitor was far more than just another pretty face; she was Kate Warne and who would become the world's first woman Private Investigator.

Though Pinkerton was clearly impressed by Warne's good looks and graceful style, what really impressed him was her sense of purpose. She was looking for a job, she told him, and he should hire her. "She could go and worm out secrets in many places which it was impossible for male detectives to gain access," Pinkerton wrote years later. "She had evidently given the matter much study." Pinkerton agreed, and a legend was soon born.

Little is known of Warne's life before she became a private eye only that she was about 23 when she came to Pinkerton's office and that she had a knack for acting and undercover work. She soon proved her worth to Pinkerton, befriending the wife of a man who had stolen thousands of dollars from a railroad company and helping find the hidden cash. But her most famous case—helping evade an assassination conspiracy against Abraham Lincoln—was yet to take place.

"She was a brilliant conversationalist when so disposed and could be quite vivacious," Pinkerton later wrote, adding that "she also understood that rarer quality in womankind, the art of being silent." Whether talkative or quiet, Warne's instincts and savvy served her well.

In 1861 Pinkerton learned of an assassination plot against President-elect Lincoln, by a group of Southern conspirators who hated his abolitionist position. Lincoln, who was on a whistle-stop tour from Springfield, Ill. to Washington, D.C. ahead of his inauguration, was to be targeted along the way. But to thwart their plans Pinkerton needed more information.

That is where Kate's special skills were critical. Traveling to Baltimore disguised as a Southern widow, she managed to gain admission to the living rooms of the families of Southerners planning to kill the newly elected Lincoln. The secession ribbon, or cockade, she wore with her clothing helped her further ingratiate herself to the Southern ladies and pull off the ruse. Warne passed the rumors and hints she learned in her conversations along to Pinkerton.

But her job was far from merely gathering information. Details of the plot were eventually pieced together and it was concluded that the assassination was supposed to take place during Lincoln's scheduled stop in Baltimore, the only slaveholding city on his calendar. The President-elect would be especially vulnerable because of all the publicity that had been communicated about his celebratory journey. His only option would be to slip through Baltimore unnoticed at night.

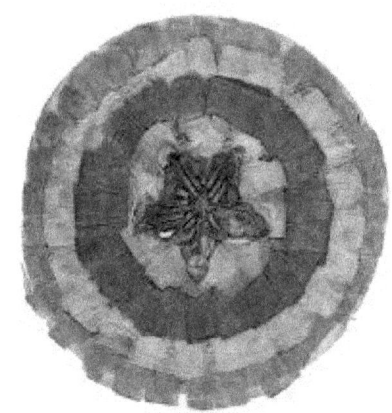

Confederate Secession Cockade

That's where Warne came in. Pinkerton arranged a complex plan that involved Lincoln traveling in the sleeper compartments of regular passenger trains to evade public notice. Warne was in charge of getting the sleeper berths and keeping them available for the future president, then helping slip him onto the train without being noticed or recognized.

Warne pretended she had a sick brother who needed complete peace and quiet on the train. She met a disguised Lincoln at the Philadelphia train station, greeted him as if he were her brother, and accompanied him to the sleeper car. Together they traveled the rest of the way to Washington, including an hour-long delay when the sleeper car had to be transported via horses through Baltimore due to a noise ordinance.

Pinkerton and Warne worked together throughout the Civil War, often posing as husband and wife and infiltrating Southern social groups and gatherings to gain important information. Warne's reputation as a detective quickly became legendary but she did not live long enough to enjoy her fame.

In late 1867 she suddenly contracted pneumonia and on Jan. 28, 1868 with Pinkerton at her side, she died. She was around 35 years of age. Warne's career may have been relatively short but she occupies a large place in history as the first female Private Investigator.

The Assassination of President Abraham Lincoln

On the evening of April 14, 1865, John Wilkes Booth, a famous actor and Confederate sympathizer, assassinated President Abraham Lincoln at Ford's Theatre in Washington, D.C. The attack came only five days after Confederate General Robert E. Lee surrendered his massive army at Appomattox Court House, Virginia, effectively ending the American Civil War. This much of the story is routinely taught and widely known among almost all Americans. But, as is almost always the case, there is considerably more to the story.

Booth was a member of one of America's most renowned families of actors. His father, Junius Brutus Booth, had a long and distinguished career and his brother, Edwin Booth, was widely regarded as the country's leading actor. John Wilkes Booth was an acclaimed performer in his own right, known for his charisma, athleticism, and good looks. However, he was also known for his wild and erratic behavior and his outspoken political views.

Booth grew up in the border state of Maryland and considered himself a Southerner. He was a passionate advocate of the slave system. Having promised his mother that he would not fight for the Confederacy, Booth remained in the North during the Civil War, but his hatred of abolitionists and Lincoln only grew.

In late summer of 1864, Booth decided on a plan to kidnap President Lincoln, take him to Richmond, Virginia (the Capitol of the Confederacy), and use him to secure the release of Southern prisoners of war.

By January of 1865, he had gathered a small band of followers, including Samuel Arnold, Michael O'Laughlen, John Surratt, Lewis Powell, George Atzerdot, and David Herold to assist him in his scheme. In March of 1865, the conspirators began meeting at Mary Surratt's boardinghouse to work out the details of their plan, which they set for March 17, when Lincoln was scheduled to attend a function at a hospital on the outskirts of Washington. Their elaborate plan never came to fruition when Lincoln abruptly altered his plans and stayed in the Capitol.

On April 9, General Robert E. Lee surrendered his large army to General Ulysses S. Grant at Appomattox Court House in Virginia signing the death-nail of the Confederacy and making Booth's plans for a prisoner exchange pointless.

On April 11, Booth was in the crowd that heard Lincoln speak outside the White House and was furious when Lincoln suggested that certain slaves should be given the right to vote. Booth felt that freeing some of the slaves was bad enough but that it was a violation of Christian principles to suggest that they should be taught to read and allowed to vote. Shortly the conspirators met again and Booth angrily proclaimed that Lincoln must be assassinated. He soon discovered that his companions' hatred of the President matched his own and they all agreed to be part of the plan Booth described – which included him killing Lincoln and the others attacking key members of his administration. He and his co-conspirators believed the simultaneous assassination of Lincoln, Vice President Andrew Johnson and Secretary of State William H. Seward–the president and two of his possible successors–would throw the U.S. government into complete disarray. Learning that the President and General Grant would be attending Ford's Theater on April 14, Good Friday, they decided that would be when they would carry out their plan.

As time grew near, they met one last time to finalize their plot. They had learned that General Grant would not be joining President Lincoln after all but it was decided that Booth would continue with his assassination of the President at the Theater. George Alzerodt, a German immigrant who had acted as a boatman for Confederate spies, was assigned to kill Vice President Andrew Johnson in his suite at the Kirkwood House, and Lewis Powell, a tall and powerful former Confederate soldier and David Herold would murder Secretary of State William Seward. All the murders were to take place at 10:15 that night.

Booth stopped by a Tavern on his way and arrived at the Theater around 10:07 p.m., making his way quickly to the private box where the Lincolns were sitting with Henry Rathbone, a young army officer and Clara Harris, his fiance'. Laughter from the audience watching the comedy helped conceal the noise created as Booth opened the door to the box. Lincoln's body guard, John Parker of the Metropolitan Police Force, had left his post so Booth faced no resistance as he drew his single-shot 44 caliber derringer and approached the President from the rear. Placing the pistol almost against Lincoln's head, he fired. Rathbone jumped to his feet and struggled with Booth, but was stabbed in the arm with a hunting knife Booth had in his other hand.

Before the audience realized what was going on, Booth jumped from the box onto the stage below, breaking his left leg just above the ankle. Swinging his knife wildly and shouting "Sic semper tyrannis" (Thus Always to Tyrants), Booth limped across the stage in view of over a thousand shocked audience members and made his way to the horse waiting for him at the back door. Climbing quickly into the saddle he rode off into the night and out of Washington.

A 23-year-old doctor named Charles Leale was in the audience and rushed to the presidential box immediately upon hearing the shot and Mary Lincoln's scream. He found the president slumped in his chair, paralyzed and struggling to breathe.

Several soldiers carried Lincoln to a boardinghouse across the street and placed him on a bed. When the surgeon general arrived at the house he concluded that Lincoln could not be saved and would probably die during the night.

Atzerodt failed to carry out his assignment and never approached Vice President Johnson. Powell managed to push his way into Seward's home and attacked him with a knife, slashing him repeatedly. Seward survived the attack but his face was permanently disfigured.

After fleeing the capital Booth and an accomplice, David Herold who had fled the scene of the Seward attack without Powell, made their way across the Anacostia River and headed toward southern Maryland.

The pair stopped at the home of Samuel Mudd, a doctor who treated Booth's broken leg. They then sought refuge from Thomas A. Jones, a Confederate agent, before securing a boat to row across the Potomac to Virginia.

Lincoln was pronounced dead at 7:22 AM on April 15. Secretary of War Edwin M. Stanton famously pronounced, "Now he belongs to the ages" (or "to the angels"; witnesses disagree).

Immediately after Booth left the Theater authorities began a frantic search for him. Eventually it would become one of the largest manhunts in history with approximately 10,000 federal troops, detectives, and police feverishly working to track down the assassin.

In Washington on April 17 investigators led by Lafayette Baker of the National Detective Police got a tip that led them to Lewis Powell, the former Confederate soldier who had attacked Secretary of State William Seward the same night Booth shot Lincoln. Later that day they arrested four other alleged conspirators: Mary Surratt, Michael O'Laughlen, Edman Spangler and Samuel Arnold.

On April 18 Union troops questioned Dr. Samuel Mudd and his wife and searched their home, where they found a boot with Booth's name written inside. Concluding that Booth had gone into southern Maryland and was probably headed for the Potomac River and Virginia, Sec. Stanton sent more troops to the region and ordered every available Union warship to patrol the Potomac south of Washington.

Lincoln's funeral took place at the White House on April 19, with thousands of mourners lining the streets to pay their last respects. The following morning soldiers arrested George Atzerodt in Maryland. Atzerodt had been assigned to kill Andrew Johnson but had spent the evening of April 14 drinking in a bar instead. Now only three of the prime suspects remained at large: Booth, Herold and John Surratt. Secretary Stanton offered a staggering $100,000 reward for their capture—the equivalent of some $1 million today. Enticed by the reward, hundreds of private citizens joined the search.

While all this was going on Booth and Herold were hiding out in a thicket of trees near the Zekiah swamp in Maryland where they would spend a total of five days. While hiding Booth kept a diary in which he recorded his amazement at the almost universal condemnation of his actions. He had expected to be heralded as a hero.

On the night of April 20 they attempted to row across the Potomac River but got lost in the fog and wound up back in Maryland. They finally got to Virginia on April 24 after crossing the Rappahannock River on a ferryboat with the help of several Confederate soldiers and made their way to a farm owned by Richard Garrett.

Members of the 16th New York Cavalry regiment eventually traced Booth and Herold to Garrett's farm and in the early morning hours of April 26 surrounded the tobacco barn where the two fugitives were hiding. A brief standoff ensued and the soldiers set fire to the barn in an attempt to smoke the two men out. Herold surrendered but Booth refused and was shot by one of the soldiers, Sgt. Boston Corbett. Carried out of the building alive Booth lived for about three hours before gazing at his hands and uttering his last words: "Useless, useless."

President Johnson ordered the eight defendants accused in the Lincoln assassination conspiracy to be tried by a military commission and testimony began on May 12 at the Old Arsenal Building in Washington. By order of Secretary Stanton the defendants (except Mary Surratt and Samuel Mudd) wore canvas hoods covering their heads during the trial. To the War Department the trial was an opportunity to prosecute not just the alleged conspirators themselves but also Jefferson Davis and the rest of the Confederate leaders who they believed had encouraged such conspiracies in a desperate attempt to salvage the war effort.

Of the eight defendants Powell, Herold, and Atzerodt had been deeply involved in Booth's plot to kidnap President Lincoln, and had played direct roles in the violent events of April 14. Mary Surratt, the owner of the boarding house where Booth and the other conspirators met, was accused of sheltering the conspirators and helping them plan the killings; her son, John Surratt, was one of Booth's main co-conspirators and had introduced the actor to both Herold and Atzerodt. He was not in Washington during the assassination, and in the confusion afterwards fled the country, living as a fugitive in Europe while his mother stood trial.

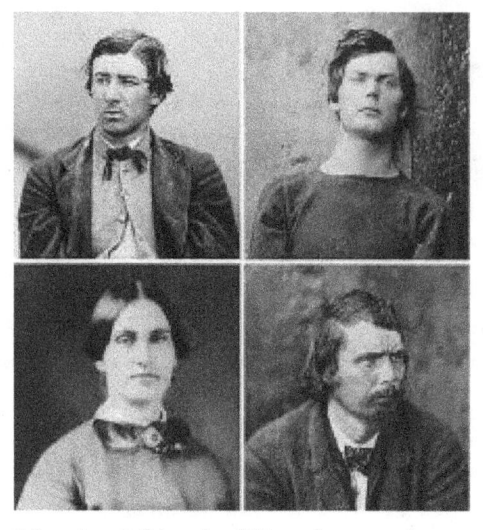
The other four defendants had weaker connections to the conspiracy. Arnold, a longtime friend of Booth, was tied to the original kidnapping plot by a letter he wrote to Booth in March 1865 but later backed out and was not in Washington when the assassination took place. Mudd, a staunch Confederate sympathizer, was approached by Booth in connection with the kidnapping plot but claimed not to recognize him when he showed up at his southern Maryland farm on April 15. He treated the actor's leg (which he broke when he jumped to the stage at Ford's Theatre) and sent him on his way. Spangler, a stagehand and carpenter at Ford's, had been enlisted to hold Booth's horse outside the theater, while O'Laughlen, another Maryland friend of Booth, was also tenuously linked to the kidnapping plot.

Justice was served quickly against the Lincoln conspirators. On June 30, after meeting in secret session, the commission delivered its verdicts: Powell, Herold, Atzerodt and Mary Surratt were sentenced to death; O'Laughlen, Arnold and Mudd received life sentences; Spangler got a six-year prison term. A week later, on July 7, Powell, Herold, Atzerodt and Mary Surratt were executed by hanging in the courtyard of the Old Arsenal Building. Arnold, Mudd and Spangler were all eventually pardoned by President Johnson and released. O'Laughlen died in prison of yellow fever in 1867. The final conspirator, John Surratt, was captured in Egypt in 1866 and tried before a civilian court the following year. The jury was unable to reach a verdict and Surratt was released. He lived until 1916.

Over the years critics have argued that the procedures, verdicts, and sentences of the Lincoln assassination conspiracy trial were unfair and unduly harsh, and by modern standards they certainly may have been. The decision to execute Mary Surratt, who despite public protests and a petition to President Johnson for clemency would become the first woman put to death by the federal government, and give a life sentence to Dr. Samuel Mudd were particularly controversial. "But for a war-torn and grieving nation, stricken by the violent murder of its leader just as the difficult work of rebuilding the Union was beginning—perhaps it could be no other way". (history.com)

Epilogue:

With the assassination of President Lincoln we are left with some important and persistent questions:

Who was really behind the conspiracy to assassinate the President and his cabinet?

Who might also have been involved in some way?

What might they have really been trying to accomplish?

These and other questions have lingered, been discussed, debated, and argued over for more than a hundred years. As we might expect, conspiracy theories abounded, then and even now.

- Several members of Congress and Mary Todd Lincoln herself were certain that Vice President Johnson knew about the conspiracy and did nothing to alert Lincoln or stop it. It is known that seven hours before the assassination John Wilkes Booth stopped by the Kirkwood House and asked to see Johnson. After learning he was not in he left a message that read "Don't wish to disturb you. Are you at home?" Johnson and Booth had known each other and were sometimes associates at least back to 1862 when Johnson served as the Military Governor of Tennessee and Booth was an actor in Nashville.

- Many people believed then and now that the assassination was part of a large and elaborate Confederate conspiracy involving many players with the purpose of retaliation and the resulting chaos that Booth had hoped for. In the winter of 1864 Pres. Lincoln authorized a bold plan, led by Brig. General Hugh Judson Kilpatrick, to raid the Confederate prison in Richmond, Virginia and rescue the 1,500 Union Officers and 10,000 enlisted men held captive there. After a series of mistakes and high water in the James River thwarted their plans papers were discovered in the pocket of Union Col. Ulric Dahlgren, who was killed by Confederate soldiers as the Union raiding party withdrew, indicating the real reason for the raid was to kill Confederate President Jefferson Davis and burn Richmond. It is known that this information was shared with Confederate General Robert E. Lee and others in the Confederate Government. Proponents of this theory paint Booth as a rebel agent working under the orders of Judah Benjamin, the Confederate Secretary of State.

- Some theorists point to the Rothschilds and International Bankers as being behind the assassination of Lincoln. To these theorists Booth was a hired hit man for powerful British Bankers upset with Lincoln for turning down their offer to lend money to the Union (at high interest rates sure to make them millions) and to more frugally acquire the needed funds elsewhere. To make matters worse, as they saw it, many of Lincoln's documented plans for post-war America were sure to destroy their commodities speculation. With Lincoln out of the way, it is said, they saw an opportunity to exploit the young nation so desperately in need of funds to rebuild.

- In 1856, Lincoln successfully defended a rebellious priest against the Catholic Church in Chicago. It was seen as a significant victory for the priest but a major black-eye to the Catholic leadership. The priest, Chiniquy, visited Lincoln in the White House on several occasions and warned him that he feared the Jesuits, who resented Lincoln, might attempt to kill him. In a sworn statement in 1906 Chiniquy swore that the Jesuits trained Booth as an assassin and used him to get their revenge. In 1963 Emmett McLoughin's "An Inquiry into the Assassination of Abraham Lincoln", claimed that Pope Pius IX may have been the instigator of the plot to kill President Lincoln.

- And finally – some theorists believe that John Wilkes Booth, with the help of accomplices, actually escaped his pursuers and lived out his days elsewhere, perhaps in Europe. Those championing this theory say that the man killed in the barn in Virginia that fateful day wasn't Booth, but someone posing as him.

Historical Footnote:

Mary Todd Lincoln went mad after that terrible night in Ford's Theater and was confined in an asylum for some time. She was eventually released but never fully recovered from the shock.

Major Henry Rathbone, wounded by Booth's knife as he attempted to stop the assassination, married Clara Harris, the other person in the theater box that night, A few years later he went mad, attempted to kill her and their children, and spent the rest of his life restrained as a violent maniac.

Boston Corbett, who received praise as the man who shot John Wilkes Booth also went mad and was confined to an asylum.

Secretary of War Edwin Stanton was also under suspicion as a member of the conspiracy to assassinate Lincoln. He immediately began a movement to impeach Andrew Johnson, now president, because of his suspected role in the assassination. Johnson advised Stanton that his resignation as Sec. of War was accepted and had him forcibly removed from office. Not long afterwards Stanton was found dead – allegedly by his own hand.

The Lost Confederate Gold

In early April of 1865 Confederate President, Jefferson Davis, was attending a church service in Richmond, Va. when he received an urgent message from General Robert E. Lee. Lee's important message warned Davis that he and the rest of the Confederate Government should evacuate Richmond immediately or risk being captured by advancing Union troops.

Late that night two trains left Richmond heading south. One carried President Davis and other Confederate Officials along with important documents. The other, under the guard of Confederate Navy Captain William H. Parker, was heavily loaded with Confederate treasure. The cache included cash, gold and silver, bank notes and a large amount of jewelry donated by Confederate women. Exactly what the value of the treasure on the train amounted to is not precisely known but rumors among both the Confederate and Union troops estimated millions. The fleeing Confederates also carried about $450,000 in Richmond bank gold, but wouldn't touch those funds as they didn't belong to the Confederate government.

By early May both Davis' party and the remaining fortune had reached Washington, Georgia. Whatever they had started with had been depleted to some degree by travelling expenses and payments to the troops.

On May 4, Davis made the decision to disband his government. He entrusted $86,000 of the remaining treasury funds to two Confederate navy officials and charged them with smuggling it out of the country to Britain. It never got there. Some historians speculate that one of the officials, James A. Semple, spent part of the money on his love affair with Julia Tyler, the widow of President John Tyler, as well as a failed plot to provoke war between Britain and the United States. Another portion may have been stolen by someone along the way.

After depositing the Richmond bank funds in a local vault in Washington for safekeeping, Davis continued heading south with his wife, Varina, their children and a few others. According to William Rawlings, a researcher and writer on Confederate topics, they split what remained of the treasury's funds with a second group they planned to meet in Florida. But on May 10, when members of the 4th Michigan Cavalry captured Davis' group near Irwinville, Georgia, they had only a few dollars with them.

What happened to the money is the unclear and has fueled legends, rumors, and countless treasure hunts ever since. One theory suggests it was stolen by the Michigan Cavalrymen. Another one says Davis and his group hid it. Rawlings himself has seen evidence of what appeared to be part of that buried Confederate loot. One of his readers showed him a Mexican silver coin dating to the 1850s which he said was uncovered by a logging crew in the 1940s near a Georgia spot where Davis' party is known to have camped.

As for the Richmond bank gold, it quickly fell into the hands of Federal troops, who occupied Washington within days after Davis left. Valued at nearly half a million dollars, the gold was loaded onto wagons heading north, in the custody of U.S. government officials. But on the night of May 24, as the group made camp for the night near Danburg Crossroads in Lincoln County, Georgia, a group of approximately 20 armed men on horseback attacked the camp and carried off as much gold as they could carry. Federal soldiers were eventually able to recover about $140,000 of what was taken. The rest of the missing money, according to some, may have been the basis for several local fortunes in the Danburg area.

Rumors and stories about the fate of different parts of the missing Confederate treasure persist to this day, and tales of discovery are sometimes whispered from rural Georgia to Michigan.

The Aftermath of the Civil War

When the Civil War was over in 1865 America was left with new problems she had never before faced as a Nation. Bridges, railroads, roads, industries, and most of the basic infrastructure in the South had been damaged or completely destroyed. Approximately 258,000 Southerners had been killed during the war, and another 100,000 wounded. This number included an estimated 50,000 civilians. Those Confederate Soldiers who had survived the war were immediately confronted with this grim reality as they made their long and difficult march back home to their towns and homes.

Even though most of the Northern Cities escaped the devastation experienced by those in the South the Union States were also heavily impacted by the long, brutal conflict. An estimated 360,000 Union Soldiers had been killed and approximately 275,000 wounded. Resources had been diverted to supporting the war effort and infrastructure was in bad need of attention in the North as well. And then there was the daunting challenge of how to rebuild the Union.

To manage the reconstruction process the eleven former Confederate States were divided into 5 large military zones, each under the control of a U.S. Army General. Approximately 200,000 Union Troops were stationed in the South to help control the Southern Populace and enforce the decisions of those in charge. Their presence was seen by Southerners as a constant reminder of the Union oppression that they had so long resisted and fought to avoid. "Yankee Rule", as they referred to it, was the realization of their worst fears – and sometimes even worse than they could imagine.

Ironically, before his assassination, President Lincoln had already begun to work on plans to "reconstruct" the South. His vision was to employ a much gentler approach to mend the lingering divisions than those devised and employed after his death. Even though Lincoln's successor, Andrew Johnson, himself a Southerner, encouraged leniency Congress and many powerful decision makers in the North were more interested in revenge than healing. The situation was made even worse by Northern Businessmen and scoundrels (Carpetbaggers) who saw an opportunity to use deception, corruption, and lies to personally gain from the terrible situations that remained throughout the South for many years following the War.

Officially Reconstruction lasted 12 years and by 1870 each of the Confederate States had been readmitted to the Union. However, civil unrest and related violence continued in many places for much longer as Southerners continued to resist and even subvert many of the laws and decrees imposed on them. The last of the Union Troops were removed in 1877 but it would take several generations for most of the old mistrust and animosity to be gone.

The Story of Hagan Hall

HAGAN HALL, 1976

The above picture clearly reveals that the years have taken their toll on the once majestic Hagan Hall. But to all who can look past the obvious decay there is also ample evidence of the amazing mansion it once was. Constructed from bricks molded and fired on the site, it contained 17 rooms, 2 baths, and was heated by steam. Elegant furnishings included an ivory piano, Persian rugs, expensive velvet drapes, beautiful ornate furniture, silk wall-paper, and an impressive library. The original painter and paperer, Harry Smith, signed his name on the bared plastered wall in the top front bedroom in 1864. As impressive as the mansion was, in every respect, the people in the story of Hagan Hall were even more so.

Joseph Hagan was a man of remarkable gifts and talents. Of landed gentry, he had been a student for the priest hood in Ireland, studied engineering, medicine, and law. As a resident of Richmond, Va. he was very well respected and responsible for surveying a large portion of the City. The first deed recorded to Joseph Hagan was August 30, 1833, when William Thompson and Bernard Hagan of Richmond, executors of the will of William Lamb, sold to Joseph and Sarah Purcell of Richmond 200,000 and 100,000 acres in Russell County, 12,328 acres and 3,155 acres in Monongalia County (now West Virginia), a number of small lots and tracts in the city of Richmond and Henrico County and any other tracts found to belong to William Lamb." On Dec. 29, 1839, a power of attorney is recorded by Joseph Hagan of the city of Richmond, empowering William Richmond of Scott County to act for him in land negotiations to the quantity of 2,000 acres, and in the county's sixth deed book, William Neal of Giles County deeded to Joseph Hagan a tract in Hunters Valley below Buckner's Ridge in 1838.

The story is told that Joseph Hagan was walking down a Richmond Street during a land sale for delinquent taxes and heard the auctioneer ask for bids on 35,000 acres. Without asking its location, he allegedly entered a high bid of $25 and walked away a Southwest Virginia landowner. This tale seems to be essentially true as records in the Scott County Clerk's Office show that in 1841, Thomas G. Martin, commissioner of delinquent and forfeited lands, deeded to Joseph Hagan of Scott County, 50,000 acres on Stock Creek under the Western Lands title Law. The high bid of $28 was reduced to $26.32 for prompt payment, and the money was to be turned over to the Virginia Literary Fund, the taxes being delinquent from 1815 to 1833. When it was discovered that the land contained springs of sulfur water, Joseph brought his invalid wife to live here in hopes that she would recover, for at that time sulfur water was believed to have miraculous healing powers. After building a log house on his new land in Hunter's Valley, of Scott County, Va. Joseph sent for his nephew Patrick Hagan who had made his way from Ireland to America.

Patrick Hagan was born in Ireland on February 2, 1828 and came to America in 1844, at the age of 16. After arriving here, he traveled to New York, Philadelphia, Norfolk, and Richmond, where he went into partnership with his brother in a grocery business. Soon he made his way to Hunter's Valley to join his Uncle Joseph.

Patrick learned from his uncle the fundamentals of philosophy, Latin, and English and he went to Tazewell, Va., to study law in the office of Col. Joseph Strass. He began law practice in Estillville (Gate City), where he was admitted to the bar in 1854 at the age of 22. He practiced law in Wise County's first county court in 1856. Patrick was said to have possessed the most thorough legal education of any man in the area. He was particularly interested in land law and made it his specialty, soon becoming known as one of the foremost land lawyers in Virginia. He was involved in many cases, some that went before the Supreme Court of the United States.

Hagan is said to have inherited his uncle Joseph Hagan's vast tracts of land and during his lifetime acquired even more, eventually owning thousands of acres. His land holdings covered most of the Jefferson National Forest area, the Stonega Coke and Coal Co., and the Clinchfield Coal Corp., boundaries that included parts of Wise, Russell, and Dickenson as well as Scott Counties. Through the success of his law practice he added to his inherited wealth and invested in other coal and timber lands. He became a resident of Lee County and was twice elected Commonwealth's Attorney there before moving back to Scott County to continue his law practice. He was also active in community affairs and gave the nearby community on the Clinch River, at Osborne's Ford, the name Dungannon in honor of his birthplace in Ireland.

Patrick married Mrs. Elizabeth Young Grubb and in 1860 the couple built Hagan Hall, some distance in front of his Uncle Joseph's log home. It took 6 years to complete. They had 8 children, four sons and four daughters.

Hagan Hall had numerous servants, cooks, maids, and even butlers, and a large colony of Negroes that worked the farm. Patrick treated them all with the respect he showed everyone else, providing them with both a school and church for their use.

In the heyday of Hagan Hall many social functions and important meetings took place there, with lawyers, politicians, governors, etc. coming from far and wide to enjoy the hospitality, the mineral water, and to consult Patrick on legal matters. Patrick was a devoted Catholic and a true gentleman. He lived when a good man's word was his bond. As the years went by his land holdings and reputation both continued to grow.

His declining years were spent contently at Hagan Hall, where he died in his 90th year, Feb. 23, 1917. He was buried in the family cemetery about 300 yards from the Hall on a little knoll. Patrick Hagan's monument has a Celtic cross on it and unusual inscriptions. Several members of the Hagan Family are buried there as well.

Patrick Hagan - A life well lived. His, oldest son, Charles F. Hagan, took charge of his affairs

Sadly, Hagan Hall was struck by lightning and burned in 2004.

Back of Hagan Hall

These pictures give us a glimpse of the former beauty of Hagan Hall.

The Hatfield & McCoy Feud

Probably no other feud in America's history is better known than the one between the Hatfields and the McCoys. But beyond the initial recognition of this famous bloody feud most people know little about the details.

William Anderson Hatfield, known as "Devil Anse", was a rough mountain man who by the 1870s was also a successful timber merchant who employed dozens of men, including some from the McCoy family. Randolph, "Old Ranel" McCoy, was the patriarch of his family and owned considerable land on which he raised cattle. Both families were involved in the illegal production and selling of moonshine.

Both families were large and included 13 children. And both lived along the Tug Fork of the Big Sandy River which wound along the boundary between Kentucky and West Virginia. The two families had complex kinship connections and allegiance. Family loyalty was often determined not only by blood but by where they lived and who they worked for. The families even intermarried and sometimes family loyalties changed, even after the feud had started.

Some historians mark the first event in the decades-long feud as the 1865 murder of Randolph's brother, Asa Harmon McCoy, by the Logan Wildcats, a local Confederate militia group that included Devil Anse and other Hatfields among their members. Asa was not well liked. He had served in the Union Army during the American Civil War and many people, even members of his own family, regarded him a traitor. Other historians view this incident as a standalone event without connection to what came later.

Regardless, relations between the two families continued to smolder over the next decade and flared again over a seemingly small matter - a dispute over a single hog. In 1878 Randolph McCoy accused Floyd Hatfield, a cousin of Devil Anse, of stealing one of his pigs, a valuable commodity and a serious offense in the poor mountain region. Floyd Hatfields's trial took place in McCoy territory but was presided over by a cousin of Devil Anse. The case primarily was determined by the testimony of a single witness, Bill Staton, a McCoy relative who was married to a Hatfield. Staton testified in Floyd Hatfield's favor, and the McCoys were furious when Floyd was cleared of the charges against him. Two years later Staton was violently killed in a fight with Sam and Paris McCoy, nephews of Randolph. Sam stood trial for the murder but was acquitted on a verdict of self-defense.

In 1880, within months of Staton's murder, at a local election day gathering, Johnse Hatfield, the 18-year-old son of Devil Anse, had a chance meeting with Randolph's daughter, Roseanna McCoy.. According to the story, Johnse and Roseanna immediately hit it off, disappearing together for hours. Supposedly fearing retaliation from her family for mingling with the Hatfields, Roseanna stayed at the Hatfield residence for a period of time, despite the ire of the McCoys.

Although they certainly shared a romance, it was short lived and it soon became clear that Johnse was not about to settle down with Roseanna. Several months later he abandoned the now pregnant

Roseanna and moved on. In May 1881 he married Nancy McCoy, Roseanna's cousin. According to a possibly romanticized legend, Roseanna was heartbroken by these events and never recovered emotionally.

The real turning point in the feud, according to most historical accounts, occurred on another local election day in August 1882. On that day three of Randolph McCoy's sons got into a violent dispute with two brothers of Devil Anse. The fight quickly erupted into chaos as one of the McCoy brothers stabbed Ellison Hatfield multiple times and then shot him in the back. Authorities soon arrested the three McCoys, but on the way to the Pikeville, Kentucky jail, the Hatfields kidnapped the men and took them to Hatfield territory. After receiving word that Ellison had died, they tied the McCoys to some pawpaw bushes. Within minutes they fired more than 50 shots, killing all three brothers.

Though the Hatfields felt their revenge was justified, the law felt otherwise, and quickly returning indictments against 20 men, including Devil Anse and his sons. Despite the charges the Hatfields eluded arrest which left the McCoys boiling with anger about the murders and outraged that the Hatfields still walked free. Their cause was taken up by Perry Cline, an attorney who was married to Martha McCoy, the widow of Randolph's brother Asa Harmon. Years earlier Cline had lost a lawsuit against Devil Anse over the deed for thousands of acres of land and many historians believe this left him looking for his own form of revenge. Using his political connections Cline had the charges against the Hatfields reinstated and announced rewards for the arrest of the Hatfields, including Devil Anse.

The media became aware of the feud and started to report on it in 1887. Their accounts of the families usually portrayed the Hatfields as violent backwoods hillbillies who roamed the mountains looking for trouble. Their usually sensational coverage turned the local story into an enduring national legend.

The Hatfields were not happy about the bounty on their heads and devised a plan to attack Randolph McCoy and his family in an effort to put a stop to the harassment once and for all. Led by Devil Anse's son Cap and Jim Vance a group of Hatfield men ambushed the McCoys' home on New Year's Day in 1888. Randolph fled and escaped into the woods. His son Calvin and daughter Alifair were killed in the crossfire. His wife Sarah was left badly beaten by the Hatfields, suffering a crushed skull.

A few days after what became known as the New Year's massacre, bounty hunter Frank Phillips chased down Jim Vance and Cap Hatfield, killing Vance. Phillips rounded up nine Hatfield family members and supporters and hauled them off to jail. Years of legal wranglings followed as a series of courts tried to sort out the legal case against the Hatfields. Eventually, the case went all the way to the U.S. Supreme Court which decided that the Hatfields being held in custody could be tried.

The trial began in 1889 and when it was over eight of the Hatfields and their supporters were sentenced to life in prison. Ellison Mounts, who was believed to be the son of Ellison Hatfield, was sentenced to death. Nicknamed Cottontop, Mounts was known to be mentally challenged and many viewed him as a scapegoat even though he had confessed his guilt. Although public executions were against the law in Kentucky thousands of spectators gathered to witness the hanging of Ellison Mounts on February 18, 1890. Reports claim that his last words were: "They made me do it! The Hatfields made me do it!"

Following the verdict the feud that had cost at least 20 and perhaps near 100 people their lives, began to fade and both family leaders attempted to escape into relative obscurity. Randolph McCoy became a ferry operator. In 1914 he died at the age of 88 from burns suffered in an accidental fire. By all accounts he continued to be haunted by the deaths of his children. Devil Anse Hatfield, who had long expressed his skepticism about religion, confessed Christ and was baptized at age 73, joining the Baptist Church.

Devil Anse Hatfield

Old Ranl' McCoy

The White-Caps Movement

Following the Civil War a number of social and economic trends put poor white rural citizens at serious disadvantage. With slavery abolished black laborers competed in the market with whites for jobs. At the same time a depressed agricultural economy and falling prices thrust farmers into great stress and debt, sometimes resulting in the loss of their land to foreclosure. "Within this generally unsettled time, many felt the need to reassert the old ways and to do so with violence and terrorism if necessary", according to Historian Matthew Hernando.

About 1873 a secret society, usually referred to as the White-Caps or Night Riders, began in Indiana. The group which primarily consisted of white males sought to impose their version of justice against whomever they felt was violating their interpretation of community standards and values. As newspapers picked up the story, the movement soon spread, and groups were organized and active in carrying out their vigilante justice in many different states.

Men who neglected or abused their families or were excessively lazy, drunkards, women who bore children out of wed lock, etc. were prime targets of their retaliation. Dressed similarly to those who were members of the Ku Klux Klan, their night-time visits often consisted of whippings, drownings, lynching, shooting into houses, arson, or other forms of bullying. Victims usually had little support from either the community or legal authorities.

On May 4, 1893 a group of 75 armed men surrounded a courthouse in Jackson, Mississippi to disrupt an ongoing trial. The mob consisting mostly of poor farmers and laborers, assembled to intimidate the presiding judge, who had jailed members of the community without bail. Mississippi law did not permit bail for criminals charged with severe crimes like arson and attempted murder, but the crowd was uninterested in the finer legal details.

The Morning Herald of December 23, 1896 reported on such an incident in Lee County, Va.

"The Lee County, Virginia White-Caps whipped _____ and _____ , fallen women, last night. Each was given 50 lashes on the bare back. The women fled after the whippings."

And the movement was not entirely limited to men.

"During the winter of 1892, a group of prostitutes from Knoxville moved into the Emert's Cove neighborhood of Sevier County, Tennessee, and began entertaining the men of the area. The wives of the community, angry that their menfolk's attention had turned away from the hearth, formed a mob to protect their families and homes. Urged on by several men the women went to the dwelling of each prostitute one night and laid bundles of hickory switches at the front doors with a note telling the occupants to leave the neighborhood or suffer a beating during a later visit. The messages were signed "White Caps." (Knoxville Tribune, 18 May 1892)

The movement continued into the early 1900's in some areas before the legal system began to take it more seriously and deal more harshly with those involved.

Some 19th Century Civic & Political Leaders of Southwest Virginia:

Benjamin Estill

Benjamin Estill was born on March 13, 1780 at Hansonville (now Russell County). He received an academic education and attended Washington Academy (now Washington and Lee University). He studied law and was admitted to the bar, settling in Abington to practice. His home was on Main Street in Abingdon and occupied a quarter acre parcel of land.

He became the Commonwealth's Attorney for Washington County and represented the County in the Virginia State Legislature from 1814-1817. During this time he proposed and assisted in the formation of Scott County, and was instrumental in naming it for General Winfield Scott, a man he greatly admired and with whom he agreed in politics. The county seat of Scott was given the name Estillville (now Gate City), to honor his work in its formation.

From 1825-1827, he was elected to the 19th Congress receiving almost every vote cast in the election.

Beginning in 1831, he served as 15th Judicial Circuit Judge for the counties of Lee, Scott, Russell, Washington, and Tazewell. Standing six feet tall and broad at the shoulders, Judge Estill was an imposing figure in the court-room. While serving as a Circuit Court Judge Benjamin was known for his eloquent speeches. When Lewis Preston Summers wrote *the History of Southwest Virginia* at the turn of the century he noted that persons now living make the statement that citizens of Abingdon would close their businesses and homes and crowd the courthouse on the first day of his court to hear him deliver his charge to the grand jury. He served in this position until his retirement in 1852, at which time he moved to Oldham County, Kentucky. Judge Estill died there on July 14, 1853 at the age of 73.

David Campbell

David Campbell was born on August 2, 1779 at Royal Oak (now Marion, Va.). His family moved to Hall's Bottom in Washington County when he was eight. His education was limited as was the norm for a frontier settlement.

At age 15 he was appointed ensign in Captain John Davis' company of militia. In 1799 he was commissioned a Captain of a company of light infantry assigned to the Seventieth Regiment of Militia, and in the fall of that year he married his cousin, Mary Hamilton. He later studied law and was licensed but never practiced.

In 1802 he was appointed Deputy Clerk of Washington County Court and served for ten years.

In 1812 he was commissioned a Major in the U.S. Army's 12th Regiment of Infantry and served throughout the War. His distinguished military service led to his appointment as General of the 3rd Brigade of the Virginia Militia in 1815. And from 1820 to 1824 he served in the Senate of Virginia.

In 1824 he was elected Clerk of the Court for Washington County, Va. He held this position until 1837, when he was elected the 27th Governor of Virginia, serving from 1837 to 1840. In his first message to the General Assembly he proposed the establishment of a common, or public, school system.

He died on March 19, 1859 and was buried in the Sinking Spring Cemetery in Abingdon, Va..

William J. Dickenson

William J. Dickenson was born on December 3, 1827 in Russell County. He was a lawyer by profession. When Wise County was established there were no lawyers in the county. Six lawyers from surrounding counties were given the oath to practice law in Wise County. William Dickenson was one of these first six.

In 1859, when he was 32, he lived in Lebanon, Va.

Dickenson was a delegate to the General Assembly from Russell County in 1880, part of the Re-adjuster Party. The Re-adjusters key political proposal was to re-adjust the existing state debt rather than pay it in full. The Re-adjusters stretched out payments on the debt rather than paying off previously incurred debts. This allowed them to fund new schools, roads, etc. Most of the debt was incurred prior to the Civil War. As a delegate, Dickenson played a major role in establishing a new Southwestern Virginia County. Due to his efforts, the county was named Dickenson , in his honor.

John A. Buchanan

John A. Buchanan was born on October 7, 1843 near Groseclose in Smyth County. He attended the "old field" school and local academies at Chatham Hill and Marion.

During the Civil War he served as a Private in Company D, Virginia Infantry, Stonewall's Brigade of the Confederate Army. He was captured at the Battle of Gettysburg and remained a prisoner until February of 1865.

After the war, he attended Emory and Henry College, graduating in 1870. He then studied law at the University of Virginia and was admitted to the bar in 1872. He began his law practice in Abington.

From 1885-1887, he was a member of the State House of Delegates. He was elected to both the 51st and 52nd Congress from 1889-1893. He declined to be a candidate for election to the 53rd Congress.

He returned to his law practice and was elected Associate Judge of the Court of Appeals of Virginia in 1895. Judge Buchanan served in this position until his term expired in 1915.

Retiring from public service, he engaged in agricultural pursuits until his death at age 77 in Emory, Virginia and was buried in the Old Glade Spring Presbyterian Cemetery, Glade Spring, Va.

Henry Carter Stuart

Henry C. Stuart was born on January 18, 1855 at Wytheville, Va.. His family owned thousands of acres of ranch land in southwest Virginia, acquired over generations. He graduated from Emory and Henry College and studied law for a year at the University of Virginia.

After leaving the university he began to raise livestock. Upon their father's death in 1893, he and his brothers Alexander ("Zan") and Dale Carter Stuart took over their father's salt company (which by then had become a cattle company). They built Stuart Land & Cattle into the largest cattle company east of the Mississippi River, with 50,000 agricultural acres in four counties. The company and other Stuart enterprises also controlled extensive coal and timber reserves.

Henry married his cousin, Margaret Bruce Carter in 1896, but they had no children.

He eventually acquired a mansion in East Rosedale, which one of his maternal ancestor had purchased from Patrick Henry in 1774, and which had been a fort guarding the Clinch River valley during the American Revolutionary War. His paternal grandfather, Archibald Stuart, a lawyer and U.S. Congressman, had several sons, one of whom (Henry's uncle) became Confederate Civil War Cavalry Commander Jeb Stuart.

Stuart became involved in politics in 1901, when he served as a member of the State Constitutional Convention. The following year he was appointed to the State Corporation Commission, where he served until 1908.

In 1913 he ran for and was elected Governor, serving from 1914-1918, during World War I. One of his priorities was preparing the state's war machinery. He was a member of the price-fixing committee of the War Industries Board. In 1917 President Wilson appointed him Chairman of the National Agriculture Advisory Committee. Throughout his career he was known for his encyclopedic mind and his extensive knowledge of agriculture.

Henry died on July 24, 1933.

After his death, the mansion he built and lived in, in the valley of the Elk Garden River, remained in the Stuart family until 1945. Sadly, "East Rosedale" burned to the ground after a lightning storm in 2002.

Colonel James L. Shoemaker

Colonel James L. Shoemaker was born near Lebanon, Russell County, Virgina, December 7, 1809. His grandfather, James S. Shoemaker, was of a good family in England and immigrated to America in 1749. When the American Revolution began he enlisted in the American Army and fought valiantly under Colonel William Campbell, of Washington County, at the battle of King's Mountain, in South Carolina.

Soloman Litton, his other grandfather, was born December, 24., 1751, in Washington County, Virginia. In 1778, while the Revolutionary War, was raging and the Americans were being assailed by the "red-coats" on one hand, and the "redskins" on the other, Mr. Litton and his wife and two daughters were taken prisoner by the Indians while traveling near Harrodsburg, Kentucky. The four prisoners were taken to Quebec, Canada and held until the close of the war when they were exchanged for other prisoners.

Colonel Shoemaker was happily married on July 5th, 1842, to Miss Aurelia Paxton Salling, daughter of Dr. Henry Salling of Scott County, Virginia. Sometime afterwards the couple moved to Lafayette County, Missouri where twelve years later his father, Joseph Shoemaker, died. His mother, Elizabeth Shoemaker, did not long survive the loss of her husband and died at the Shoemaker homestead in Missouri the next year.

Opportunities for acquiring an education at that time were very meager. Like a great many young men of his time his only chance to prepare for the responsibilities and duties of life was simply to assume them and learn by experience. How well he did this is demonstrated by his success in business and the philanthropic disposal of a life-time of earnings.

He began business in Estiville, (now Gate City, Va.) a member of the firm of Alderson and Shoemaker. Afterwards he bought Alderson's interest and continued the successful business in his own name. He was not a politically ambitious man chosing instead to serve the people of his county in less remunerative though probably more important ways. He was enumerator of the census of 1840 and 1850, land assessor several times, postmaster for a number of years, and County Court Clerk. In all these positions his integrity and accurate business methods made him a trusted official. The papers submitted by him as assessor were declared by the officials at Richmond to be the best in the state.

This quiet, business-like, patriotic citizen always remembered his own difficulties in securing a limited education and was determined to help ensure that others might have greater access. Seeing the need of increased educational facilities in the region, he began to cherished the idea of giving his wealth to found an institution of learning to be called "Shoemaker." It was his oft-expressed plan to give $5000 for the erection of a building, and the remainder of his estate for an endowment fund, the proceeds of which were to be used to pay the expenses of deserving students, who financially were unable to help themselves. He decided that the institution should be located in Scott County, among the people he had loved, and with whom he had labored so diligently. To use his own words: "I have made my money here in Scott county and I want these people to be the

Shoemaker College - Harold B. Peter's Photos

beneficiaries of it when I am gone."

After his death, on January 9th, 1894, it was ascertained from his will that the principal part of his large estate was to be given to the cause of education. After some litigation over the particulars, only $7,500 of his estate was obtained by the people of his chosen county. "With this amount, supplemented by popular subscription, a handsome and commodious building, costing about

$13,000 was erected. It was known as Shoemaker College. The doors of the institution were thrown open for the education of both sexes, on October 22, 1897". As of 1902, "six successful sessions have been completed, and the prospects for the coming session are the brightest of her history".

Epilogue:

Shoemaker College served students of the area from its inception until 1906, when it was discontinued and the building used as a High School. It was used for this purpose until 1923.

In the early morning hours of November 21, 1957, Ezra McNutt, the school janitor, went to the furnace room to check a fire he had started an hour earlier. He immediately discovered flames, initially confined to an area "behind a boiler" which were eating their way to the ceiling. The janitor said he ran to a near-by school building and told another janitor to call the Fire Department. He said the alarm was finally sounded by an unidentified soft drink salesman who was making a delivery at the school.

The Gate City Volunteer Fire Department responded in the freezing cold with two trucks and about six men and were later joined by some 18 others. For about 2 hours the flames remained confined to the basement and first floor, and volunteers were able to save quite a bit of furnishings and files. But once they had gained headway in a wide natural draft between the walls, they quickly consumed the three-story building.

The remains of the old building were demolished and, later, Shoemaker Elementary and Junior High School were built on the same campus.

Author's Note: Material for this story was taken primarily from the sources listed below and paraphrased and edited for clarity.

THE SHOEMAKER SENTINEL, (February 1, 1938) which was taken from the Shoemaker Catalog of 1902-1903.

The Pocahontas Mining Explosion of March 13, 1884

When the night shift entered the Laurel Mine around 1:00 a.m. they were expecting it to be just another hard night's work, like every other shift in the mine. They knew they would have to wait until the blasting crew finished their work to enter certain areas of the mine and they used their time to ready their gear and talk about goings on in the Camp and Town of Pocahontas. Little did anyone expect what was about to happen and how it would impact the entire area and the coal mining industry itself.

Actual documents from the period tell the story best:

Southwest Virginia Improvement Co.
Laurel Mine Explosion

Pocahontas, Tazewell County, Virginia
March 13, 1884
No. Killed - 112

Note: The photo of the memorial marker indicates 114 died in this disaster, however, the total on the official form is 112.

(From the U. S. Bureau of Mines Bulletin 20, pp. 20, 29)

The night shift was in the mine at 1 o'clock in the morning when the explosion shook the ground and dwellings for half a mile around the mine. None of those in the mine survived. The mine consisted of five openings from the outcrop in a ravine into the hillside.

Cars, timbers, and debris were hurled from the openings with awful force. The fan, the mine buildings, and surroundings on the surface in front of the openings were demolished. Fire succeeded the explosion in the mine, and all that could be done was to seal the openings as the fire and smoke rapidly increased.

After the sealing steam was conveyed into the mine from five boilers. The mine was flooded then opened and the bodies were recovered in April. It was thought that dust with possibly

some gas, was fired by blasting. Gas could not be found in the mine after the explosion although some claimed to have found it while working there before the disaster. The mine was considered non-gassy and no safety lamps were used. Ventilation was of a low order. Blasting was done at the end of each shift. Shooting was "off-the-solid," using excessive amounts of black powder. The mine was very dry and dusty.

For months after this explosion, its causes and possible preventive measures were argued in newspapers, and technical journals. This disaster, with those at Crested Butte, Colorado and West Leisenring, Pennsylvania caught public attention; a mine inspection bill was introduced in the Virginia Legislature but failed to come to a vote. Several committees investigated the circumstances, and the published conclusions stated that fine coal dust in mines was a serious explosion hazard when coupled with firing of heavy charges of black powder without first undercutting the coal.

The question of whether the coal might be ignited without any gas being present was not clearly answered, although experiments had indicated that it might occur (48, pp. 28, 29).

Source:

Historical Summary of Mine Disasters in the United States - Volume I

The Mountain Cracked by the Force of the Explosion
Plattsburgh Sentinel, New York
March 21, 1884

The victims of the mine disaster at Pocahontas, Va., last week, leave 97 widows and orphans. There were five distinct explosions, and their force was so great that the mountain was cracked. There were no expert gas men employed in the mine, and no safety lamps used. The officers say the explosion was not caused by a lamp, but probably by a blast which opened up a large quantity of gas. Two-thirds of the men were white, and more than fifty had families. The actual number killed is 184, of whom fifty were negroes, forty Hungarians, and the remainder Germans and natives. Ten mules were also killed.

The night relief went into the mines at the usual hour on Wednesday night. A little after midnight the town was startled from its sleep by a noise that sounded like the rumbling of an earthquake, followed by a clap of thunder. Soon a messenger came from the mines, three-fourth of a mile away, with information to the superintendent that there had been a terrible explosion there. The superintendent and others hastened to the mines, and the scene presented to their view was indescribable.

The entrance to the main shaft was entirely torn out and scattered pell-mell for hundreds of feet. The little train track was torn and twisted, and shapeless timber and ties were mixed in confusion all around. The cars were taken up bodily and torn apart, and their iron wheels were shivered. They were thrown across a ravine five hundred yards, and buried in the mountain beyond. The mountain itself was upheaved by the force of the explosion and in several places near the entrance of the mines enormous crevices were made in the earth. In many places near the entrance of the mines enormous crevices were made in the earth. In many places on the mountain coal dust has settled an inch thick. Immense trees were uprooted four hundred yards from the mine. Three dwelling houses near the mines were demolished by the falling of cars and debris on them. Two colored women and a child were in one of the homes, and were literally torn to pieces. Rocks were thrown through the workshops, and every object that stood in the direct course of the forced air was demolished. Several workmen in the shops were injured. The shops, as well as the locomotive house, were leveled with the ground.

The furthest entry effected was by a Hungarian whose son was buried in the ruins. Nearly crazed by grief he could not be restrained, and penetrated to a considerable distance, but was eventually compelled to retire. He reported seeing a number of bodies congregated in one chamber indiscriminately, torn and mangled beyond recognition. One of the victims was a youth, 13 years of age, who was employed as a door boy, and was the pet of the mining camp. The little fellow had just entered the mine when the explosion occurred.

The management, to prevent the possibility of any fresh disaster, will flood the mine. It may be therefore several weeks or months before any attempt can be made to reach the bodies of the unfortunate miners.

The Pocahontas Disaster
Bringing the Bodies of the Victims to the Surface
The New York Times, New York
April 12, 1884

Lynchburg, Va., April 11 -- After everything had been got in readiness at Pocahontas yesterday evening a police force was placed on guard at the main entrance to the mines in order to keep back the crowd which had been attracted by the notice posted by Superintendent Lathrop announcing that the bodies would be reclaimed, and then Mining Engineer Moody, in charge of a rescuing party, entered the mines to note the situation of affairs. When the party emerged from the mines it was announced to the crowd that the damage was less than had been supposed and that little trouble would be met with in recovering the bodies of the victims.

Two bodies were recovered yesterday in a horribly mutilated condition. They proved to be those of Boon Maxey, a white boy, and Jim Crim, a negro. The work of recovery was then postponed until this morning, when it was resumed under the direction of Engineer Moody. A still larger crowd than that of the day previous congregated at the entrance, and ropes had to be stretched around to prevent too near an approach to the entrance. The crowd, however, observed proper decorum, and no undue excitement was manifested, a spirit of great solemnity seeming to pervade the assemblage.

The bodies, as they were recovered were placed in boxes on the inside of the mine, and several of them were brought out together on a car. A number of miners well acquainted with the victims were placed at the entrance for the purpose of identifying the bodies, if possible, but of the 16 recovered so far only 6 have been identified. These are Jim Crim, recognized by a bell he wore; Isham Maxwell, by his boots; George Maxwell, by being found with his brother; William Slusher, identified by a patch on one of his boots; Young Jewell, by his hair and the location in which his body was found, and a German who was recognized by his wife.

Many of the bodies are horribly mangled, some with the heads blown off, others with arms and legs torn from the sockets, and still others with the entrails torn out entirely. An arm and a leg were found in the main entrance, but the body to which they belonged could not be found. A thrill of horror passed through the crowd in front of the mines as the rescuing party brought out the charred remains of a miner with his dinner bucket clasped in his arms. He was probably just partaking of his midnight meal when the explosion occurred. Several miners were found with picks in hand, and the positions of these bodies indicated that death was instantaneous to all in the mines. At 3:30 o'clock the announcement was made that no more bodies would be removed before 9 o'clock Saturday morning. The remainder of the day was occupied in getting out the carcases of mules, which, being too heavy to be dragged out, had to be quartered and taken out. Very little excitement prevailed at the mines any times during the day. As soon as the announcement was made that no more bodies would be taken out until Saturday the crowd quietly withdrew.

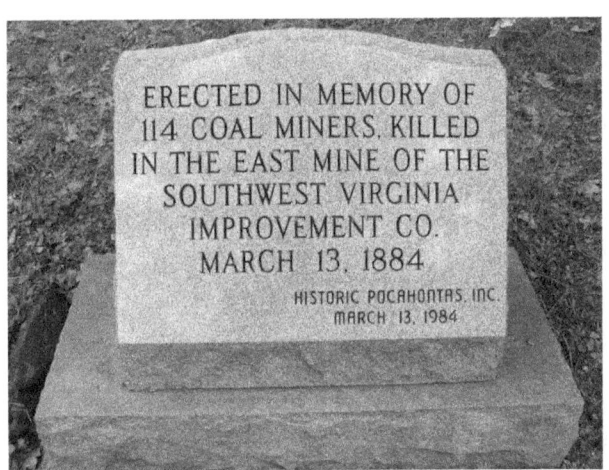

The Pound Gap Massacre

Dr. Marshal Benton Taylor
"The Red Fox"

Marshall Benton Taylor was born in 1836, in Taylor Town of Scott County, Virginia, the oldest son of William P. and Mary (Stallard) Taylor. His family was well known in the area and also well respected. As a young man he became interested in medicine and studied under his Uncle, Dr. Stallard, of Lee County, VA, when conventional medical schools were few and far removed from the Southwest Virginia area. He also was fascinated by the use of various healing herbs and became quite skilled at harvesting them from the mountains and fields and using them to treat various common ailments. According to many of his patients he was well regarded and his services often sought.

Doc Taylor was also always interested in mysticism and religion and often mixed both of them with his medicine and herbal treatments. It is said that he professed to be able to talk with spirits, contact the dead, and to see into the future. But it is also true that he considered himself a preacher and that people would walk for miles to listen to his mesmerizing, almost hypnotic sermons. Despite his mystic ways the people of the community did not immediately consider him a quack as many swore that his method worked to make them feel better. Those same mystic ways that led people to respect him as a healer also caused them to fear him.

After practicing medicine for a few years he volunteered for the Confederate Army, serving in the 64th Virginia Cavalry for four years. During the war he continued to provide medical care to the members of his company. When the war ended he returned to the region and resumed his medical practice especially in the remote mountains and hollows along the Virginia/Kentucky border near the Pound Gap area of Wise County. With his flaming red hair and bright blue eyes he soon was given the nickname – "Red Fox". Over the years his reputation grew as did the legends told about him.

In 1876 an event took place that seemed to significantly change the course of his life. Late one night Robert Moore, a noted local outlaw, was shot and killed in his home and Red Fox was one of the prime suspects. The evidence was not conclusive but most of his neighbors felt he was guilty. He was eventually arrested and charged with the crime but was acquitted in a trial where no direct testimony was given. The Law was satisfied but not the people of the community.

Following the trial Red Fox began to dress in an all black suit with pistols on each hip and cartridge belts hanging over his shoulders. His Winchester rifle was always close by as well, and often a 5 feet long telescope. He made quite a mysterious and intimidating figure as he traveled the mountain roads armed with both his guns and his Bible. Over the years he gained an incredible knowledge of the remote mountains and the many trails that criss-crossed them. This knowledge would serve him well.

Ira Mullins

Ira Mullins was the fourth child born to John Mullins and his wife Martha Potter on February 8, 1857. He was raised in Pike County, Kentucky with his siblings: Ruben, Nancy, Amanda, Sarah, Hulda, John, and Mary. Throughout their early life John worked as a farmer and shoemaker to feed his family. The 1870 Census lists his real estate value at $100 and his personal belongings to value $200.

On June 30, 1870, when young Ira was only 13-years-old, John disappeared out into the woods, planning to tan hides for his leather work as he had done so many times before. But this time he never came back. He was murdered.

On May 10, 1879, Ira married Louranza Estep. The couple moved to Virginia where he became an established farmer and merchant who also had a side job: Bootlegging.

It has been said that Ira operated his businesses and life much in the style of a modern day mafioso, using his money and his connections to keep him out of trouble and control the way the laws affected him. The authorities certainly wanted a piece of Ira and set out to bust his operations at every corner. But stopping Ira Mullins, they would discover, would be anything but easy.

While Ira was busy operating his moonshine stills and distributing his goods across the state boarders, Taylor had been busy making career moves that would allow him to do something about the Mullins mob and their unlawful deeds. He became deputized as a Federal Marshal. One day, while at his post in the old Wise County courthouse, Taylor caught sight of the Mullins' covered wagon rolling by. He wanted Ira Mullins as much as he wanted the goods contained inside the wagon which he knew would be unstamped bottles of white lightning. Calling his men into action, the deputies drew their guns and began firing on the cart. Nearly 200 shots were fired within a few minutes. The commotion sent the horses drawing the wagon into a wild dash through Town but not before the driver was hit. Ira and another man who was traveling with him leaped from the wagon and returned fire on foot. The raid failed to accomplish its intended purpose that day as the only person stopped was the man whose dead body was carried away with the fleeing horses. Ira Mullins merely packed away his gun and casually walked down the street unscathed.

Doc Taylor was severely reprimanded and ultimately stripped of his badge and removed from the Police Force. The reasoning behind his firing was said to be because he was unstable. But it was very likely that Ira, through his connections, had Taylor removed by men in prominent positions who did business in the shadows with the bootlegger. After all Ira usually got what he wanted. But this was not enough for Ira and he never forgave him. The bitter feeling of hatred and resentment between the two lingered often erupting in mutual threats and challenges. This was an incident neither Mullins nor Taylor would ever be able to put behind them.

On July 6, 1883 Ira Mullins received a land grant and had 100 acres of land surveyed in Pike County KY on Elkhorn Creek beside land owned by Henry Vanover, Louranza's maternal uncle. Henry Vanover had served in the Union Army during the Civil War and as payment for his services the government had granted him 900 acres. Henry's land was situated on both sides of Elkhorn Creek and included what is now Burdine, East Jenkins, and Number 3 Hollow. Vanover sold the timber felled on his land and used the profit to purchase more land. He wanted to continue to expand his property line and was rather upset to find that Ira had settled his own homestead against his property line - and even more upset that Ira ran a moonshine distillery there. Vanover accused Ira of settling on land that he had claimed for himself. Ira had the survey papers to prove he was within the lines of his own property but that wasn't good enough for Henry Vanover. The two men would dispute this land claim for years to come.

Another detail that played a hand in the feud between Vanover and Mullins was the company Vanover kept. Doc Taylor was a known close friend and frequent visitor of the Vanover home, as were Calvin and Henan Fleming with whom Ira had long-standing problems. On the evening of May 28, 1885, just after having come in from a long day of timbering, Henry was resting in his home when someone on horseback raced down the creek firing shots at the house. Protecting his wife and kids who were inside, Vanover shot back, knocking the lone rider from his horse and killing him with a shot to the head. It was discovered that the attempted assassin was James Roberts, from Ohio, who had been staying at the home of Ira and Louranza Mullins. Vanover was convinced the dead man was a hired gun for Ira Mullins sent to kill him in an attempt to steal the land from his wife after he was gone. Henry was tried for killing the would-be assassin but was acquitted of the crime.

Sometime later, on June 18, 1887 Henry Vanover and his wife were working in their field in Rocky Hollow when again an armed rider galloped past, firing at Henry. This time the assassination was successful and Henry's wife was left with nine children to provide for on her own,

Initially Clifton Branham and his brother, Tandy, were charged with the killing of Henry Vanover. They were given a hearing before Judge Hogg the week of August 19, 1887. During the hearing Ira Mullins was also implicated in the murder. A few minutes before the trial John Venters and George Belcher, who were working as guards at the jail, helped Mullins escape.

On an April night in 1892 shots were fired through Ira's bedroom window. Ira, who was now bed-ridden from injuries he had received, was laying in his bed and the bullet narrowly missed him, becoming lodged in his bedclothes setting the bed on fire. He understood the shot to be a warning from Taylor. As Ira was now invalid and unable to return fire or retaliate himself, he took other measures to handle the problem. It was rumored that Ira had paid a friend of his $300.00 to do it for him.

Taylor heard about the target that had been placed on his head. He argued that he couldn't have shot into Ira's house because he was doctoring that night in Kentucky but even having an alibi was not enough to satisfy Ira or make Taylor secure in his safety. Fearing for his own life now the Red Fox packaged himself into a shipping crate and had himself boarded onto a freight train to Bluefield, West Virginia where he hid out at his son's house. Taylor later fled to Kentucky and waited the movements of the moonshiners.

On May 14, 1892 the Mullins family had travelled to Leasburg, Virginia on a business trip to sell a tract of land Ira owned there. By late morning, the sale had been made, money collected, and the family started on their way from his brother-in-law, Wilson Mullins, who lived at the mouth of Cane Creek Branch in Kentucky to their home in Pound. Heading a group of eight people they dropped off Wilson's eleven year old daughter Mindy, at her grandmother, Patsy (Potter) Mullins' house. She cried to go with them and Wilson stopped at a store and bought a can of peaches to soothe her. Wilson told Mindy to be a good girl and that they would be back soon. Mindy remained with her grandmother and this was the last time she saw her father alive.

Louranza (Estep) Mullins

Now seven in number the group continued on along the rutted mountain road planning to cross the mountain by way of Pound Gap. The gap, originally called "Sounding Gap," is a high pass at the head of Elkhorn Creek, near where the present day town of Jenkins, Kentucky is now located. Wilson, who was a son of Marshall "Big Foot" Mullins and had married Ira's sister, led the procession riding on horseback. John Chappel, a mentally challenged handyman who worked for Ira, was driving the wagon, and Ira's wife, Louranza (Estep) Mullins, sat beside Chappel on the wagon seat. Ira Mullins was partly reclining on a quilt that was spread over straw filling the bed of the wagon. Two young boys, Ira's fifteen-year-old son, John Harrison Mullins, and Greenberry Harris, the son of Jemima Harris were walking just behind the wagon. Wilson's wife, Jane Mullins, rode on horseback beside or just behind the boys.

Travel over these steep rough roads was slow and laborious but they had made good time. Though they had stopped two or three times during their trip it was just after noon when the party neared the crest of the mountain.

Henan and Cal Fleming

Information came out later that The Red Fox had enlisted the help of Henan and Cal Fleming and possibly the rifle of Mean Henry Adams and that they hid on top of Pine Mountain to keep and eye on the road leading from Kentucky that Ira would have to take. With his long spyglass Doc soon sighted the wagon lumbering over the rough road toward Pound Gap and atop a bed of straw was Ira Mullins. Quickly Red Fox and the Fleming men covered their faces with green cloths to hide their identities and dropped down the south side of the mountain where they hid between two rocks near the right side of the road waiting for the approach of the wagon.

Eventually the wagon came into sight winding its way slowly up the steep northwestern slope of Pine Mountain arriving at the Gap about noon, then beginning its descent along the old Fincastle Trail toward Pound, Virginia. It was around one o'clock in the afternoon when the Mullins family neared the site that is today known as "Killing Rock," across the mountain from Jenkins, Kentucky, on the Virginia side of the border about one fourth to one half mile from the top of the mountain.

Everything seemed to be going well. They felt assured that no revenue officers were near and perceived no other danger. Only the sound of the birds sang over the creaking of the wagon and groaning leather harnesses of the team. Suddenly a thunderous roar of gunfire exploded from behind the rocks near the road and time seemed to stand still as events happened at a pace difficult to take in. Masked men unexpectedly rose from the cover of the rocks beside the road, firing rapidly into the group with repeating rifles. The air was filled with the pungent odor of the black powder smoke from the guns. As in a dream state they watched as one after another of the group was hit and went down. Even the team of horses pulling the wagon was struck by the gunfire and fell to the ground dead. Blood ran from the bodies of the Mullins family and the animals covering the dirt road. Shot after shot was fired until the revolvers and rifles were all emptied. The startled group had no time to react, the look of disbelief on their faces. Astonished and confused at the happenings they watched the scene unfold unable to defend themselves. Within a matter of only a couple of minutes five members of the Mullins party were killed,

Ira Mullins died almost instantly as he was hit by eight bullets. Louranza Mullins was struck by several bullets to her body. Their fifteen year old son, John Harrison Mullins, was walking with Greenberry Harris just behind the wagon when the firing began. In the chaos he saw one of the horses go down and Wilson desperately seeking cover about fifteen feet up the road when he was struck, staggered and fell to the road. Terrified, he dived into the thick brush beside the road and somehow managed to escape, running as fast as he could in the direction of the town of Pound.

When the firing began, Jane Mullins was either thrown or got off her horse on her own, the terrified animal running off down the road. She saw one of the team horses go down and turned to see her husband start to run then fall. She ran to him and turned him over on his side trying to ease his pain.

The Killing Rock

Louranza managed to climb out of the wagon and crawl under it as the lead rained down on them. Mortally wounded she yelled for Jane to come to her and amid the melee of gunfire Jane hurried as quickly as possible to her aid. She helped Louranza to a sitting position with her back up against the wagon. As she looked into Jane's eyes Louranza managed to utter her last words, "They have killed me."

Terrified Jane began to try to determine if any of the others were still alive. The air was heavy, filled with black powder smoke from the still blazing guns and it was hard to see. During a slight pause in the gun fire she looked toward the rocks where the shooting was coming from and as the smoke cleared she saw three men standing twenty to twenty-five steps from the wagon. They were concealed behind the rocks wearing veils that covered their faces. She could see them from the waist up and the lower part of their faces were visible.

She screamed, "Boys, for the Lord's sake, don't shoot anymore, you have killed them all now. Let me stay here with them till someone finds us."

The men called out to her three or four times cursing and threatening her. Jane thought she heard three voices yell and took the first voice to be Calvin Fleming's. She thought one of the voices she heard might have been Doc Taylor. One of the men, possibly Henan Fleming, asked that her life be spared, then another of the killers yelled, "G-- D--- you, take to the road and leave or we will kill you too."

Terrified, Ira Mullins' sister, Jane, took them at their word and ran from the grisly scene of the murders as fast as she could go fleeing for her life with bullets still flying past her and many piercing her outer clothing. She ran all the way back to her home in the Camden section of Jenkins which is on Elkhorn Creek. She mournfully cried – ""Everyone has been killed but me."

John Harrison Mullins, the only other survivor of the deadly ambush, somehow managed to escape and make his way to Pound by around 2 o'clock. There he located Jemima Harris, the Mother of Greenberry, and George Francisco telling them of the terrible events on the mountain. Jemima immediately started to the place where the shooting had occurred and on the way passed the house of Floyd Branham. She stopped at the Branham house and asked Floyd's wife, Elizabeth, to go with her.

When Jemima Harris and Elizabeth Branham arrived the killers were gone and the site they came upon was almost beyond description. The wagon was filled with bullet holes and both the horses pulling it had been killed. They lay bleeding in the road still hitched. Ira Mullins' body was still atop his pallet in the wagon, his bullet riddled body covered in blood. Then Jemima's eye's fell on the body of her son, Greenberry, lying in the wagon shot twice in the head. The body of John Chappel was also in the wagon, his body showing evidence of six shots. Wilson Mullins was lying on his face in the road about fifteen steps from the wagon. Everywhere they looked was more carnage.

Louranza Mullins was found about five feet from the wagon lying flat on her back with her apron thrown up over her head. Her little handbag in which she had carried approximately $1,000.00 in cash was gone and the money pocket attached to a string belt and worn under her dress was also taken. It was later disclosed that the killers had hidden all the money except $100.00. Each of them took $25.00 to buy themselves a new suit of clothes. The purse was found cut to pieces but the lost bag of money was never recovered.

Robert Mullins lived about three miles from Pound Gap and arrived at the scene about an hour and a half after the killings. Jemima Harris and Elizabeth Branham had already been there. John Vint Bentley, who lived in Kentucky, was also at the scene that same afternoon. They examined the body of Ira Mullins and determined that they looked like Winchester or pistol wounds but they could not tell the size.

A Posse was quickly organized and began scouring the mountains around the Gap. After finding nothing for three or four days they eventually disbanded.

The Fleming brothers managed to escape and avoid arrest for years before being captured and tried for their crimes. Intercepted letters in the mail revealed to authorities that the brothers had left the area and were presently working at a saw mill in Boggs, West Virginia. A posse of heavily armed men met up with the brothers at their local post office in West Virginia. Immediately a violent shoot-out began. When the shooting stopped and the smoke cleared it was discovered that Calvin Fleming lay dead and one of the armed agents was fatally wounded. Henan Fleming was immediately arrested and tried for murder on behalf of the agent who died in action there but was acquitted. He was then extradited back to Virginia to face trial for his part in the Pound Gap Massacre. As fate would have it the only witness able to testify to seeing Henan Fleming, Jane Harris, by this time had died from complications two weeks after giving birth to a son by a second husband. With no witness to testify against him Henan was acquitted of a second murder charge and was set free.

While the Fleming men were working their way into West Virginia the sly Red Fox managed to stay one step ahead of attempts to find him. On one occasion he returned to his own home in the town of Wise one night and hid in his attic remaining there for several days. Then one night his son Sylvan, a respected businessman and surveyor living in Norton, five miles from Wise, took his father to his home. The son insisted his father leave the mountains and go to Florida although the son testified in court later that his father wanted to stay and stand trial.

The Red Fox decided to take his son's advice and outfitted in new clothes mounted an empty boxcar standing on the yard at Norton and rode to Bluefield, WV where he intended to hobo another train going south. But somehow the Wise County Commonwealth Attorney, Robert Bruce, heard of Red Fox being in a boxcar bound for Bluefield and wired the Baldwin Detective agency to apprehend him when he left the train. They did and he was returned to Wise for trial.

Doc Taylor was indicted for the slaying of the Mullins family and was found guilty. In an attempt to avoid a hanging death his first plan of defense was to plead insanity. The entire community was fully aware of the eccentric character he was, delving in spiritualism and using spirits from the "Great Beyond" to aid him in his healing practices. He had already convinced the people of the area that he could move faster than the speed of light, appearing and disappearing in the blink of an eye, so he was confident his plan would work. But if it was not successful he felt they might be convinced he could escape all attempts to confine him and might as well let him go free.

His friends and family asserted that Doc Mullins was insane and circulated a petition asking the governor of Virginia to pardon him, if not spare him death with a life sentence behind bars. Very few people signed the petition however. Even more damaging to his insanity claim was the fact the sitting judge heard him suggesting questions to ask specific witnesses. The judge reasoned that no insane man would have the clear mind about him to counsel his attorney about law and questioning so he refused to accept the argument of insanity.

Taylor then appealed the judgment on the grounds that his gun could not have possibly fired the killing shots. The casings found at the site of the massacre were rim-shots, meaning the pin hit the rim of the casing rather than the center. The execution was put on hold while an investigation was done. A closer look at Doc Taylor's gun revealed that it did indeed fire at the center but only because it had recently been tampered with. Red Fox, the ole "sly fox" wasn't so smart this time. His tampering with evidence only expedited a new hearing rather than grant him forever freedom. This didn't worry the Red Fox as much as one might expect. The old Fox had yet another idea, an almost unbelievable scheme that some witnesses say he did in fact carry out. An idea, they say, that worked.

On the night before his hanging the Red Fox ate a hearty supper and slept soundly until daylight. It was further reported that twenty-five heavily armed guards stood outside the jail. Doc asked to preach his own funeral and was allowed. From an upstairs window in the courthouse he called down to a large crowd citing the Revelations 3:20 from the Bible: "Behold, I stand at the door and knock: if any man hears my voice, and opens the door, I will come in to him, and will sup with him, and he with me."

Taylor was taken back to the Wise County Jail and went up to the scaffold at 2 o'clock in the afternoon. He once again read from the Bible and said one last prayer. As the Sheriff affixed the white cap Doc fell victim to a panic attack, dropping hard to the floor shaking in tears. Renfro and the other men quickly raised him to his feet and adjusted the rope around his neck. At 2:20pm Jailer Renfro cut the ropes to the trap door and Taylor fell through the floor of the box, the rope straight and tight in the view of onlookers. Eighteen minutes later the physicians gathered inside the box and under the floor, out of view of spectators, pronounced Dr. Marshall B. Taylor dead. His body was turned over to friends whom he had asked to keep it until the following Sunday. Three days were given in waiting to honor Taylor's last wishes and testament which were that his loved ones keep watch over his body for three days, where like Christ, on the third day, he would rise again. Naturally nobody honestly expected him to resurrect from the dead but they did keep watch over his body as requested. On the third day the coffin was then given a proper burial.

Epilogue:

- The "Killing Rock" can be reached by following the newly developed "Red Fox Trail" which starts on old Route 23 between the Pound and the top of the Gap. "Killing Rock " is about 1 1/2 miles up the trail along Rocky Branch.
- The family and neighbors made arrangements to recover the bodies of those slain and took them to Wilson's home. There wasn't enough room inside so some of the bodies were put on the porch. They then built a big fire to keep the flies away from the bodies. Ira's sister Nancy was married to William Potter who allowed the family to bury the victims in the nearby Potter Cemetery.
- Family members of Marshall B. Taylor are certain that the Sly Red Fox was not executed that day at the courthouse. Many swear that when his body dropped through the floor of the scaffold he landed on the ground and was quickly released. It is said Taylor was given a disguise to help him blend in with the other physicians who were in the boxed off portion under the scaffold to pronounce his death. Dr. Cherry, one of the physicians present inside the box at the execution, stated that the attending doctors carted out an empty coffin and released it to the Taylor family, allowing Taylor time to flee to Missouri where he is rumored to have lived out the rest of his days. This theory is quite possible considering that Doc Taylor's mother lived there and evidence exists of his children and grandchildren packing up and moving to Missouri from Virginia as well.

The Gallows on which Doc Taylor (the Red Fox) was hung – or so they say?

The gallows encased by a house. The man at the top is adjusting the rope.
Photo courtesy Southwest Virginia Museum.
272

Works Cited

https://vocal.media/criminal/killing-rock-massacre-the-story-of-doc-taylor-and-ira-mullins

"Preached His Own Funeral Sermon".The Times-Picayune. (New Orleans, Louisiana), 28 Oct 1893, Sat • Page 7.
https://www.newspapers.com/clip/8599334/marshall_benton_taylors_life_and_death/

Jillson, Willard Rouse. The Kentucky Land Grants. Vol. I-II. Louisville, KY, USA: Filson Club Publications, 1925.

"A Red Handed Demon Hung". The Morning News. (Savannah, Ga.), 28 Oct. 1893, Saturday. Page 1. Chronicling America: Historic American Newspapers. Lib. of Congress.
https://chroniclingamerica.loc.gov/lccn/sn86063034/1893-10-28/ed-1/seq-1/

A Visit to Southwestern Virginia in 1855
By *Appalachian Magazine*

On June 20, 1855, The Richmond Dispatch published the following account of a recent visit to Southwestern Virginia:

Saturday, June 9. – We had a good night's rest at the Lick – a night of sweet sleep, induced without rocking, and continued without interruption, until the golden light of the sun had tinged the sky of the beautiful valley. The charming songs of the birds and the cheerful chatter of the feathered domestics of the homestead, were peculiarly delightful to ears unaccustomed to them`, and helped rapidly to dissipate the lingering drowsiness of sleep. We arose refreshed and invigorated, feeling ready for another day of active observation.

Immediately after breakfast, our whole party mustered, and accompanied by our kind host, Col. Preston, and Mr. Robertson, we stared on our route homeward. We ascended Little Walker's Mountain – which rises immediately behind the mansion of the Lick – while the stages proceeded without passengers. Reaching a prominent point in the oblique road on the mountain side, we took a last view of the Salt Valley. Oh, how lovely it was! It was one of those enchanting scenes in nature which one always wants dearest friend to be at his side and with him to admire. It was such an one as we see not often in our pilgrimage, and is not soon to be forgotten...

In a few miles we crossed both the Walker mountains – neither of which is large – seeing some very pretty farms, and travelling through fertile lands all the way. Our road ran within a few hundred yards of the Chilhowie Sulphur Springs, which we visited. They are about four miles from Seven Mile Ford, and perhaps two from the line of the Va. And Tenn. Rail Road. We found them remarkably strong with sulphur – an analysis making them as strong as the White Sulphur of Greenbrier. They have not however, the elevation and bold flow of that yet unparalleled fountain. But the Chilhowie is very strong sulphur, and might become a much frequented watering place. It is understood to be in market, and with a reasonable expenditure and some trees, which have to be planted to supply the place of these the heedless axeman has cut down, might be made a very pretty place.

Here we parted with Col. Preston, sincerely grateful for his kind and courteous hospitality. ..

We entered the Abingdon Road about two miles from Seven Mile Ford, and there we bade adieu to our kind friend Mr. Robertson, who had treated us so hospitably, and had contributed so much to promote the pleasure of the Southwestern tourists...

At last, we turned our horses' heads directly homewards, and soon reached Seven Mile Ford, where we swapped the rough and rugged mud pike for the excellent Macadamised Road. Getting our dinners at a somewhat early hour, and taking a last look at the grand valley of the Holston, we were again on our journey, and retraced our way over the road – the three culverts which are under the embankment of the railroad – through which gush the cool, pure waters of a mountain stream and where our company on the outward voyage, with the aid of spirit rappers, took the mysterious third degree – thence by Marion, Mt. Airy (Rural Retreat), and our good old friend Aker's, to Wytheville. As we passed his house, Jonathan Aker was ready to greet us.

Ten gentlemen jumped out of the stages and besieged the doors of Rural Retreat. The landlord appeared with three large cakes of the sugar and a hammer to break it up – the ten gentlemen seized him – he scuffled his way to the block before the house, and there laying down two cakes, they were immediately seized upon by two of the ten, who fled and others after them, while the third cake was broken up by our host and distributed among those who remained. Never did school boys show such avidity for maple sugar.

Getting the needed information and exchanging hearty good wishes with the landlord of Rural Retreat, we hurried on to the store, where stood forth a sign upon which was writ the long name of some of the numerous family of Hisers...

We arrived at Wytheville Saturday night about 9 o'clock, after a week of as much activity and real enjoyment as ever it fell to the lot of a company of gentlemen...

There being no train in Wytheville on Sunday, the 10th, we rested there on that day. In the afternoon, by invitation of Mr. E. McGavocl, a portion of our party drove down the farm called "Fort Chiswell," on the Macadamized Road, nine miles from Wytheville. It is owned by his brothers and their two sisters. It is a very large estate of remarkable fertility and beauty, having upon it one of the finest mansions in the West. It is noted for having been the site of a Fort, (whose name the place bears,) occupied by the British in Braddock's war. Here resided Col. Chiswell, an Englishman, under whom before the revolution, the Lead Mines of Wythe were worked. Some remains of a brick office, the brick for which are said to have been brought from England, are still seen on the farm.

"General" John Salling the Last Confederate Veteran?

Was John Salling the oldest living Confederate Veteran at the time of his death? That is a question that is unlikely to ever be completely settled. What we think we know is that he was born on May 15 in either 1846 or 1858 to Caroline Matilda Salling, when she was 14 yrs. old. His Father was a slave on her grandmother's farm. He had 3 siblings. It is said that Salling spoke with a Chaucerian lilt common to the people who migrated from Elizabethan England and were land-locked around the Bristol, VATNarea. He died on March 16, 1959 in Kingsport, SullivanCo., TN.

Salling was officially enlisted in Company D, 25th Virginia Infantry of the Confederate Army but did not see military action. He spent the term of his enlistment in his native Scott county, Va., digging for saltpeter needed for Confederate gunpowder. He said that he never had a uniform because uniforms were scarce. The title of "General" was unofficially added late in his life by those wishing to recognize and honor his unique service.

His home was a 35-acre mountain farm on the Clinch river, near Slant, Va. He was born on the farm and lived there all his life, even while in service. Over the years he worked as a farmer, logger, horse trader, and moonshiner. Several years before his death he told fellow veterans at a Confederate reunion in Mobile, Ala. that he had to get back to tend his corn crop which he expected to run three gallons to the acre. He smoked a daily cigar until he broke his hip at almost 100 yrs. of age. He chewed plug tobacco and admitted he liked an occasional nip of mountain liquor. A lanky, rawboned man, his hair remained black and he still had many of his own teeth when he died.

John filed for a Confederate pension with the Commonwealth of Virginia in 1933 stating that he was 84 years of age, born in Scott Co., VA, and that he was in a branch of the service that dug Saltpetre. He further stated that he enlisted in the DeKalb district of Scott County under Capt. James Collins and worked with him in the mines, along with Houston Darnell and Billy Ervin, both of whom were dead at the time. He reported that he worked under the direction of J. Monroe McConnell of Scott County, Virginia. John was granted a Confederate pension beginning in 1933.

John claimed to be the second-oldest surviving Confederate Veteran of the American Civil War, though his claim of being born in 1846 has since been found to likely be in error. In 1991 William Marvel examined the claims of Salling and several other "last Civil War veterans" for an article in the Civil War History magazine Blue & Gray. Marvel found multiple instances of census data that indicated Salling was born in 1858 rather than 1846.

At the time of his death John Salling was officially considered the next-to-the last Confederate veteran. Walter Williams of Houston, Texas was frequently listed as the last Confederate veteran. Shortly before Williams died in late 1959, however, a New York Times report cast strong doubt on his claim.

The John Salling case gained attention and interest after Guinness World Records listed him as the "oldest soldier" of all time, erroneously as 113 years and 1 day old. It was later found that John claimed shortly before his death to have been born in May 1846, not March 1846, as Guinness had mistakenly reported. Thus, Salling's age was first dropped from 113 to 112, and then a census search suggested that he was really 'only' 100. In any case no documentation to support his claim to being a veteran was ever produced and in 2006 Guinness pulled their recognition of John.

The last authenticated Confederate veteran was Pleasant Crump, who was 104 when he died on December 31, 1951.

It is very likely that John Salling did serve the Confederacy as a Petre Monkey during the Civil War as he attested. Records of such service were often very difficult to come by. Whether he was the oldest surviving Confederate Veteran we may never know for sure. But we do know that he was the oldest and last one in Virginia.

(Material for this story from: https://www.findagrave.com/memorial/49607043/john-b_-salling edited for clarity.)

Navigation on the Clinch, Powell, and Holston Rivers

"A few yards from the edge of the Tennessee Valley in Bland County, Va., two small streams rise and flow toward the southwest for just over a mile. There, at the community of Sharon Springs, the streams join and continue a meandering course among hills and through pastures, picking up water from creeks along the way. These are the headwaters of the North Fork of the Holston River." (Dan Kegley, for the Smyth County News & Messenger, August 2001)

Haywood states the Indians called the river "Cootcla;" and elsewhere says that it was known by the Cherokee as "Watauga." J. G. M. Ramsey states that from the Little Tennessee to the French Broad the river was called by the aborigines "Cootla" and above "Hogohegee". The French called it the Cherokee. Many early explorers and settlers referred to it as the "Indian River". Eventually it became officially known as the Holston River. However it is referred to it has always been a very important waterway throughout Southwest Virginia and Northeast Tennessee for both transportation and commercial purposes.

In 1748 Steven Holston, a noted long-hunter and explorer, settled about 8 miles east of what is now Marion, Va., approximately thirty yards from the large spring that eventually became the Middle Fork of the Holston River. Not long afterwards he made a famous canoe voyage from near his home downstream all the way to Natchez, Mississippi. The information he gained on this voyage added much to what was known about the territory and probably resulted in the river system being named for him.

The North Fork of the Holston River was navigable by flatboats for about 110 miles, from an iron works and boat yard at Chatham Hill, a major industrial center in the early 1800's, in what is now Smyth County, Va. But the major port on the upper reaches was Saltville at mile 83. From here many different products including maple sugar, loosely woven material called homespun, wool, pig iron, gypsum, lead, beeswax, apples, spirituous liquors, etc. were shipped downstream to Kingsport, Tn, a distance of 83 river miles, and sometimes beyond. Of these the big business was clearly salt which was packed in barrels at Preston's and King's salt works and shipped in small flatboats downstream to the confluence of the three forks of the Holston at Kingsport. There it was often transferred to bigger boats that were floated down the main channel of the river into the Tennessee River, and on to the Ohio and eventually the Mississippi.

The South Fork of the Holston River was navigable for at least 72 miles, as far as the mouth of the Middle Fork, and perhaps higher at times. A Corps of Engineer's report in the 1930's says boats had descended from as far upriver as Big Creek (mile 50.5) and log rafts from as far up as Big Jacob Creek (mile 59.9).

The Middle Fork of the Holston River was probably only navigable commercially for a few miles above its confluence with the South Fork, despite plans to extend it 32 miles, to Seven Mile Ford. No proof has been found of the project being completed or its being used by flatboats that far upstream.

The Clinch River, which early accounts say was named for a long hunter by that name, lies to the north of the Holston, in Southwest Virginia. Commercial use of the river, primarily for timber, began later than on the Holston around 1880. It was navigable by flatboats from as high as Nash's Ford, at mile 279 (77 miles above the Tennessee line). It was often also used to float large flotillas of logs which sometimes came from as high up as Raven, in Tazewell County, Va., at mile 315. An article by Roy and Logan Osborne says the rafting "had to be done in the cold weather of winter and spring. Hardy young men were required. Many times they would have to swim out through floating ice and spend the night around a camp fire. Food was stored on the raft and cooked there on a hearth of mud and stone or sometimes in a small cook stove. The bunks were built in the middle of the raft, and straw was carried for bedding." The much smaller North Fork of the Clinch was apparently never used commercially.

Powell's River (as it was spelled during the 19th Century) was named for Ambrose Powell, one of the explorers who accompanied Thomas Walker on his famous trip through the region in 1750. It was navigated by flatboats as far up as Shaver's Ford, in Lee County, Va., (153 miles above its mouth and 37 miles above the Tennessee line).

Commercial traffic on each of these rivers was primarily by way of flatboats which were built at several locations along the upper stretches of the rivers, from the tall straight poplar trees growing in abundance. According to Goodridge Wilson's Smyth County History, (1932, p. 173-174), "these boats were usually from 60 to 90 feet long and up to 16 feet wide. These long, narrow craft required skillful handling in the rapids of the turbulent, swollen stream." Flatboating and rafting on the rivers was a one-way trip. Boats were built, loaded, and launched where they were needed and sold for lumber when they had reached their destinations. Many older homes near these downstream ports still contain lumber originally cut far upstream and used in these old boats. Crews were then left to make their way back home anyway they could, often walking and camping along the way. Keelboats, which were up-swept and pointed at both ends were able to navigate upstream when the currents weren't too swift, but were less frequently used on any of the rivers of the area.

Each of these rivers contained dangerous currents, shallows and rocky shoals that could easily wreck a boat or break up a log raft, threatening the lives of the crew. Consequently most commercial traffic occurred during the "Tides" of early Spring when the rivers were high and could more safely float the boats above these natural and man-made hazards. When such opportunities presented themselves there was a flurry of excited activity as the boats began their long and arduous journey. People would often line the river banks to watch the flotilla of boats stream by for hours. However the swift turbulent water during that time of year added its own dangers to the trip and many boats and lives were lost to the swirling, muddy water over the years.

Until the coming of the railroads most commercial traffic and a good deal of general transportation in the S.W. Virginia and N. E. Tennessee area was on the various waterways as roads were few and difficult and travel was often limited to only foot and horseback.

Rafting Down the Clinch River
By Roy L. Osborne and Logan Osborne

There are yet many people in Scott County who remember the days of rafting on the Clinch, but for the sake of those who shall yet crave to know something about the days when we were much more in the backwoods than we are today, we write this story.

Most of the fine timber in Scott County was gone before a good market existed. Perhaps a better price should have been paid for the logs that went down the river. The rafting began about 1880 and continued until the completion of the C. C. & O. Railroad about 1909. It would be difficult to estimate the millions of feet of the County's best timber that was sold in this way.

In the beginning, Mr. James Brickey from near Ft. Blackmore bought all the timber on the ridges along the Clinch from Ft. Blackmore to Russell County. He paid one to two dollars a tree. The best walnut brought two dollars. This timber was easily logged. Much of it could be rolled or skidded with little effort to the edge of the river. Mr. Brickey used two or three yokes of oxen for the entire boundary. The oxen cost about $65.00 a yoke. A good driver received a wage of fifty cents or $10 a month.

Some other timber was later cut that had to be hauled a short distance to the river. All the timber close to the river was gone when the Railroad was built. One large boundary in the mountain above Ft. Blackmore was manufactured at Ft. Blackmore after the completion of the C. C. & O. and earlier than that another large set was sawed out at the base of the High Knob on the Stoney Creek. Reforestation will now begin in this area with the organization of the Lake-mountain National Forest and we hope to see a Civilian Conservation Corps Camp established on the Scott County side of this Forest.

The technique of raft making will soon be a lost art. It has probably served its day and will never be revived. Yet it was an economical way to get the timber to the markets. Much of the timber was delivered at Clinchport to men who tooled it on down the Clinch into the Tennessee to Chattanooga or Clinton. A crew of ten men brought the rafts through the rough waters from Dungannon on the Clinch to Clinchport. Here men were turned back and still others as the work became less hazardous. These rafts were made up of 150 to 250 logs and contained 50 to 100 thousand feet. The rafts were started as single rafts, but after the worst water was passed two were tied together to form a double raft. These rafts were steered by large oars. A nice slim chestnut of sufficient strength was used for an oar stem. This tem was 25 to 35 feet in length. The paddle was a well seasoned 16 foot board, three inches thick at the end which fastened in the stem, and shaved to a thin edge to make it "flip" as the stroke was completed.

The logs were bound together with young hickory saplings. These were split in the center. At first spikes were tried, but these were not satisfactory. Wooden pins were used for successful rafting. The holes for these pegs were made with a two-inch auger through the binder and one-and-one-half inch auger into the log.

These rafts were not always brought through the rough waters, such as the Slate Cliff and the Blue Cliff above Dungannon, Stoney Creek Shoals at Ft. Blackmore, and Ervins Bend at Hill Station. Many rafts were torn up in these places, and most of the logs lost. Men were hurt and some killed. Hop Duncan was killed while trying to swim out of a wreck in the Stoney Creek Shoals. Sometimes a wreck was tied up until the tide went down and was repaired to be floated again on the next ride. This was sometimes the following winter. These wrecks were relatively few, for these expert steermen knew the tricks of the river, and when the tide was high enough and not too high. When the tide was too high they would have to tie up and wait.

Steersmen to Clinchport through the bad waters were P. H. Osborne, B. F. Osborne, Logan Osborne, Kenny Ramey, and David Sluss. These men would direct the hazardous work of drifting the rafts out of Russell County and upper Scott County. John Catron, John Church, Isaac Horton, and Tom Neff were steersmen on to Chattanooga.

This work had to be done in the cold weather of winter and spring. Hardy young men were required. Many times they would have to swim out through floating ice and spend the night around a camp fire. Food was stored on the raft and cooked there on a hearth of mud and stone or sometimes in small cook stoves. The bunk was built in the middle of the raft, and straw was carried for bedding.

Steersmen were paid two dollars a day and other hands one dollar a day. The round trip to Clinchport took about a week. The trip on into Tennessee was slower and usually took about a month.

We wish it were possible to collect the stories of the experiences of the men who rode these rafts through the rapids of the Clinch. Z. D. Collins at Dungannon had all his money tied up in two large rafts. These rafts were approximately 300 feet long. P. H. Osborne was steering one and David Sluss the other. The rafts started out from Sandy Point at Dungannon. Each raft was worth about $1,000. Bill Bryant, Will Collins, Evan Collins, Hoge Osborne, Fleet Osborne, and Loge Osborne were on the two rafts. The rafts were very heavy and they had been forced to tie up frequently. The cable had worn out. They got through and were nearing Clinchport. The oars were broken in an effort to tie and the ropes would not hold. It looked like the rafts would be lost by running into the railroad bridge at Clinchport. Three attempts were made to tie. P. H. Osborne and Z. D. Collins broke a boat loose nearby and paddled with all their strength ahead to get a rope. They overtook two men from Chattanooga, who had two ropes. Collins said, "I cannot tie my rafts and all I have will be lost. Loan me a rope for a few minutes." "We will do no such G___ D___ thing. We are taking care of ourselves; you do the same." "Sell me a rope," Collins begged. "Nothing shaking," the other replied. "Now you get to hell off here before I cut your head off with this axe." "You put that axe down or I will kill you," Collins said, "if you will not loan nor sell we will take a rope." At that a fight started and P. H. Osborne untied a rope and they started back up the river with cursing and threats from the owner. The raft which was now a double raft, was tied up just in time to keep it out of the bridge. The rope was returned and the owner forced to take pay for its use.

One winter Kenny Ramey was steering a raft for Jim Marcum and Marion Stapleton. Loge Osborne, P. H. Osborne, and Charlie Wheatley were on the bow. "Happy" Blevins and Kenny Ramey were on the stern. The raft was loaded and cut loose at Isaac Porter's at Sinking Shoals. A good start was made. But Kenny saw a friend on the bank and began "hollering" to him. The friend was Lonzo Semones. This joking and fun took the steersman's eye and mind off the job. Sinking Shoal Cliff was just ahead. When Kenny was aroused to the danger he gave the command, "Quick, up! Lay her over to the right." It was too late. The raft hit the cliff, tore off the oars and ripped the binder back half way. Many of the best logs were lost. On down through the rapids, ripping, bumping with loose logs rolling under the raft, men screaming, but not daring to leave the wreck. What was left reached an eddy and was tied up, and rafted for the next tide.

Many trips were made on many a tide in the roughest weather down the Clinch. And many are the stories that these old rafters still tell to the children and grandchildren around the winter fires, while tides come, but the rafts float no more. The oxen are found no more in the woods, the powerful truck hauls the logs to the market, or to the railroad station. The railroad came and had its day like the rafting tide, and now the good highway and the auto-truck. But nothing today compares in adventure to those days of logging with the oxen and the floating of the mighty rafts down the Clinch.

Truly the history of man's progress is the history of transportation. But do we have better men with it all? Have we in Scott County builded men as we have builded roads and school houses? The nation's security depends not upon these material things but upon the character of men. In the shadow of the monument of material success we seek a way out. Plenty of railroads, too much cotton, too much wheat, too many hogs, too much clothing in warehouses, too much money in the banks, too many school houses and teachers, too many churches and preachers, too many colleges. The wealth of plain and mountains, of soil and mine are still here.

Yet we lost something and that loss has brought us down into the trough of the greatest "depression" in the history of our country. What had we lost? We had lost that quality that enables men to trust each other.

From the Gate City Herald, clippings in the possession of E. B. Broadwater.

Historical Sketches of Southwest Virginia, published by Southwest Virginia Historical Society, Publication 8, June 1974, pages 1 to 4.

Major Roads in Virginia During the 19th Century:

In the 1800s the major transportation and migration roads running through Virginia included:

The Kings Highway

The Fall Line Road

The Great Wagon or Great Valley Road

The Wilderness Road

"King's Highway" was the principal inland route of the Colonies and it ran from Charleston, SC to Boston, MA. In Virginia this Highway ran from Suffolk through Williamsburg and Fredericksburg to Alexandria as follows:

Suffolk Norfolk

Hampton Yorktown

Williamsburg New Kent

King William Bowling Green

Fredericksburg Alexandria

The "Fall Line Road" ran from Alexandria to Fredericksburg on the Kings Highway and then broke off toward Richmond following the general "Fall Line" above which travel on rivers required portage around the "river falls".

The "Great Wagon Road" or "Great Valley Road"

Ran from Philadelphia down through Winchester, Va and along the "Great Valley" of Virginia to Fort Chiswell in present day Wythe County.

In Virginia, the "Great Wagon or Great Valley Road" ran through:

Winchester

New Market

Staunton

Lexington

Fincastle

"Big Lick" (now called Roanoke)

Ingles Ferry, and

Ft. Chiswell

- It was extended to the Long Island of the Holston in 1760.

The "Wilderness Trail/Road", blazed by Daniel Boone and others in 1775, went from the "Great Wagon or "Great Valley Road" through Scott and Lee Counties in Virginia, through the Cumberland Gap into Kentucky and up into the Ohio River Valley. It was widened to allow wagon traffic by 1800.

Major Railroads in Virginia (from 1827-1861)

- Baltimore and Ohio (1827)
- Winchester & Potomac (at Harpers Ferry)
- Winchester & Strasburg
-- North Western RR to Parkersburg, WV
- Manassas Gap (1850-54)
- Orange & Alexandria (1848)
- Virginia Central (1836)
- Virginia & Tennessee (1850s)
- Richmond, Fredericksburg, and Potomac to Alexandria (1834) & Fredericksburg & Charlottesville RR
- South Side or "Petersburg & Lynchburg RR" (1849-54)
- Richmond & Danville (1847-1856)
- Petersburg & Roanoke River (in NC)
-- Richmond & Petersburg
- Norfolk and Petersburg (1853)
- Seaboard & Roanoke River (in NC) or "Portsmouth and Weldon RR" (1835)

Built in the 1850s, the Virginia & Tennessee Railroad ran completely through southwestern VA along the length of the Great Valley of Virginia. The railroad extended westward from its Junction with the Orange & Alexandria RR at Lynchburg, through a gap in the Blue Ridge Mts near the town of Big Lick (the present-day city of Roanoke); there, it turned southwestward and followed the Great Valley to Bristol, TN, a total distance of 204 miles.

From Bristol, it continued to Knoxville, TN and was known as the Tennessee & Virginia Railroad Principle Railroad In Southwest Virginia:

Selected Counties & Incorporated Towns in the Appalachian Mountain Region of Virginia

Washington County Virginia (1776, from Fincastle Co.) (Named for Gen. George Washington)

- Abingdon – (County Seat – 1778 named by Martha Washington for her home town).

- Damascus – (1886 – named for the ancient capitol of Syria).

- Glade Spring – (originally called Passawtami, a Native American word meaning "This is the Place", later likely named for springs outside the town).

Russell County Virginia (from Washington Co. in 1786) (Named for Col. William Russell)

- Lebanon – (County Seat – 1819 named for Cedars of Lebanon)

- Honaker – (1797 – named for Martin Honaker, renamed for Harvey Honaker)

- Cleveland – (1890 – to honor Pres. Grover Cleveland)

Lee County Virginia – (from Russell County in 1793) (Named for Gen. Henry "Light Horse Harry" Lee, a Delegate to the Continental Congress and Governor of Virginia

- Jonesville – (County Seat – 1834 named for Frederick Jones)

- Pennington Gap – (1891 – named for business leader, John W. Pennington)

- St. Charles – (1907 – named for Charles Bondurant, mine owner, and a Mrs. St. John, his secretary)

Tazewell County Virginia – (from Russell and Wythe in 1799) (Named for U.S. Sen. Henry Tazewell)

- Tazewell – (County Seat, originally named Jeffersonville to honor Pres. Thomas Jefferson, changed in 1892)

- Richlands – (began as land grant in 1785, named for rich land in the area, 1892)

- Bluefield – (first called Pin Hook in early 1860s. Renamed Harman and then Graham in 1884, then to Bluefield in 1924).

- Cedar Bluff – (originally called Indian or Mouth of Indian for Indian Creek, renamed for local scenery in 1895).

- Pocahontas - (1881 - named for the Indian Princess who aided Capt. John Smith).

Scott County Virginia (from Lee, Russell, and Washington Co. (Named for Gen. Winfield Scott, a hero of the War of 1812).

- Gate City - (County Seat - originally called Winfield for General Winfield Scott, later changed to Estillville for Judge Benjamin Estill, who helped establish the County, and in 1886 it was changed to Gate City.

- Clinchport - (named for the Clinch River, which was likely named for William Clinch, a Long Hunter who was in the area around 1745).

- Duffield - (named for either Sam Henry Duff or Robert Duff, who lived in a cabin called Duffield).

- Dungannon - (originally known as Hunter's Ford and later Osbourne's Ford, named in early 1900s by Patrick Hagan who joined his Uncle Joseph Hagan there around 1884).

- Nickelsville - (named for James Nickels, Sr. who was a local merchant and post master in the 1830s. Originally chartered as Nicholsville in 1902 and changed to its current spelling in 1938).

- Weber City - (1930s, businessman Frank M. Parker, Sr. jokingly put up a sign with the name that came from a skit on the radio show, "Amos and Andy". The name stuck and was made official when the town was chartered in 1954).

Wise County Virginia- (from Lee, Scott, and Russell Counties in 1856, originally planned as Roane, but the name was changed at the last minute to Wise in honor of the then governor of Va., Henry A. Wise).

- Wise - (County Seat - originally known as Big Glades, then Gladeville when it was incorporated in 1874, changed to current name in 1924 to match County name).

- Appalachia - (named for the mountains surrounding the town. The original name probably came from the name Appalachee, which was the name the Spanish gave to Indians in this area back in the 1500s).

- Big Stone Gap - (originally called Mineral City by northern investors who dreamed of a southern version of the steel town Pittsburg. The current name comes from the natural gap in the mountain near by).

- Coeburn - (originally known as Gist's Station when the post office was established there in the 1860's the town and the Guest River were likely originally named for Christopher Gist, an early explorer who came through the area about 1750. The name was changed in 1892, to recognize W. W. Coe and William E. Burns, partners in land development in the area.

- Pound – (probably named for The Pound, a grain pounding mill in the 19th Century).
- St. Paul – (originally planned as a "twin city" with the Clinch River as the dividing line, but the idea failed to catch on. It was also discovered that a town in Carroll County, Va. already was called by this name so Estonoa, and Indian name meaning "land of the blue waters" was chosen. Later, according to oral tradition, residents from the town bought the name from the Carroll Co. community
- The City of Norton – (originally known as Prince's Flats for William Prince, a settler in the 1780s. The first post office was called Eolia in 1883. The current name was adopted in 1890 in honor of Ekstein Norton, President of the Louisville and Nashville Rail Road).

Buchannon County Virginia –(from Tazewell and Russell Counties in 1858 and named for U.S. President James Buchanan)

- Grundy – (originally called Mouth of Slate, for Slate Creek, was named for U.S. Senator Felix Grundy of Tennessee).

Dickenson County Virginia – (Virginia's 100th and last county, from Buchanan, Russell, and Wise Counties in 1880 and named for William J. Dickenson, a member of the House of Delegates who sponsored the bill to create it).

- Clintwood – (first called Holly Creek, the current name is in Honor of Henry Clinton Wood, of Scott County, who was a member of the Virginia Senate).
- Clincho – (had its first post office in 1917, and is named for the Clinchfield Coal Company, incorporated in 1990).
- Haysi – (originally called Mouth of McClure, eventually named for two store owners, Charles M. Hayter and Otis L. Sifers).

Editor's Note:

Much of the information in this book about incorporated town names comes from "*Southwest Virginia Crossroads: an Almanac of Place Names and Places To See* ", by Joe Tennis and

"*Far Southwest Virginia: A Postcard and Photographic Journey*", by Frank Kilgore copyright 2014 by Frank Kilgore.

Other Works By The Author:

"Pathfinders, Pioneers, & Patriots" (Volume 1) - at Lulu.com

https://www.lulu.com/search?adult_audience_rating=00&category=History&q=Danny+Dixon

The story of the amazing people who settled and defended the Appalachian Frontier during our nation's most precarious years until 1800 - featuring a 34 page historical time-line and over 100 pages of stories about the people and events highlighted in the time-line.

"When Courage Was Common" - Lulu.com

https://www.lulu.com/search?adult_audience_rating=00&category=History&q=Danny+Dixon

The amazing courage displayed by the settlers of the Applachian Frontier as they crossed the stormy Atlantic Ocean, cleared and settled America's First Frontier, and defended it against all enemies during the French & Indian War, The American Revolution, etc. - featuring many first hand accounts, journals, documents, etc. form the era.

"Echoes From the Past" (a unique site on Face Book) featuring rare historical pictures and brief historical clips about days gone by in America.

www.ingramcontent.com/pod-product-compliance
Lightning Source LLC
Chambersburg PA
CBHW081233170426
43198CB00017B/2743